Law and Justice

**Nelson-Hall Series in
Justice Administration**
Consulting editor: **Howard Abadinsky**
St. Xavier College, Chicago

About the Author

Howard Abadinsky is Associate Director of the Criminal Justice
Program at Saint Xavier College/Chicago, and an Inspector for
the Cook County Sheriff; he was a parole officer in New York for
fifteen years. The author of several books on crime and justice,
Abadinsky holds a Ph.D. in sociology from New York University
and is the founder of the International Association for the Study of
Organized Crime.

Law and Justice

Howard Abadinsky

Nelson-Hall
Chicago

To Donna, Alisa, and Sandi

Cover Illustration: *Breakout* by Catherine Doll, 1983.
Mixed Media, 40 " × 60 " Used with permission of the artist.

Library of Congress Cataloging-in-Publication Data

Abadinsky, Howard, 1941–
    Law and Justice.

    Bibliography: p.
    Includes index.
        1. Justice, Administration of—United States—
History.   I. Title.
KF384.A7514   1988   347.73   87–12184
ISBN 0-8304-1171-2   347.307
ISBN 0-8304-1188-7 (pbk.)

Manufactured in the United States of America

10   9   8   7   6   5   4   3   2

 TM The paper used in this book meets the minimum requirements of American National Standard for Information Sciences—Permanence of Paper for Printed Library Materials, ANSI Z39.48-1984.

Contents

Preface

The course on the law, the courts, and the judicial process that I have been presenting for several years is cross-referenced as an elective for criminal justice and political science students. During this time I have been experimenting with a variety of textbooks in order to better meet the needs of both disciplines and to best fit the manner in which I present this course. None have been completely satisfying. There are texts written for criminal justice students with the focus on criminal law and prosecution; there are other texts designed for a political science audience that stress the policy aspects of law and the politics of justice. The use of a book from one or the other category requires a number of supplementary readings, which, while not an untoward imposition on students, is something that I (and perhaps many other educators) prefer, if possible, to avoid.

There has also been a tendency for materials on the law and justice to be presented without historical references. But law and justice without history leaves an educational void. Consequently, I have attempted to place law and justice in their historical contexts, and an entire chapter is devoted to an examination of the history of American law and justice. Another chapter provides an analysis of the development of the legal profession, bar associations, and legal education as the necessary prerequisite for understanding law and the administration of justice in the United States.

Chapter 1 examines the problem of defining law, the types of law, and how they are applied in the American system of justice.

Chapter 2 provides a history of the development of law and the justice system from colonial times into the twentieth century.

Chapter 3 examines the practice of law, the development of bar associations and restrictions on the practice of law, and legal education, and the case-method revolution at Harvard University. The chapter also looks at differences between law schools, at the law school curriculum, and at the stratification of the legal profession.

Chapter 4 discusses the history and development of court systems, their policy-making functions, and the variety of ways in which they are organized. A major portion of the chapter examines the appellate courts, particularly the operations of the United States Supreme Court. The chapter ends with a discussion of court administration and reform.

Chapter 5 looks at the key actors, the lawyers: judges, prosecutors, attorneys for plaintiffs, and attorneys for defendants in criminal and civil cases. The role of the trial judge is described, and methods for the selection of judges are compared and contrasted. The office of the prosecutor, including the ways in which it can be organized and their implications, is examined. The discussion of the criminal-defense attorney—private counsel, public defender, court appointed—focuses on the very difficult problems encountered in the practice of criminal law. The chapter is completed by a discussion of attorneys practicing public interest law.

Chapter 6 begins with a review of the due-process guarantees to which every criminal defendant is entitled. The trial process is examined from pretrial activity to the *voir dire* hearing to the judge's charge to the jury. The differences between the indeterminate and various types of determinate sentences are reviewed as a prelude to the presentence report and the sentencing hearing.

Chapter 7 contrasts the civil process with the criminal trial and ends with a review of juvenile justice system and the important Supreme Court decisions that have affected the juvenile court.

Chapter 8 provides an in-depth examination of the method most frequently used to decide criminal and civil cases—negotiation. The chapter ends with a discussion of alternative methods of dispute resolution in both civil and criminal matters.

The author would like to thank the educators who reviewed and critiqued earlier versions of this book, and whose suggestions improved the quality of the final work. A special acknowledgment and thanks is extended to Jon R. Waltz, Northwestern University School of Law, who reviewed the legal materials contained in the book.

Special recognition goes to editor Ronald F. Warncke for his confidence in the author, Kristen Westman and Dorothy Anderson for their attention to production details, and for that most proficient copy editor, Barbara Armentrout.

1

An Introduction
to the Law

In this chapter we will examine the law—its attributes and definition—and the variety of ways in which it can be operationalized. We will move from the concept of natural law to capitalism's need for rational law. This chapter will compare common law and the use of codes, and the American case-law process. We will also distinguish among inquisitional and adversarial systems and mediation and arbitration as a way of introducing the reader to more detailed examinations and comparisons of the law, the courts, and the judicial process.

Law: The Problem of Definition

Although most books on the law do not define the phenomenon—as if the obvious need not be defined—the definition of law can be as complex as its enforcement. The term *law* is believed to be derived from one of two Old Norse terms, *log* or *lag*. The former means to lay down or determine; the latter refers to a team, the concept of binding people together (Aubert 1983). Although central to social functioning, *law* has defied authoritative definition. Wallace Loh (1984: 23) points out that even lawyers and judges have no generally agreed-upon definition of law: "For them it is simply what they practice and what courts do." Jerome Frank (1970: xiii) admits that he "seriously blundered" in offering a definition of the word *law* because "that word drips with ambiguity," and efforts at definition are futile.[1]

Lawrence Friedman (1973) states that law is simply a body of rules governing a social order. But social scientists disagree over the point at which law can be said to exist in a society. Jay Sigler (1968) raises the question, How is *law* to be distinguished from social rules and customs, the norms of a society?

A *norm* indicates societal expectations of what is right—or "normal"—in short, of what ought to be. According to Max Weber (1967: 14), laws are "norms which are directly guaranteed by legal coercion." In other words, conduct that violates a social norm may be impolite or perhaps eccentric and it can cause the violator to be shunned by those who are aware of the norm-violative behavior. Behavior that violates the law, however, draws punishment.[2] Punishment, if it is to be "lawful," must be imposed by persons specifically authorized by society; thus, law represents the rules of conduct backed by the organized force of the community (Abraham 1975). E. Adamson Hoebel (1974: 276) points out that "law is distinguished from mere custom in that it endows certain selected individuals with the privilege-right of applying the sanction of physical coercion."[3] Benjamin Cardozo (1924: 52) adds the necessity of *regular enforcement by courts of law.* Law, he says, "is a principle or rule of conduct so established as to justify a prediction with reasonable certainty that it will be enforced by the courts if its authority is challenged." That norms require a formal mechanism for enforcement admits to the possibility that there may be those who do not, or will not, support them in all instances.

In sum, law appears to have four components:

1. norms,
2. regularly enforced by coercion,
3. by persons authorized by society,
4. as stipulated by courts of law.

Some laws compel conduct while others serve to facilitate voluntary actions by providing guidelines for them. Wallace Loh observes:

> It is useful to think of law as comprising a set of authoritative and prescriptive rules for conduct. Some rules instruct persons in what they must or must not do (for example, "pay your taxes"; "do not segregate public school pupils on the basis of race"); others tell people how to do what they wish to do so that their actions are legally enforceable, that is, backed by the power of the state (for example, "this is how to make a valid contract"; "follow these steps in setting up a partnership"). (1984: 24)

Natural Law

When Moses stood on Mount Sinai and received a code of law, its origins were clear to all who accepted its mandates. Even so, the Bible relates that Moses and the divine code of law he attempted to enforce encountered stiff opposition on a number of occasions. Thus it is easy to understand how law from less lofty origins can be ignored, opposed, and violated.

In the code revealed to Moses on Sinai—for example, thou shalt not steal, thou shalt not murder—we can find elements that more contemporary observers refer to as natural law. *Natural law*, while not requiring belief in a deity, refers to a higher law or law of nature—in other words, rules for living that are binding on all human societies and reflected in such concepts as "natural rights." Edwin Schur (1968: 52) points out: "The theory of natural law is always grounded in the assertion that through reason we can know the nature of man and that this knowledge should be the basis for the social and legal ordering of human existence." However, there is a strain of natural law that stresses the importance of the promptings of conscience. Recurring themes appearing in the natural-law tradition are an appeal to nature and human nature as sources of objective standards for ethics, politics, and law (Sigmund 1971). Roberto Unger (1976: 79) writes of "a higher or natural law distinct from, and superior to, the customs of particular social groups and the commands of earthly sovereigns."

Often seen as a liberalizing force, natural law stresses moral and rational elements in the legal process. The natural law exists whether or not there is a specific enactment by the authority of government and, thus, transcends all formal human constructs; any law contrary to the natural law is based on the coercive force of the state, not the voluntary compliance of the governed. According to the *Commentaries* of William Blackstone, any human law contrary to natural law has no validity. However, stalwarts of natural law often had no difficulty arguing that its protections did not apply to certain "nonpersons"—Indians, blacks, women, children. Until the Civil War, it was not natural law, but property law, that defined the fate of slaves in the United States (*Scott v. Sandford* 1857). Natural law, notes Paul Sigmund (1971: 206), "has been used to defend slavery and freedom; hierarchy and equality; revolution and reaction."

The development of a theory of natural law can be traced from fourth-century Greece, the Stoics and Aristotle, to Roman law. In fourth-century Greece, writes Roberto Unger (1976:76–77),

> men came to realize that societies which could not easily be dismissed as primitive cherished different and even conflicting customs. This shattering discovery provoked a search for universal principles of conduct, based upon human nature, that might underlie the variety of customs and serve as criteria for their assessment. The philosophic doctrines fashioned in the course of the quest for these overarching norms were used by Roman lawyers.

These doctrines were incorporated into a Christian framework by Thomas Aquinas who, in his *Summa Theologica*, argues that law that violates the natural law is not law but a corruption of law (Sigmund 1971). During the Middle Ages the concept of natural law served the interests of the Church in its dealings with the secular powers, and in the hands of the papacy it was an impediment to the growth of nation states (Aubert 1983). The concept of natural law was later used by an emerging middle-class in their efforts to counter the power of the feudal nobility and later the divine right of the monarch: "they hoped to preserve an area of individual freedom and initiative secure from interference by the state," notes Malcolm MacDonald (1961: 4). Natural law necessarily places limits on political power and in England was embodied in the common law.

In the United States the natural-law concepts of John Locke (1632–1704)—by nature men are all free, equal, and independent and, thus, no one can be subjected to the political power of another without his own consent—were incorporated into the Declaration of Independence: "all men are created equal" and "governments are instituted among men, deriving their just powers from the consent of the governed." While Locke referred to the natural-law right of "life, liberty, property,"[4] Thomas Jefferson enumerated the inalienable right to "life, liberty, and the pursuit of happiness." There is, however, an inherent conflict between natural law, which restrains and limits human enactments, and *positive law,* human enactments resulting from the popular consent of individuals who form themselves into a sovereign people. According to Locke, the people may delegate lawmaking to a governmental agency (legislature) which is limited to those ends authorized by the people; natural law, however, limits the ends which the people may authorize. "If legislatures should act beyond or against such ends, even with popular consent, their acts would not be valid. Thus, the laws that must be established by positive human authorities are in turn limited by natural law" (Smith 1985: 68). Natural law stands as a bulwark against totalitarianism, even that brought about by democratic means or the popular will (for example, Fascist Italy and Nazi Germany). The natural law doctrines limiting the power of government prepared the way for the institution of *judicial review* by the Supreme Court (Smith 1985; Sigmund 1971) which will be discussed in Chapter 2.

Rational Law

In contrast to a rational legal order—the application of general norms to specific cases—Weber (1967: 63) describes irrational lawfinding, that is, when decisions are "influenced by concrete factors of the particular case as evaluated upon an ethical, emotional, or political basis rather than by general norms." Irrational lawfinding may prevail when laws have theological origins and are enforced by agents of the prevailing religious order. Weber uses Islamic *kadi* justice as an example of highly particularized law. Decisions are rendered by the religious judge, or *kadi,* without recourse to generalized principles of law but, rather, according to what is morally correct in each case. Decisions are made on a case-by-case basis, and their legitimacy is dependent upon the charisma of the individual judge.[5]

Under such a legal system a modern capitalist economy cannot develop: "For modern rational capitalism has need, not only of the technical means of production, but of a calculable legal system and of administration in terms of formal rules" (Weber 1958: 25). Modern rational capitalism requires a legal order that is both prompt and predictable, one that is calculable in accordance with rational rules and guaranteed by the strongest coercive power. Weber notes that the development of capitalism occurs under rational legal orders wherein contractual obligations will be enforced not only between the primary parties, but also their agents. He says:

> Every rational business organization needs the possibility, for particular cases as well as for general purposes, of acquiring contractual rights and of assuming obligations through agents. Advanced trade, moreover, needs not only the possibility of transferring legal claims but also, and quite particularly, a method by which transfers can be made legally secure and which eliminates the need of constantly testing the title of the transfer. (1967:122)

Without such guarantees, an economy must remain on the primitive level of barter or under control of the state.[6] Thus, for example, a merchant of the medieval period who placed his trust in a contract was in a quandary. There were several kinds of law, and the merchant would be uncertain as to which court had enough power to make the opposite party pay up or deliver the goods (Tigar and Levy 1977).

As opposed to laws and legal systems having divine or "natural" origins, the rational-law systems governing Western nations proceed from five postulates described by Weber (1967):

1. Every legal decision involves the application of an abstract legal proposition to a concrete factual set of circumstances.
2. Every concrete case can be decided on the basis of abstract legal propositions derived by means of legal logic.
3. The law constitutes a gapless system of legal propositions, one that can deal with any and all possible concrete cases. In other words, there are no gaps in the legal system that render certain disputes outside the pale of law.
4. Every social action of human beings is construed as either an application or a carrying out of legal propositions, or as an infringement thereof.
5. Whatever cannot be decided legally in rational terms is legally irrelevant.

In sum: *A system of modern or rational law involves the application of general principles to specific facts (cases).*

Common Law

England's rational system of law is based on judicial lawfinding. Prior to the Norman conquest in 1066, principles applied in local Anglo-Saxon courts broadly reflected the customs of local communities as declared by the freemen of those communities who were the judges. In 1086 William the Conqueror sent commissioners throughout the realm to make a record of the names of towns, number of persons, cattle, and houses as well as the customs and norms of the population. The Norman kings gradually wielded these local customs into a single body of general principles. In applying these principles, judges placed great reliance on previous judgments given similar cases, a procedure that gave rise to the doctrine of judicial precedent. Toward the end of the thirteenth century, arguments of the barristers (lawyers) and the rulings of the judges were written down and circulated. These documents became the forerunners of the published *Law Reports* that are the basis for common law.[7]

"The common law of England evolved from spontaneously observed rules and practices, shaped and formalised by decisions made by judges pronouncing the law in relation to the particular facts before them," notes the British Central Office of Information (1976: 4). *Common law* involved the transformation of community rules into a national legal system. The controlling element is precedent. "When a group of facts come before an English Court of adjudication . . .," observes Henry Maine (n.d.: 24), "it is taken absolutely for granted that there is somewhere a rule of known law which will cover the facts of the dispute now litigated, and that, if such a rule be not discovered, it is only because the necessary patience, knowledge or acumen, is not forthcoming to detect it."

Basic to understanding common law, Edward Re notes, is the notion that a judicial decision serves a dual function:

> First, it settles the controversy, that is, under the doctrine of *res judicata* [final conclusive judgment] the parties may not relitigate the issues that have been decided. Second, in the common law system, under the doctrine of *stare decisis,* the judicial decision also has precedential value. The doctrine, from *stare decisis et non quieta movere,* "stand by the decision and do not disturb what is settled," is rooted in the common law policy that a principle of law deduced from a judicial decision will be considered and applied in the determination of future similar cases. . . . [This doctrine] refers to the likelihood that a similar or like case arising in the future will be decided in the same way. (1975a: 2)

However, the common law was not a "gapless system" capable of resolving *all* concrete cases. Common law remedies were confined almost entirely to money damages, and the procedures became increasingly complex and inflexible. As Charles McLaughlin notes:

> Common law judges are averse to deduction of particular rules from basic princi-
> ples; the process is rather the inductive one of letting the general rule emerge
> from a succession of individual cases. Yet the courts do not respond with notable
> flexibility to social change because of the firmly held principle of binding judicial
> precedent. (1984: 104)

As a result, an alternative system of law—equity—developed alongside common-law courts.[8]

Equity

Equity, from the Latin *aequitas,* meaning equality or justice, was a Greek contribution to Roman law; it referred to a concern for fairness or equality of treatment (McDowell 1982). The Roman concept of equity appears to have influenced English custom where equity developed out of the practice of asking the king to intercede in the name of justice on behalf of a petitioner. In the early days of English common law, litigants were refused a hearing if their suits could not be settled by a narrowly drawn writ or order, so petitioners who argued that they could not find justice in courts of common law often begged the king to follow his conscience rather than cause them to suffer because of the technicalities of common-law procedures. The king typically referred these petitions to his chancellor—a combination executive secretary and chief of staff. In time, petitioners went directly to the chancellor, the keeper of the king's conscience, for relief; from this practice came the chancery courts, or courts of equity.

The chancellor, usually an educated clergyman with a staff of scribes, was in a unique position to provide relief for petitioners who could not gain swift justice in common-law courts, which could proclaim duties and rights but could not compel any kind of action other than the payment of money. Equity, on the other hand, had a plethora of remedies. For example, the injunction could be used to command a person to do some specific act or to refrain from something he might be doing or planning to do. Injunctions were enforced by the chancellor's power to declare something in ''contempt'' and ordering summary imprisonment. Henry Abraham (foreword to McDowell 1982: xii) notes that equity ''begins where law ends; it supplies justice in circumstances not covered by law.'' While the common law provides for money damages, it cannot easily deal with nonmonetary issues such as divorce, administration of estates, civil rights, and labor disputes. Equity, however, had power over persons (*in personam* jurisdiction), not over things (*in rem* jurisdiction). For example, notes Friedman (1973:22), it could not force a transfer of land, although it could jail for contempt the party that refused to make such a transfer.

Because the chancery courts were empowered to settle controversies on the basis of general notions of fairness—equity—their decisions were often contrary to one of the principles of a rational system of law: the application of abstract legal propositions to concrete cases. The outcome of any dispute became difficult to calculate and predict with any certainty. The tensions between common-law courts and chancery courts were relaxed by the end of the seventeenth century as chancery judges also began to use precedent—called *maxims*—in rendering decisions.

In England, for about four hundred years before 1776, either the common-law judges or the lord chancellor handled legal problems as they arose. "Because litigation produced substantial revenue for the judges, which branch got which piece of the fee-generating action depended on which branch got interested in the subject first and had the political muscle to seize jurisdiction" (Neely 1985: 38). While England still has different courts and judges for issues of law and equity, in the United States equity did not develop into a separate system of justice; instead, in most states, judges were empowered to hear cases of law *and* cases of equity. The Constitution "guarantees the right to a jury trial in all cases that would have been tried in law courts at the time of the Revolution, but not in cases that would have been tried in equity courts at that time" (Neely 1985: 38). Since England did not provide for jury trials in cases of equity, in the United States there is no constitutional right to a jury trial in equity cases, although some states, such as Texas and Georgia, provide for such juries. In most states and the federal system the judge makes a determination "in good conscience," often granting a restraining order or injunction to prevent further or future harm to the plaintiff.

Relief granted through equity is considered extraordinary and, thus, used only when there is no satisfactory remedy at law. Some states, however, have a separate chancery division, for example, in Delaware there is a Court of Chancery which has historically provided a speedy and clear resolution for corporate litigation, thus attracting major corporations. Today most major U.S. companies are incorporated in Delaware,[9] which gives the Court of Chancery an importance beyond the borders of the nation's second smallest state.[10] Corporate takeovers and disputes involving management and stockholders are routinely adjudicated by the Delaware Court of Chancery, whose four chancellors (a chief and three associates) are appointed for twelve-year terms (Grunson 1986). Richard Neely points out that in addition to the injunction, equity is often used in stockholders' derivative suits: "A stockholder brings a derivative suit on behalf of the corporation not to redress a wrong done him individually, but to obtain recovery or relief in favor of the corporation for all similar stockholders and to compensate the corporation as a collective entity for some wrong done to it by management" (1985:39–40). Typically, in such actions, a group of stockholders seeks to enjoin the corporate directors from certain actions such as selling off assets. Corporate directors have a fiduciary responsibility to the corporation, and as trustees—

persons obligated to act for the benefit of others—they can be held accountable in equity.

Toward the end of the nineteenth century, the injunction was frequently used to enjoin strikes, a practice that continued until federal legislation favorable to labor unions was enacted during the New Deal era of the 1930s. Since the 1960s the courts have used their equity powers to impose themselves in broad policy areas; for example, they have reorganized the management of mental institutions and welfare agencies, and for several years courts presided over the operation of the Alabama prison system and South Boston High School in order to remedy the violation of constitutional rights. Equity was used by the Supreme Court in the decision of *Brown v. Board of Education* (1954), which marked the beginning of the end of de jure segregation in the United States (McDowell 1982).[11]

Civil Law Codes

While common law and equity are products of English history and tradition, other European nations use civil law (such as France, and Germany) and have comprehensive codes that supersede earlier law—precedent is absent as a legal concept. The roots of civil law (as distinguished from ecclesiastical or canon law) are found in Roman jurisprudence—which "has the longest known history of any set of human institutions" (Maine n.d.: 18)—as interpreted by lawyers in the middle ages. Roman jurisprudence descends from the Twelve Tables—a written code—and thus differs from the English common law, which is descended from an age-old unwritten tradition.

The civil law is a detailed enumeration of rules and regulations, a code that provides the basis for settling all possible disputes. After the Roman Empire became permanently divided, the Emperor Justinian I (483–565) in Constantinople appointed a team of scholars to systematize Roman law. The resulting *corpus juris civilis,* or simply Code of Justinian, was relegated to obscurity with the fall of the Eastern Empire in 1453. Interest in Roman law re-emerged during the Renaissance, but until the French Revolution it was largely in the form of a body of academic text and commentary rather than a set of statutory enactments. The idea of a code was reformulated by Napoleon beginning in 1804,[12] but the Napoleonic Code was never a complete and exclusive body of statutory law (Shapiro 1981). In his egalitarian zeal, Napoleon wanted laws so clear that they could be understood even by peasants with limited education. The civil-law judges were to apply the provisions of the code literally to the cases that came before them.

Civil-law codes are the products of scholars who draft the statutes to be as clear as possible. Accordingly, the function of the judge is to discover the applicable provisions of the code and apply them to the cases under consideration, without discretion (Murphy and Pritchett 1986). Martin Shapiro (1981:26) notes that in practice, however, no civil system is so complete as to make unnecessary judicial discretion: "A code law judge would be almost completely bound by preexisting rules if his code were complete, consistent, specific, produced by a single authoritative legislator, and capable of rapid amendment by that legislator to meet changing circumstances. No code can fully meet these conditions." John Dawson (1961: 26) states that a "purely deductive method in which decisions are explained merely by citing some code provision may seem to be simple, but it disguises the real choices that are inevitably involved." Ray Henson (1960: x) argues that "it would be intellectually, as well as practically, impossible to decide a case without reference to prior decisions, and this is true even of jurisdictions using extensive codes rather than a common law basis."

Harold Berman (1958: 371) points out that differences between English and American law and French and German law with respect to the predictability of the outcome of cases and the degree to which judges exercise discretion in adapting the law to changing conditions "are not significantly attributable to differences in the respective techniques of legal reasoning. They are attributable to differences in the political and social role of the judiciary, differences in constitutional structure, and differences in basic attitudes toward law." Martin Shapiro (1981: 135) argues that differences between common law and civil law are often overdrawn; he observes that while the Continental judge "purports to be drawing a series of definitions, doctrines, and conclusions from the code by logical exegesis, in reality he is acknowledging the body of legal doctrines built up around the bare words of the code by previous cases." While the civil-law judge may avoid citing previous cases, other judges and lawyers are able to discern which prior cases are being followed, and some decisions will contain references to prior cases. Thus, while the importance of *stare decisis* is not given official recognition in civil-code countries, there are hundreds of volumes of published decisions, and Continental lawyers frequently cite them when presenting their arguments in court.[13]

Courts and Judges under Common Law and Civil Law

In the United States judges are typically attorneys who have been active in the political arena. In civil-law countries, judges are civil servants who are educated and trained specifically for the position. Walter Murphy and C. Herman Pritchett (1986: 11) write that "students decide to become judges at the end of their professional training, and, if their grades are high enough, immediately enter into a largely anonymous civil service in which promotion is dependent upon a mixture of seniority and professional skill in interpreting the relevant codes." The opinions that they render are unsigned and there is an absence of dissent.

In the United States judges sit in either trial courts or appellate courts. The trial court is a fact-finding body having original jurisdiction in criminal and civil (meaning noncriminal) matters. The fact-finding responsibilities of a trial court may be carried out by a jury or by a single judge in what is known as a *bench trial.* The trial court has primary responsibility for the enforcement of norms; its decisions respond to the single case at issue. Appellate courts do not use juries (they render decisions on issues of law, not fact), and (except in certain specific cases) they hear cases on appeal only after they have been decided by a trial court. The decisions of an appellate court are typically elaborate documents that outline the issues presented by the litigants and the rationale underlying the court's decision—the *ratio decedendi.* Since these published decisions are available to other judges and lawyers and can be used to buttress issues litigated in other courts, appellate courts serve to make policy decisions, something very rare for trial courts. There are trial courts and appellate courts on the state and federal levels, with the United States Supreme Court being the preeminent appellate court. (The federal and state courts are the subject of chapter 4.)

Continental courts do not use juries in civil cases, but they have become widely used in criminal proceedings. In Continental Europe there is not a clear distinction between trial courts and appellate courts. A single judge using simplified procedures has jurisdiction over minor cases, while a second level of courts hears serious cases and appeals from the lower courts. Judges in these courts sit in panels of three, and their decisions may be appealed to courts at a third level, whose judges sit in panels of between three and seven. These courts may also conduct trials in special circumstances, or when the matter is particularly serious. At the highest level is a single supreme court, whose judges sit in panels of seven or more. The European appellate process allows for consideration of questions of fact *and* law; new evidence can be introduced, and often the appellate tribunal will hold a new trial (trial *de novo*) (Shapiro 1981).

Common Law and Codes in the United States

The American colonies and United States after the Revolution inherited the English system of common law. Americans found, however, that common-law procedural requirements were not only too rigid for their purposes, but there was also an absence of uniform rules for the commencement of a particular action in law or equity. The formal language of the *pleadings* (the formal written statements that constitute the plaintiff's cause of action and the defendant's grounds for defense, or in short, the statements of the litigants' positions outlining the area of dispute) was antiquated and verbose, and an action could be lost for failure to adhere to numerous technical details despite the merits of the case. There was a need for codes of civil and criminal procedure that could simplify and standardize the commencement of legal actions. The establishment of such a code is largely the result of the efforts of David Dudley Field (1805–1894).

The Legacy of David Dudley Field

Field, a prominent attorney who practiced in New York, campaigned vigorously for a uniform code of procedure for both civil and criminal matters. He advocated legislative enactments that would simplify both the substance and the language of pleadings. His efforts were opposed by those who were attached to the common law by education and training and who favored the slow organic growth of the common law as opposed to the swift legislative remedy. Conservative opponents argued that substantive changes in legal development should come from judges—the judicial branch of government—and not from the legislature, which was prone to follow the whims of an electorate that might be bent on radical social and economic reformulations.

Nevertheless, Field's code of civil procedure was enacted in New York in 1848 and served as a prototype for other states in codifying their rules of civil, and later criminal, practice (Feldstein and Presser 1984). The codification movement died down about the time of the Civil War (Gilmore 1977). During the 1890s, however, the American Bar Association set up an affiliate, the National Conference of Commissioners on Uniform State Laws, that worked to codify various aspects of commercial law. These efforts resulted in the Negotiable Instruments Law (NIL) promulgated in 1896 and eventually enacted in all American jurisdictions. The NIL and other commercial codes drafted by the conference were eventually replaced by the Uniform Commercial Code, which is now in force in all jurisdictions except Louisiana. Its major architect was the legal scholar Karl Llewellyn. Morton Horowitz (1977: 265) points out that codification resulted in the merger of law and equity: "it marks the final and complete emasculation of Equity as an independent source of legal standards." It was the rationalization of civil and criminal procedure, a move away from "natural justice" to formalism.

Statutory Law

In addition to its procedural rigidity, common law was criticized as being *ex post facto* (that is, making an action done before the enactment of a law prohibiting that action criminal and punishable as a crime). If it is left to judges to determine what actions are criminal, the individual will often be left without guidance, ignorant of what the law enjoins as a duty or prohibits as a crime (Horowitz 1977). While common law continues to provide certain avenues of civil redress, particularly in state courts (for example, claims of public services being applied unfairly; see Haar 1986) the major sources of law governing the United States are the Constitution (constitutional law), appellate judicial decisions (case law), and legislative enactments (statutory law).

Statutory law is the province of legislative bodies—the Congress of the United States, state legislatures, county boards, municipal councils—that enact statutes. In general, one or more legislators introduce (sponsor) a bill into the house of which they are members. Serious bills (as opposed to those introduced solely to score points with certain constituents and which have no hope of passage) are usually introduced into both houses by a legislator in each body and referred to the appropriate committee (or committees) for consideration. Bills reported out by committee are referred to the entire upper or lower house for consideration. Legislation that passes both houses (in bicameral legislative bodies) is sent to the chief executive—president, governor, county board chairman, or mayor—for his or her signature or veto. The signing of a legislative enactment, or the overriding of a veto, makes the bill a law.

All federal and state statutes and regulations (rules promulgated by administrative agencies pursuant to statutory authority) and all county and municipal ordinances are published in full. Federal statutes, the enactments of Congress, appear in several forms, the most convenient being the compilation authorized by Congress in 1925 and referred to as the *United States Code* (U.S.C.). There is also the *United States Code Annotated* (U.S.C.A.), which includes commentary on judicial decisions relating to the statutes contained in the code. State statutes are first published in volumes called session laws because they are prepared at the end of each legislative session. They are later printed in volumes that are arranged by subject matter and have different names in different states: Statutes, Statutes at Large, Compiled Statutes, Consolidated Statutes, Revised Statutes, Code, or Revised Code.

Statutory law includes both criminal and noncriminal enactments. The criminal or penal law (or code) defines those behaviors that are criminal and prescribes punishment, while civil law is concerned with resolving noncriminal disputes and carrying out government functions—for example, the budget. In all criminal proceedings in the United States, the government is the plaintiff (*United States v. Smith* or the *State of California v. Jones*), while litigation in civil disputes is typically brought by private persons, although government may be a defendant or a plaintiff in a civil action. In some instances a criminal violation can result in damages and a civil action, or the government can bring a civil action against certain defendants in order to seize property that has been secured through the proceeds of criminal behavior.

The criminal law grades crimes in descending order according to their seriousness. For example, the *Illinois Criminal Law and Procedure* classifies all crimes into eight categories: felonies as classes X, 1, 2, 3, 4, and misdemeanors as classes A, B, C. The *New York Penal Law* classifies crimes into seven categories: felonies as classes A, B, C, D, E, and misdemeanors as classes A and B. Both states also have numerous lesser offenses such as violations or infractions of, for example, local (municipal or county) ordinances prohibiting jay walking or littering and traffic-related violations.

Edward Levi (1955) points out that legislative enactments are the result of political compromise, and controversial laws may be deliberately ambiguous to protect legislators voting for them. Legislators tend to avoid controversial issues since they generate negative publicity and may antagonize the media and turn off campaign contributions (Neeley 1981). They often vote for bills about which they know little or nothing—following the party leadership—so bills are often the result of political compromise, not rational lawmaking (Rembar 1980). Furthermore, much, if not most, of a legislator's energy is expended on getting elected and reelected. As a result of these realities, legislation is often ambiguous, confused, or contradictory. The courts are often left with the responsibility of cleaning up the legislative act.

Levi (1955: 5) points out that ambiguity is inevitable in both statutes and constitutions. No statute, he writes, no matter how clearly written and intended, "can be completely unambiguous and applied as intended to a specific case." Because of this ambiguity, the practice of judicial review emerged. The words of a legislative enactment are not always easily applicable to all cases; the courts must interpret legislative intent with respect to each specific case. This may entail a review of the committee reports, debates, or earlier drafts of the final bill (Levi 1955). Richard Posner (1985: 5) points out that the court has access to information denied the legislature—that generated by the parties to disputes: "The legislature passes a rule, thinking it knows what the effects will be, but cannot have a precise understanding of them in advance of the actual application of the rule. The judge has the advantage of seeing the rule in operation, and he can deal with problems of application that the legislature did not foresee."

Administrative and Regulatory Law

Statutory law is rarely self-implementing, and it may create an administrative agency to carry out a particular function—for example, to administer Social Security or unemployment insurance. These agencies are most frequently part of the executive branch, but there are also numerous independent administrative agencies. Both kinds of agencies are the creation of the legislative bodies whose statutes they implement—for example, independent regulatory agencies such as the Federal Communications Commission (FCC), and executive branch agencies such as the Internal Revenue Service (IRS). These agencies make *regulatory law,* and the bureaucrats enforcing these laws are governed by *administrative law.* For example, FCC rules limit the number of commercial broadcasting stations a company may own, and IRS rules determine which groups need and need not pay taxes. As Lief Carter (1983: 37) observes, "The IRS creates tax law, and the FCC makes communications law."

Governments in colonial America, (discussed in chapter 2) often combined the executive, legislative, and judicial functions, a practice that came to an end when our Constitution created a clear delineation of authority; this has become a basic doctrine in American government. Nevertheless, many administrative agencies still enjoy a combination of these powers. For example, Carl Auerbach notes that the federal Environmental Protection Agency (EPA) in the executive branch

> exercises legislative powers when it issues rules and regulations to minimize industrial pollution of the air. These rules and regulations have the force of laws passed by Congress. The EPA exercises executive powers when it monitors and publicizes pollution levels throughout the nation and subsidizes the construction of municipal waste treatment plants. It exercises judicial powers when it determines whether a business firm has violated certain of its antipollution rules and regulations and then imposes penalties for the violation. (1983: 74–75)

Many administrative agencies provide a mechanism for adjudicating disputes arising out of regulatory law, usually in the form of administrative hearings—the equivalent of a trial court. Instead of a judge, however, there is usually a hearing officer empowered to take testimony and either render a decision or make a recommendation to the agency's governing board. The decision of an administrative agency may sometimes be appealed to a specialized tribunal, for example, in tax disputes, to the Tax Court or the Courts of Appeals (discussed in chapter 4). "Congress gave Courts of Appeals special responsibility to review the actions of federal regulatory agencies and to reconcile their conduct with law," notes J. Woodford Howard, Jr. (1981: 6). Courts of Appeal may hear petitions to review or enforce the orders of such agencies as the National Labor Relations Board or the Securities and Exchange Commission.

Case Law and Legal Reasoning

In place of English common law, judicial lawfinding in the United States developed into case law guided by precedent. Case law is embodied in judicial decisions, particularly those of appellate courts where the justices usually provide a written explanation of how the decision was reached. The principle upon which justices decide a case—the *ratio decedendi*—is based on a given set of facts: the evidence presented by the litigants. The decision embodies a principle that will govern this set of facts and other similar ones (Rembar 1980). Thus, a court is bound by its own previous decisions and by those of all higher courts; the role of the judge is to apply existing rules of law to the facts of each case in the deductive method known as *stare decisis*.

Stare decisis operates in two dimensions (Carter 1984), vertical and horizontal. The *vertical dimension* requires judges to honor the rulings of the highest court in any jurisdiction and, of course, those of the United States Supreme Court, while the *horizontal dimension* refers to prior decisions of the same court.

Richard Wasserstrom (1961) states that the use of precedent is justified by four factors:

1. *Predictability.* The doctrine of precedent allows for consistency of application and thus for a degree of certainty—order and uniformity—vital to a rational legal system.
2. *Reliability.* People rely on the fact that courts will follow precedents.
3. *Equality.* Similar cases are treated in a similar fashion.
4. *Efficiency.* If justice is not to be interminable, judges must have a source for the timely resolution of cases.

The law must harmonize and reconcile two ideals: stability and change. Edward Re (1975a: 1) observes that "stability requires a continuity with the past, and is necessary to permit members of a society to conduct their daily affairs with a reasonable degree of certainty as to the legal consequences of their acts. Change implies a variation or alteration of what is fixed and stable. Without change, however, there is no progress." In a discussion of common law, Arthur Hogue (1966: 8–9) notes: "The doctrine of *stare decisis* assumes that court decisions have been reasonable, that what was reasonable in one century may be reasonable in another—even though in the meantime the most revolutionary social and political changes may have occurred. The important word here is *reasonable*."

The system, however, is flexible. If the case at hand is to be governed by a particular precedent, it must be similar enough to the facts of the case that established the principle, and it is up to the judge to determine similarity or difference. If the case is not essentially similar to an earlier case (usually cited by one of the litigants), or the reasons for that earlier decision are not good ones, the court is not bound by the precedent. Thus, judicial interpretation provides flexibility in the system of case law.

Ronald Dworkin (1986: 24–25) distinguishes between two legal doctrines of precedent:

1. The *strict doctrine* "obliges judges to follow the earlier decisions of certain other courts (generally those courts above them but sometimes at the same level in the hierarchy of courts in their jurisdiction), even if they believe those decisions to have been wrong."

2. The *relaxed doctrine* "demands only that a judge give some weight to past decisions on the same issue, that he must follow these unless he thinks them sufficiently wrong to outweigh the initial presumption in their favor."

Dworkin (1986: 26) points out that "differences of opinion about the character of the strict doctrine and the force of the relaxed doctrine explain why some lawsuits are controversial. Different judges in the same case disagree about whether they are obliged to follow some past decision on exactly the question of law they now face."

The basic pattern of legal reasoning in the system of case law is *reasoning from case to case,* that is, reasoning by example. It is a three-step process in which a preposition descriptive of the first case is made into a rule of law and then applied to a next similar situation. The steps are described by Edward Levi (1955: 1) as the following:

1. similarity is seen between cases;
2. the rule of law inherent in the first case is announced;
3. the rule of law is made applicable to the second case.

For example, in 1913 the Supreme Court ruled in *Hoke and Economides v. United States* that the Mann Act, which prohibits the interstate transportation of women "for the purpose of prostitution, or debauchery or for any other immoral purpose," was constitutionally valid since the Court had already upheld the right of Congress to prohibit lottery tickets, diseased cattle, and obscene materials from interstate commerce (Levi 1955).

In order to apply the rule of precedent, the judge must analyze a case and distinguish between holding and dicta. The *holding* of a prior case refers to the rule or principle that was absolutely necessary for the resolution of the factual and legal issues actually litigated and decided. Any other remarks or observations in the decision are *obiter dicta;* dicta, at best, may have persuasive authority, particularly if the judge who authored the dictum has a reputation for legal scholarship (Re 1975a).

Case law is embodied in the published opinions of state and federal appellate courts. State decisions are found in the *National Reporter System,* which is divided into seven regional volumes, such as Atlantic or South Western, and additional volumes for New York and California. Federal appellate decisions are found in a series commissioned by the United States Supreme Court, *United States Reports.* The most important case law decisions, those of the United States Supreme Court, can also be found in other publications such as the *Supreme Court Reporter.* The use of computerized information systems has dramatically enhanced the use of case law.

Judicial and Legal Realism

At about the time of the First World War, a number of national law schools began to revise their curricula in a way that challenged the case (law) method of instruction that had become predominant after being introduced by Christopher

Columbus Langdell at Harvard University in 1870 (see Chapter 3 for a full discussion of the case method and legal education). Instead of using the case method, which focused exclusively on the *ratio decedendi* of appellate court decisions, a number of schools, most notably Yale and Columbia, introduced courses on legislation, comparative law, and the social sciences.

These changes did not merely affect legal education, they had much wider implications. Well-known legal scholars were asserting that deciding cases on the narrow grounds of precedent was both reactionary and illogical. These critics became known as *judicial realists*. Edwin Schur (1968: 43) notes that "they asserted, with varying degrees of emphasis, that judges *make law rather than find it.*" Judicial realists were critical of the proposition that judges are simply engaged in lawfinding, that they merely apply the facts as presented by litigants to known and certain principles of law. Instead, the realists argue, judges exercise considerable discretion in rendering decisions.

Richard Wasserstrom (1961: 17) states that "it is one of the curious features of Anglo-American case law that regardless of the way in which a given decision is actually reached, the judge apparently feels it necessary to make it appear that the decision was dictated by prior rules applied in accordance with the canons of formal logic." Even when a judge decides to overrule a previous case—to disregard precedent—he often finds it necessary to confine the case to its particular facts—to "distinguish away," which is a legal device that allows the judge to ignore precedent without stating that the previous decision was incorrect. The realists state that this is simply an effort to protect the dogma of the infallibility of the courts. The skillful judge will not be bound by the past, but will use precedent to maximize freedom of decision-making (Llewellyn 1951). Thus, states Jerry Frug (1986: 28), judges "need to find a way to impose their own views on the text without thinking of themselves as doing so, and they disguise their role by attributing what they say not to who they are but to what they read."

Oliver Wendell Holmes, (1841–1935), Benjamin N. Cardozo (1870–1938), both justices of the Supreme Court, and Roscoe Pound (1870–1964), a judge and dean of the Harvard Law School, argued that the proposition that judges merely find law was ludicrous; they held that judges choose between competing political, social, and economic values. Law, they argued, cannot be separated from social forces, but instead acts as a controlling and stabilizing force in a changing society. According to the realists, law has to be understood in the context of the social sciences: sociology, political science, economics, and history. (Judicial realism is sometimes referred to as *sociological jurisprudence.*) Judicial realists also hold that judges, in effect, *create* law (Murphy and Pritchett 1986). The judge, as lawyer, is schooled in disregarding precedent that does not support his or her case, while citing in capital letters cases that do (Llewellyn 1951).

The dissent of Justice Holmes in the 1905 case of *Lochner v. New York* provides an example of the realist critique. In *Lochner* five of the nine justices of the Supreme Court held that a New York statute that provided maximum hours for bakers was unconstitutional; they held that it interfered with the baker's right to "liberty of contract"—the baker might want to work more than ten hours a day, sixty hours a week. "Liberty of contract" is not found in the Constitution; it is a judicially created concept. Justice Holmes pointed out, however, that in 1896 the Court had upheld the constitutionality of a similar law for miners in Utah. In a bitter attack, Holmes accused his colleagues of embracing the philosophy of social Darwinist Herbert Spencer.[14] The Constitution, he wrote, "is not intended to embody a particular economic theory, whether of paternalism and the organic relation of the citizen to the State or of laissez-faire."

Judicial realism was extended by the *legal realists,* particularly Karl Llewellyn (1893–1962) and Judge Jerome Frank (1889–1957). They argued that judicial decisions are not controlled by prior rules of jurisprudence, but are simply value-laden choices of the judges. Rather than search for precedent to determine the outcome of a case, Frank (1970) stated that in practice, judges arrive at a decision first, no matter how tentative, and then seek the justification for it. If sufficient justification cannot be found, that decision will be dropped (unless that judge is arbitrary or mad), and the process of seeking a justifiable decision continued. Conclusions, he argued, determine a judge's reasoning. Thus, according to Frank, the stimuli that lead a judge to justify a particular decision are what need to be studied and explained. In addition to variables such as the economic and political background of the judge (items stressed by judicial realists), Frank pointed to individualistic elements: the personality factors that influence a judge's decisions. Jerry Frug notes:

> By attributing the cause of their actions to others, these lawyers and judges establish legal rules without taking responsibility for what they are. They hide—even from themselves—the extent of their own role in choosing what these rules are. And, by presenting themselves as experts, they reinforce the average reader's sense that only a professional can make legal judgments. (1986: 28)

Frank (1970: xxiii) states that personality factors are usually beyond discovery except by the judge's own introspection—*psychoanalytic jurisprudence:* "The conscientious judge will, as far as possible, make himself aware of his biases . . . and by that very self-knowledge, nullify their effect." The legal realists urge a system of law based on the social sciences that is designed to meet the needs of contemporary society.

In an extension of the realists' approach, *critical legal studies* (CLS) became popular during the 1960s, when Americans were struggling with issues of civil rights and the war in Vietnam. Many who took this approach viewed law from a neo-Marxian perspective. They pointed out that laws and their application are not neutral, but represent the interests of a dominant elite to the disadvantage of the less-powerful masses; they challenged the ability of the judicial system to dispense "true justice." (See, for example, Kirchheimer 1961; Wasserstein and Green 1970; Lefcourt 1971; Balbus 1973; Auerbach 1976; Kairys 1982a; the entire issue of the *Stanford Law Review* 36, January 1984; Unger 1986.) For example, in the prevailing pro-business climate of the nineteenth century, judges interpreted *tort law* (which governs cases of personal injury; discussed in chapter 2) in a manner that clearly favored business and industry at the expense of the public (Friedman 1973), while the courts were routinely used to harass and weaken the ability of workers to organize and strike. The courts allowed corporate America to be essentially free from legal liability in the pursuit of profits, while workers were kept under strict legal control (Michalowski 1985).

Appellate court justices, cognizant of the realists' critique, often provide reasons for the policies that underlie the legal rules they fashion and use (Feeley 1984). David Kairys points out, however, that

> *stare decisis* neither leads to nor requires any particular results or rationales in specific cases. A wide variety of precedents and a still wider variety of interpretations and distinctions are available from which to pick and choose. Social and political judgments about the substance, parties, and context of the case guide such choices, even when they are not the explicit or conscious basis of decision. (1982b:14)

Harold Berman places the arguments of those who stress the importance of precedent and the judicial/legal realists in perspective (edited):

> Not only is *stare decisis* not absolute but it also has no clear meaning. The *ratio decedendi* of a case is never certain. Moreover, the doctrine of precedent has different values in different fields of law. In dealing with questions of property law or commercial law a court is reluctant to overturn the holdings of previous cases since the community relies upon the stability of court decisions in making property or business transactions. In dealing with questions of tort law, on the other hand, courts have less reason to be reluctant to overrule precedent or to "distinguish away" past cases; presumably if a driver of a car proceeds carelessly through an intersection when another careless driver is approaching from the opposite direction, he does not do so in reliance on a rule that the contributory negligence of the other driver will bar the latter's recovery. Nevertheless, predictability of judicial decision is a factor to be considered in tort cases as in any other, if only for the reason that the lawyers for the parties rely on past decisions in bringing suit or in defending. (1958: 373; edited by the author)

Inquisitorial and Adversarial Legal Systems

Common law, case law, and legal codes can be operationalized in several ways. The term *inquisitorial* (or inquisitional) *system* carries negative connotations of the papal ecclesiastical courts established in 1233 and the notorious courts of the Spanish Inquisition established in 1478, which often resorted to torture to compel cooperation in their investigation of heresy. However, the inquisitorial system is actually a judicial procedure in which the judge is at the center of the fact-gathering process. This system is used on the European continent in civil law countries. The parties must provide all relevant evidence to the court, and the judges, not the attorneys for the plaintiff or defendant, call and actively examine witnesses, although the attorneys may suggest questions to the judges. Nancy Goldberg and Marshall Hartman describe the inquisitorial system:

> Under this system, the parties must inform the court of all relevant facts as well as available proof. Subsequently, the court calls the witnesses, and experts examine them regarding the evidence. The European trial is considered more like an investigation than competition between two opposing sides. Underlying the theory of this system is faith in the fairness and good will of the judges. (1983: 69)

Continental legal systems are staffed by professional bureaucrats who typically employ lower-ranking judges to gather and prepare the evidence in written form and to present it to judges of higher rank. As the case proceeds, there are continuing written additions to the file. Martin Shapiro (1981: 149) notes that "the parties have many opportunities to enter new evidence and argument and to respond to written pleadings filed by the other side." Finally, the entire process ends in what appears to the unknowing observer to be a "trial," but it is simply the time when the court finally decides the case that has been developed by the opposing attorneys and lower judges during the preliminary proceedings.

The *adversarial system,* that used in Anglo-Saxon countries, developed out of trial by combat. Each side is represented by an attorney, its advocate, while the judge is neutral, a referee who enforces the rules of "combat." In trial courts, a jury of citizenry, of one's peers, determines issues of fact: guilt or innocence, or blame in civil cases. In appellate courts, however, the justices typically directly question the attorneys in a process that resembles an inquisitorial system.

Martin Mayer points out that

> under an adversary system of law the lawyer is not supposed to see the resolution of these disputes as a question of what might be best for the society as a whole. He is an advocate; his function is to see the possible resolution of a controversy in terms of his client's best interests (though he is not obliged to accept his client's view of what these best interests might be). (1967: 82)

There are, however, systems of law whose goal is the resolution of disputes in terms of what might be best for the society as a whole, or at least what is best for the disputants: mediation and arbitration.

Mediation and Arbitration

The goal of both inquisitorial and adversarial systems is the determination of "truth" so that blame or guilt can be assigned. The outcome clearly favors one or the other side of the dispute—a zero-sum outcome. Mediation and arbitration, on the other hand, have as their goal reconciliation between the disputants. In mediation the disputants assign a neutral party, who, after hearing from both sides, recommends a settlement. Arbitration is a similar process, but the decision of the arbitrator is binding on the parties. Mediation and arbitration are legal forms frequently found in more primitive (e.g., tribal) societies or less developed countries (see, for example, Gluckman, 1955; Elias 1956). In contemporary America, however, mediation and arbitration have gained support as alternatives to the traditional adversarial systems; their use will be discussed in chapter 8.

Now that we have looked at the attributes and definition of the law, we can move to chapter 2 and review its historical development and its implementation.

Notes

1. For a full discussion of the elements that comprise "law," see Hart 1961.
2. William Evan (1962: 176) notes that there is an "increasing tendency for the norms of private legal systems to be judicially recognized, as for example, in a medical malpractice suit in which the code of ethics of the American Medical Association is invoked; in a suit involving the internal relations of a trade union in which the union's constitutional provisions are accorded legal status by the court; or in a suit by a student against a college or university in which the institution's disciplinary rules are judicially recognized." The once private nominating practices of political parties are now rigidly governed by (public) law.
3. Edwin Schur (1968: 75) finds this definition problematic because it fails to distinguish between law and government: "Not only does this seeming indistinguishability make their separation for analytical purposes impossible, but also it renders the notion of a government *subject* to law meaningless."
4. The protection of property was a primary concern of John Locke, and it obviously influenced the Constitutional Convention, see Beard 1913.
5. For a different rendition of *kadi* justice, see Shapiro 1981, chapter 5.
6. John T. Noonan, Jr. (1976) states that a modern legal system in America made bearable the institution of slavery. The legal process depersonalized participants to such an extraordinary degree, that it was possible to deal with slaves using legal principles and processes that applied to the sale, transfer, and inheritance of property.
7. Arthur Hogue (1966: 7) notes: "If the modern layman is bewildered by the language of the legal profession, he can blame William the Conqueror for his confusion, for the Norman Conquest made French the language of the royal household and the language of the royal courts. Anglo-French, or 'law French,' was used in pleading in the English courts, and the lawyer was forced to learn it as a second language. He had to

learn Latin as well, for Latin was the language employed in the Middle Ages for formal written records. Anglo-French was a dialect from which the English legal profession first developed a precise vocabulary for the expression of legal concepts. Words such as *plaintiff* and *defendant* are of French origin.''

8. For a detailed history of the common law, see Plunkett 1956.

9. Congress has never provided for federal incorporation, and, accordingly, there is a separate, although similar, body of corporation law in each of the fifty states, the District of Columbia, and Puerto Rico (Loss 1961).

10. In 1985 there were 166,000 corporations registered in Delaware that paid the state about $140 million dollars in fees and taxes.

11. Gary McDowell (1982: 4) argues that judicial activism under the guise of equity ignores its history and distorts its purpose: ''The [Supreme] Court, in using its 'historic equitable remedial powers' to impose its politics on society, is often forced to ignore or deny the great tradition of equitable principles and precedents, which had always been viewed as the inherent source of restraint in equitable dispensations.''

12. The *Code Civil des Frances* was proclaimed on March 21, 1804. In 1807 the title was changed to *Code Napole'on,* but the original title was restored in 1816 with the fall of the Napoleonic regime. Napoleon III (1852–1870) restored the reference to Napoleon (Weber 1967).

13. For a full discussion of the differences between common law and civil law systems, see Merryman 1969.

14. Herbert Spencer (1820–1903) was an English philosopher and early sociologist whose ideas were influential in the United States in the latter part of the nineteenth and early twentieth centuries. Building on Darwin's theory of natural selection, Spencer argued that the suffering of the poor was an inevitable price of evolutionary progress: the struggle for existence will end in the survival of the fittest and, accordingly, the elimination of the unfit, i.e., the poor. His social Darwinism provided the wealthy with a justification for not helping the poor (Andreski 1971).

2

A History
of Law and Justice
in America

Law and legal structures reflect the complexity of a society at any given time in its development history. As a society grows larger and the economy expands, relationships become more distant and law and justice become more formal. This relationship between societal complexity and legal formalism has an ancient history; one example can even be found in the Bible (Exodus, chapter 28). When Jethro, the father-in-law of Moses, visited the camp of the Hebrews, he saw that "Moses sat to judge the people; and the people stood about Moses from the morning unto the evening." After the departure from slavery in Egypt, life had grown more complex for the Hebrews; the informal system used by Moses to deal with matters of law was no longer adequate. Jethro advised Moses to establish a formal system of courts and judges, to choose able men "to be rulers of thousands, rulers of hundreds, rulers of fifties, and rulers of tens. And let them judge the people at all seasons; and it shall be, that every great matter they shall bring unto thee, but every small matter they shall judge themselves." Martin Shapiro (1981: 5) notes that as societies become more complex they tend to substitute law and public officials—judges—who can impose a resolution for consensual third-party dispute resolution.

The primitive life of the early American colonists was dominated by issues of survival. As time passed and life became more secure, the economy expanded, agriculture and commerce thrived; important issues were not simply those of survival, but also ones of more complex social and economic relationships. As the population increased, so did the complexity of relationships. The shoemaker no longer dealt directly with the farmer, exchanging shoes for milk, meat, and vegetables. Now the farmer sold these items to a merchant who in turn sold them to the shoemaker. But what if there were defects or spoiled goods? Who was liable: the original producer, the merchant, or was the ultimate buyer without recourse? The Puritans of New England could simply consult the Bible for guidance in matters of law and justice. But as Boston became a great seaport and commercial center, the greater complexity of society demanded greater rationality than that offered by the Bible.

The Law in Colonial America

British colonialization in America began in 1607 (during the reign of James I), a time when common law was quite formal and strict—equity and the Court of Chancery were still in a developmental stage. As Roscoe Pound (1953) notes, the common law of that period was heavily laced with Latin and French legal jargon developed in the Middle Ages and unfit for a wilderness society that stressed individualism. The original colonies were corporations chartered by the king, and their legislative powers were limited to making bylaws and ordinances. Colonial charters required legislation to conform to the common law, and those deemed contrary could be reversed by an appeal to the Privy Council in England. Furthermore, royal governors often interfered with the decisions of the colonial courts, much as the Crown had done in England when judges ruled against its wishes or interests. "There could be little legal development under such a system," notes Pound (1953: 134).

While colonial law was clearly subordinate to English law, it was not clear which acts of Parliament and which court decisions were binding on the colonists. While each group of settlers brought with them an English legal heritage, each colony was founded at a different time (there was one hundred years between the founding of Massachusetts and Georgia), and they differed in economic and political development. Moreover, not only did each colony differ from the others, but within each there was a commercial center, a seacoast, and a hinterland. Richard Morris (1964: 20) points out that "the rugged independence which was born of the frontier brought about the scrapping of important common-law practices incompatible with life in the new agrarian communities." Indeed, on the frontier, colonists were free of English supervision and tended to disregard the authority of the common law.

Dramatically different conditions in England and the colonies resulted in differing needs and, thus, laws. For example, land was scarce in England, where it was a symbol of power and social status; it was bound up in centuries of land law handed down from feudal times. In colonial America, however, there was a shortage of people, not land. Land was important, but there were numerous landowners (Friedman 1973). Bradley Chapin (1983: 9) notes that the labor supply influenced the law: "As a matter of policy it must have seemed that no great harm was done if the hangman thinned the horde of vagrant Englishmen. In the colonies, the need for labor urged the use of penalties that might bring redemption." Consequently, the use of capital punishment was severely restricted in the colonies. "Although the colonial law of crimes against persons remained basically English law," Chapin observes, "the colonial law of crimes against property was largely indigenous," and it virtually abolished the death penalty for crimes against property, replacing it with branding, whipping, terms in the house of correction, and restitution. There were, however, several notable and historical exceptions: the banning and hanging of Quakers by Puritans in the Massachusetts Bay Colony and the subsequent witchcraft trials and executions. The Quakers of Pennsylvania eliminated capital punishment for all crimes except murder; however, blacks convicted of burglary, buggery (sodomy), or rape could still be executed (Walker 1980). In New Amsterdam the system of law resembled that of Holland, while the Puritans of New England and the Quakers of Pennsylvania sought to establish a society based on the Bible, and there was also a French influence.

"The Dutch and French influence in different colonies gradually disappeared," Samuel Walker (1980: 12) notes, "and other variations between colonies also diminished. By the time of the American Revolution, religious influence had declined noticeably" even in Massachusetts and Pennsylvania. A distinctly American approach to law and justice had emerged, based mainly on the Anglo-Saxon legal heritage as modified by the colonial experience. As colonial conditions stabilized, commerce flourished and economic growth required an increasingly commercial America to turn toward economically advanced countries for guidance in law; the only country that could provide a supply of law without the need for translation was England.

The Courts in Colonial America

Colonial courts originally assumed a wide range of responsibilities. They generally served as the legislative, executive, and judicial branches of county government, a reflection of the highly unspecialized nature of government agencies during this time (Walker 1980). For example, judges of the Superior Court of Massachusetts decided the validity of tax assessments and entertained damage suits against sheriffs, jailers, and customs officials (White 1976); and the governor of colonial Maryland and his council sat as a chancery court (Katz 1971). With significant economic and population growth, court structures moved from the simple to the more complex, from the undifferentiated to the hierarchical. Executive, legislative, and judicial powers that had heretofore not been clearly differentiated—for example, legislatures heard appeals—became more distinct. English legal models, terms, and customs became more important and more frequently used (Friedman 1973). At the same time, however, the courts were increasingly seen as tools of the Crown and mistrusted by the common people, while legislatures supported popular sentiment against the king (Chroust 1965).

In the seventeenth century there was absence of chancery courts in most colonies: Stanley Katz (1971: 262) believes that this may have been the result of the inventiveness and flexibility of common-law courts: "With the eighteenth century, however, we reach the era of more sophisticated adoption of the common law and the emergence of a distinctive colonial equity law." Some colonies established separate courts of equity, while in others equity was merged with courts of common law; in some colonies equity powers were the province of the legislatures.

While common law in England was typically used by persons of power—nobility, commercial classes, and wealthy clergy—colonial law was substantially codified law, a response to frontier conditions. As Lawrence Friedman (1973) notes, a newly settled colony cannot wait until a body of common law evolves before disputes are settled. Codes, on the other hand, can be reduced to knowable text in a single book or a short series of volumes. Common law is complex and unwieldy, while codes can be moved from one colony to another, and adopted, and until the eighteenth century some codes were borrowed in toto.

The works of Sir William Blackstone (1723–1780) were widely cited in pre-Revolutionary American courts. While law books were quite scarce, Blackstone's four-volume work, based on his lectures at Oxford, *Commentaries on the Laws of England* (1765–1769), was generally available. This most influential writer on the common law undertook to demonstrate that England's legal system was not simply a confusion of rules, justified only by their age. Blackstone organized the English common law into four areas: (1) the rights of persons, (2) the rights of property, (3) private wrongs (torts), and (4) public wrongs (criminal law). He provided the rules governing each legal topic and the logic behind them in an effort to gain support for the common law. Arthur Sutherland (1967: 23) observes that "he tried to show that Englishmen had rationally, by trial and error through the centuries, worked out a system of social regulation which produced the greatest satisfaction for themselves, [and] the justest rule for their common existence." Blackstone viewed the principles of common law as being derived from natural law or divine in origin. His work was favored by the conservative Tory party in England and gained the support of colonial lawyers for whom it provided "an up-to-date shortcut to basic English law" (Friedman, 1973: 88). Since there was a paucity of readily available alternatives, the influence of Blackstone was pervasive.

Lawyers in Colonial America

There were no law schools in the colonies, and many lawyers went to England to attend the Inns of Court in London; these were four societies of barristers in charge of legal education and admission to the upper branch of the English legal profession (the lower branch was solicitors). Roscoe Pound (1953) notes that the era of American colonialization, however, was a time when education at the Inns of Court was in decay. Many colonial lawyers learned through apprenticeship, and numerous lawyers combined their practice with being innkeepers, soldiers, merchants, or clergymen (Friedman 1973). Robert Stevens (1971) notes that only in urban areas could the apprenticeship be described as compulsory. The requirements for being admitted to the bar varied from colony to colony, and the traditional English differences between solicitors and barristers, for all practical purposes, did not exist. In some colonies each court admitted attorneys to practice before it, and admission to the higher courts was more difficult than admission to the lower courts. In other colonies admission by one court granted an attorney the right to practice in all courts of the colony. In still others, admission to practice was centralized through the royal governor or an examining body appointed by the court (Pound 1953).

Throughout the colonial era, there was hostility toward lawyers. Some colonists had had negative experiences with lawyers in England, and the poor often viewed lawyers as part of the ruling merchant and propertied class. There was opposition to lawyers from the landed gentry of the South and the clergy of the North, both of whom saw attorneys as competitors for power and influence (Pound 1953). Legislation hostile to the practice of law was enacted in many colonies from the middle of the seventeenth century to the middle of the eighteenth century (Schwartz 1974).

Commerce and increasingly complex social relations, however, increased the need for lawyers, and they began to flourish accordingly, even if many persons known as lawyers had little education or training. Lawrence Friedman (1973:83) states, "If lawyers were an evil, they were, however, a necessary evil."[1] In fact, lawyers were the most prominent members of colonial legislatures and the Continental Congress. Of the fifty-six signers of the Declaration of Independence, twenty-five were lawyers. Being aligned with the merchant and propertied class was obviously not a political handicap.

The Revolution

The Revolutionary War resulted in two bodies of law: the Crown authorized the British Army to seize goods for the war effort, to regulate prices, and to punish traitors, and the Continental Congress, driven out of Philadelphia in 1777, drafted its own legislation (Friedman 1973). The defeat of the British Army brought dramatic changes to the law and judicial process in America. Neither common law nor lawyers were any more popular in post-revolutionary America than they had been in the colonial era. However, the courts, now with patriotic judges, continued to conduct business using the only law they knew—English law, much of it based on common law. While British statutes were put aside, the importance of common law remained. Blackstone was frequently cited in American courts of this era, and popular British manuals of procedure were readily available and used in the United States. There was a brief flirtation with things French after the Revolution, and some even proposed basing the American legal system on that of the French codes. However, most Americans were unable or unwilling to read law books written in foreign tongues, so the British common law prevailed (Schwartz 1974).

Except in Louisiana, the French and Spanish civil law of the West was eventually overwhelmed by the American settler invasion, although some of these traditions were incorporated into the common-law tradition. One of the earliest American innovations was trial by jury, which was absent in Spanish and French legal traditions. A civil code enacted in 1825 in Louisiana was drawn primarily from the Napoleonic Code, and the law of Louisiana is a blend of French, Spanish, and common-law traditions (Friedman 1973). In the original thirteen states on the Atlantic seaboard, there was a continuation of colonial legal institutions and doctrines. As new states were formed, "it was generally provided in their constitutions that the English common law, as it then existed, should form the basis of judicial proceedings" (Berman 1961: 13). Most states added the parts of the common law that they found useful to their own statutes. This meant that each state had a different form of common law.

Without recourse to a standard body of common law, judges and attorneys found themselves without authoritative sources for their arguments and decisions. As Grant Gilmore (1977: 9) points out, "there can hardly be a legal system until the decisions of the courts are regularly published and are available to bench and bar." Thus, he dates the beginnings of American law from the turn of the nineteenth century, because during its first three decades, the publication of legal treatises and decisions rapidly proliferated. At the turn of the century, states began introducing the *reporter system,* which published the decisions of the state courts. By 1821 there were more than 150 volumes of such reports available (Chroust 1965). Decisions of federal courts were also being published, as well as American republications (with added local annotations) of English books and case collections (Gilmore 1977: 23). In 1879 the West Publishing Company established the National Reporting System and an overwhelming number of decisions became readily available to every lawyer; *stare decisis* became a quantitative as well as a qualitative challenge.

Lawyers after the Revolution

Anton-Hermann Chroust (1965) notes that a majority of lawyers appear to have sided with the king and either left America for Canada or England or were forced to retire from practicing law after the Revolution. In some states loyalty oaths were required before an attorney was permitted to practice law. The loyalty test required by the state of New York in 1779 resulted in so many attorneys retiring from practice ''that the bar of the state Supreme Court had almost ceased to exist,'' says Chroust (1965: 10). Many of those who left because of the Revolutionary War were the better-trained lawyers, so the post-revolutionary bar was one of limited ability (Pound 1953). Patrick Henry, for example, was admitted to the practice of law in Virginia at age twenty-four, and ''what law he knew was self-taught'' (Handlin and Handlin 1982: 71); Alexander Hamilton's preparation for the bar consisted of three months of law reading. And most judges were as unfit by training and education as the lawyers who practiced before them (Pound 1953). Despite the low status of the bar, however, lawyers continued to be prominent in American government: thirty-one of the fifty-five members of the Constitutional Convention were lawyers, as were ten of the twenty-nine senators and seventeen of the fifty-six representatives of the first Congress (Schwartz 1974). Lawyers were articulate, active in community affairs, and available to help with the myriad of increasingly complex issues affecting the newly independent United States.

Economic disarray was widespread in the years following the Revolution, and the lawyer was despised in debtor areas as a tool of monied interests. A major part of his practice typically involved legal action against debtors, many of whom were Revolutionary War veterans who had left their farms and businesses unattended to serve in the military. Unable to pay their debts, veterans found their property foreclosed and sold at auction by the sheriff. If this was insufficient to pay off the debt, the debtor was imprisoned (Chroust 1965). In 1786 these conditions resulted in a farmers' rebellion in western Massachusetts, led by Revolutionary War veteran Daniel Shays (Hurst 1950). The newspapers regularly castigated lawyers, and legislation was proposed in a number of states to curtail the practice of law or otherwise open it up to anyone who wished to practice (Chroust 1965).

In spite of the antagonism against lawyers, the profession thrived. Anton-Herman Chroust (1965: 30) notes that ''highly effective in the gradual conquest of public opinion and the common mind was the consistent and clever barrage of self-serving propaganda which lawyers levied in their own behalf.'' The portrait presented to the public was that of the noble lawyer eager to assist those who could not afford his services. Ambitious young men flocked to the practice of law as the dislocation of the Revolution expanded the need for attorneys at a time when the number of attorneys had dwindled. However, ''a large segment of the young American bar was made up of men who had but a sketchy acquaintance with the law and with the standards required of an honorable profession'' (Chroust 1965: 35).

The first American professorship in law was established by Thomas Jefferson at the College of William and Mary in 1779. This led to the establishment of other positions in law at major institutions of higher learning. Robert Stevens

(1971: 415) states that "overall, the efforts by the colleges to develop law as a scholarly study were not a success. Professorships frequently lapsed or remained sinecures. The common law content of courses was normally small, and serious professional training took place at the private law schools." (The history of legal education will be discussed in chapter 3.)

Courts after the Revolution

In post–Revolutionary War America, the concept of a separation of powers was not immediately developed. Under the first constitution, the Articles of Confederation and Perpetual Union, most functions of government were vested in a single-chamber legislature: Congress. Executive and legislative powers were not separated, and there was no national judiciary. State governments also reflected the absence of a clear separation of powers. Legislators and chief executives, often laymen without legal training, served as justices of the states' highest courts. (Friedman 1973). State legislatures began drafting detailed statutes setting out the structure and jurisdiction of the judiciary and the executive branches of government (Hurst 1950), but these were the years of legislative supremacy, and the legislatures frequently intervened in judicial activity reversing decisions and passing special laws to the advantage of certain litigants or defendants (Chroust 1965). State constitutions were viewed as inferior to legislative enactments, and the legislature had supremacy over the courts even when its enactments were contrary to the state constitution.

The state courts were characterized by extreme decentralization, a Balkanization sometimes based on territorial jurisdiction, sometimes on the nature of the case, and sometimes on both. This was caused by the need to bring the courts closer to litigants in an expanding nation where transportation was primitive. Each court played an important political and social role in the life of its community. When court convened in the county seat, it was a major event, often occurring only once a month. Large numbers of people would come into town, where they conducted business, discussed politics, and socialized with one another (Walker 1980). These were the days before radio, motion pictures, and television, and people flocked to the courtrooms to hear the oratory of noted attorneys. Courtroom oratory and successful advocacy gained an attorney a following and clients (Friedman 1973).

Of particular importance in rural America was the justice of the peace (JP) who, in colonial times, had been appointed by the royal governor and served at the county level. Requirements were minimal; legal training was not one of them, but political connections were. The JP was the basis of the states' systems for handling small everyday disputes (Hurst 1950). The JP was empowered to try minor cases, but the more serious ones were reserved for the higher courts, which met infrequently—and as a result, justice suffered. The justice-of-the-peace court was an effort to bring the administration of justice close to a scattered population with a minimum of public expense, so the office was usually operated on a fee-for-service basis.

Following the Revolutionary War, there was a trend throughout the states toward the establishment of a separate appellate branch; at the same time, there was a neglect of the lower courts, which became unwieldy, inefficient, and in many areas tied to corrupt political machines, a link that would remain a problem in many urban areas well into the twentieth century. Over the decades the appellate process improved as specialized courts developed that could review cases without recourse to a *trial de novo*—a retrial in a higher court (Hurst 1950).

From the Revolution until 1832, most states provided for both elected and appointed (by the legislature or governor) judges; in that year Mississippi initiated the popular election of all judges, and in 1846 New York did the same. Within ten years, fifteen of the twenty-nine states that then made up the Union had followed suit, and every state that entered the Union after 1846 stipulated the popular election of all or most of its judges (Hurst 1950). A number of the other states experimented with both electoral and appointment systems, sometimes, as Texas did, going back and forth (Friedman 1973).

Frontier Law and Justice

With the westward expansion, judges in the newly settled territories borrowed from a variety of state sources but primarily from those states with which they were most familiar. In many areas there was little law, justice being decided in a rather crude fashion by persons having rather limited knowledge of law and legal processes, and often acting on their own instincts. Lawyers and judges carried weapons, and duels often settled legal questions. There was a paucity of law books, and lawyers were often not law-school graduates; many had only been law clerks, and others gained their knowledge of the law through experience— and often resorted to tricks or the few technicalities with which they were familiar (Friedman 1973). Court sessions were usually held in makeshift courtrooms by judges who were ignorant of the law; some were even illiterate. Judges were chosen on the basis of personal qualities—Indian fighters were popular—rather than legal knowledge. Justice was dispensed without report to precedent or decorum, so its administration varied widely from court to court. Courts were filled with rowdy, tobacco-chewing participants. "The backwoodsman was intolerant of men who split hairs, drew fine distinctions, or scrupled over methods of reaching the right solution" notes Chroust (1965: 96). Frontier justice, while often primitive, also had some outstanding lawyers who presided over quality justice (Stevens 1971).

Out of these frontier sentiments, writes Richard Maxwell Brown (1969:156), vigilantism and lynch law "arose as a response to a typical American problem: the absence of effective law and order in a frontier region. It was a problem that occurred again and again, beyond the Appalachian Mountains. It stimulated the formation of hundreds of frontier vigilante movements.'' Brown also points out that the extralegal violence that emerged in late nineteenth and early twentieth century America—southern lynch mobs, western vigilantes, and northern and eastern ''white caps''—had the support of many leading members of the legal profession, whose

> conception of law and order in regard to the problem of criminal and disorderly behavior did not stress the method of due *process* of law but the *aim* of crime repression. In the vast majority of their actions these attorneys, jurists, and legal writers were law abiding in deed and thought. But when the disorder of late nineteenth century America confronted their devotion to the strict letter of the law, the latter gave way to their primary desire for order. (Brown 1971: 96)[2]

Lynch law was an extreme manifestation of popular local democracy—government by the people—responding to community sentiments and needs. Lynchings cut through the complexities of procedural law that thwarted ''popular justice'' and avoided the costs of jail and trial (Brown 1971). Lynch law prevented the obviously guilty defendant from escaping justice; it also imposed the ultimate penalty on the innocent, often in collusion with local officials sworn to uphold law and order. The more contemporary problem of police brutality may be seen as a continuation of this tradition.

Policy-Making and the Courts

Throughout the post-Revolutionary eighteenth century, social change was the result of legislative, not judicial, activity. As Morton Horowitz (1977: 1) notes, during this period common-law rules were not regarded as instruments of social change: ''common law was conceived of as a body of essentially fixed doctrine to be applied in order to achieve a fair result between private litigants in individual cases.''

By 1820, however, a new trend became apparent; according to Horowitz, ''the process of common law decision making had taken on many of the qualities of legislation,'' and judges began using the law in instrumental ways, framing general doctrines ''based on a self-conscious consideration of social and economic policies.'' The appellate courts began to generate case law and it was accepted without serious question that the prime responsibility of the appellate court was to declare law, rather than merely decide the case. This often meant creating law where little or none existed. Richard Posner (1985: 4) points out that during much of the nineteenth century ''legislatures concerned themselves mainly with revenue measures and local administration rather than with enacting general rules of conduct.'' He points out that, with some notable exceptions, ''they left the regulation of safety and health, trade and commerce, employment, inheritance, internal security—almost the whole range of social interactions—to be regulated by judge-made law.''

The instrumental use of law to further social and economic policy clearly reflected the growing power of commercial and industrial groups, who, in an expanding capitalist America, forged an alliance with the legal profession to advance their own interests through the transformation of the legal system. Morton Horowitz (1977: 253–54) notes that ''by the middle of the nineteenth century the legal system had been reshaped to the advantage of men of commerce and industry at the expense of farmers, workers, consumers, and other less powerful groups within the society.'' The judicial response to torts provides an example.

Torts

Prior to 1800 torts were a rather insignificant part of the law; the common law contained little on personal-injury issues. The advent of the industrial revolution, however, changed this. Tort law in America depended heavily on the English experience since the industrial revolution had its early impact there. Of particular importance to economic development in the United States were the often mismanaged railroads that devastated livestock, set fires in the surrounding countryside, and injured passengers and damaged freight. Much of the tort law involved railroad injury, and judges limited the liability of the railroads and other important industries such as mining through three common-law doctrines: contributory negligence, assumption of risk, and the fellow-servant rule (Friedman 1973).

Contributory negligence limited the liability of railroads in order to protect their economic basis for expansion. The courts rejected a competing legal doctrine, *absolute liability,* and by using instead the standard of *reasonable care*—that which could be expected of any reasonable man or, in this case, a railroad—developed the concept of contributory negligence. This meant that if the victim could be shown to have been even slightly negligent, he or she could not recover from the defendant.

Assumption of risk was a common-law doctrine that meant some occupations, such as coal mining, entailed danger by their very nature, and thus the victim of a job-related accident was said to have accepted the risk involved by agreeing to work at his or her occupation.

The *fellow-servant rule* prevented an employee from recovering damages from his or her employer as a result of the negligence of a fellow employee. The fellow employee was, of course, legally liable, but was rarely in a position to provide compensation.

There was an additional irony to judicial enactments that protected business and industry: The victim took his or her right to sue for damages to the grave with him or her; an injured victim could sue, but a dead victim's family had no legal remedy. "Insofar as there was any responsibility toward destitute workers and their families, society as a whole through its poor laws, would bear the burden, rather than leaving it to the most productive sector of the economy," notes Lawrence Friedman (1973: 414).

As the Gilded Age of the nineteenth century drew to a close, the power of organized labor began to affect the law. Statutes were enacted that changed the business bias of tort law. Moreover, judges began to alter the doctrines, using, for example, the concept of *comparative negligence* (assessing damages based on a sharing of the blame), and by the end of the century the fellow-servant rule disappeared. By the 1960s a substantial turnaround with respect to personal injury had taken place. It was no longer necessary to prove that the party who caused the injury was negligent, and under the current doctrine of products liability, "an injured person need show only that he was injured and the injury was the result of a defect in a product—the manufacturer's negligence is simply presumed" (Neely 1985: 6).

Toward the end of the nineteenth century, a reaction to the excesses of laissez faire capitalism resulted in federal and state legislation regulating railroads, ships, utilities, banks, and other vital services. The legislation created administrative agencies to set rates and oversee services. "Thus began our modern era of a privately owned capitalist economy," notes Louis Jaffe (1961: 115), an economy "subjected to government regulation at carefully chosen points." The goal was to break up monopolies in order to restore competition, "or where that was not possible, then charges and services were to be controlled in order to assure a fair price and equal treatment to customers."

Well into the twentieth century conservatives continued to express a distrust of the legislative branch, which they feared might be used to promote the redistribution of wealth for egalitarian goals; instead, they placed their faith in a judicial branch that could remain relatively aloof from the political whims of the electorate. To a greater or lesser degree, this was the situation until the years of the Great Depression. In post–World War II America, judge-made law, particularly that of the Supreme Court, furthered new social and economic ends and brought the judicial branch under attack by conservatives, whose faith shifted to the legislative branch.

The Supreme Court

Shortly after its adoption by the thirteen sovereign states, it became obvious that the Articles of Confederation was not a viable basis for governing the United States. States squabbled over interstate trade, the national currency was practically worthless, and there was real fear that European nations would take advantage of the governmental anarchy. As criticism grew, Congress reluctantly called for a convention to meet in Philadelphia in 1787 to revise the Articles of Confederation. Even though the delegates were not authorized to create an entirely new instrument of government, they obviously did. James Madison wrote (*The Federalist* No. 40) that the convention had not exceeded its authority; but even if it had, he argued, it was justified by the need to protect the welfare of the nation. Out of this Constitutional Convention emerged the cornerstone of American government, the separation of powers. A bicameral legislature (House and Senate), and a chief executive (president) was agreed upon after long and often acrimonious debate. The idea of a national judiciary was widely accepted, but the delegates could not agree on the details. While there was general agreement on the need for a Supreme Court, the advocates of states' rights opposed the creation of a system of inferior federal courts—they argued that state courts were sufficient and a single federal appellate court was adequate to protect national rights and promote uniformity of judgments.

In a compromise, the delegates approved of Article III, which states in part, "The judicial power of the United States, shall be vested in one Supreme Court, and in such inferior Courts as the Congress may from time to time ordain and establish." They left it up to the Congress to resolve the issue, which led to the Judiciary Act of 1789 that established a Supreme Court consisting of a chief justice and five associate justices; three circuit courts each made up of two justices of the Supreme Court and a district court judge; and thirteen district courts each presided over by a district judge (Carp and Stidham 1985).

The new Constitution needed to be ratified by nine of the original thirteen states, and the outcome was in doubt. A veritable war of words broke out and the press of the day was submerged with contributions from anonymous citizens writing under a variety of noms de plume (Earle 1937). "Publius"—the pen name chosen for the joint writings of the Federalists Alexander Hamilton, John Jay, and James Madison—wrote a series of eighty-five essays between October 1787 and May 1788 in support of the Constitution; collectively, these essays have become known as *The Federalist Papers*. Although designed primarily to support ratification of the Constitution in New York, *The Federalist Papers* were known throughout the states. Edward Mead Earle (1937) notes that although it is doubtful whether they had much influence in determining ratification, *The Federalist Papers* provide an illuminating discussion of intent and a basis for interpreting the Constitution.

The role of the judiciary was stated clearly in *The Federalist Papers:*

> The courts were designed to be an intermediate body between the people and the legislature, in order, among other things, to keep the latter within the limits assigned to their authority. The interpretation of the law is the proper and peculiar province of the courts. A constitution is, in fact, and must be regarded by the judges, as a fundamental law. It therefore belongs to them to ascertain its meaning, as well as the meaning of any particular act proceeding from the legislative body. (*The Federalist* No. 78: 506)

Publius argued that "limitations of this kind can be preserved in practice no other way than through the medium of courts of justice, whose duty it must be to declare all acts contrary to the manifest tenor of the Constitution void. Without this, all the reservations of particular rights or privileges would amount to nothing" (*The Federalist* No. 78: 505). In his assessment in *Democracy in America,* the Frenchman Alexis de Tocqueville (1956: 76), writing in the 1830s, stated that "the power vested in the American courts of justice, of pronouncing a statute to be unconstitutional, forms one of the most powerful barriers which has ever been devised against tyranny of political assemblies" and it is a methodological expression of the supremacy of natural law.

   The Federalist Papers noted the relative weakness of the judicial branch and its dependency on the executive branch to carry out its decisions:

> The Executive not only dispenses the honors, but holds the sword of the community. The legislature not only commands the purse, but prescribes the rules by which the duties and rights of every citizen are to be regulated. The judiciary, on the contrary, has no influence over either sword or purse; no direction either of the strength or of the wealth of the society; and can take no active resolution whatever. It may truly be said to have neither *force* nor *will,* but merely judgment; and must ultimately depend upon the aid of the executive arm even for the efficacy of its judgments. (*The Federalist* No. 78: 504)

Publius also stressed the need for judicial independence, a principle that has become a cornerstone of the federal courts:

> That inflexible and uniform adherence to the rights of the Constitution, and of individuals, which we perceive to be indispensable in the courts of justice, can certainly not be expected from judges who hold their offices by a temporary commission. Periodical appointments, however regulated, or by whomsoever made, would, in some way or other, be fatal to their necessary independence. (*The Federalist* No. 78: 510)

This warning was heeded, and all federal judges are appointed to lifetime terms.

   The Constitution was ratified by the ninth state, New Hampshire, on June 21, 1788, and the Supreme Court began operations in the Wall Street area of New York City on February 1, 1790. A federal bar began to develop and, when the capital moved, a number of more prominent attorneys settled in Washington to argue cases before the Court (Chroust 1965). The justices appointed by President Washington were all loyal Federalists, three from the South and three from the North (Washington established the traditions of appointing the party faithful and of geographic balance). The chief justice was John Jay of New York, but when he was elected governor of New York, he resigned from the Court, because the judiciary was still the least important branch of government. Several individuals declined appointments to the Court, and one, Robert H. Harrison, refused the appointment even after the Senate had confirmed him—he chose to accept a state position (Carp and Stidham 1985).

The first Supreme Court was weak and ineffective and relegated to an undignified room in the basement beneath the Senate chamber. Only two justices and John Jay were present on opening day. "Required by law to sit twice a year, it began its first term with a crowded courtroom and an empty docket. Appeals from lower tribunals came slowly; for its first three years the Court had almost no business at all," report Mary Ann Harrell and Burnett Anderson (1982: 15). When war raged between England and France, President Washington, hoping to keep America neutral, asked the Court for advice on twenty-nine questions on international law and treaties. In a precedent-setting response, the justices politely declined to provide advisory decisions. For its most important historical decision, *Marbury v. Madison,* only three of the Court's six justices showed up to hear arguments.

Marbury v. Madison

In 1800 the Court moved to a site on the Potomac. In that same year the Federalists were defeated. Chief Justice Oliver Ellsworth became ill and resigned, and Jay refused to serve again. In an effort in 1801 to save the Constitution from the "radical" Democratic Republicans led by Thomas Jefferson, lame-duck President John Adams appointed his secretary of state, the Virginia Federalist and Jefferson's cousin, John Marshall, as chief justice. In his last act before leaving office, President Adams appointed forty-two justices of the peace for the District of Columbia, which the lame-duck Senate quickly confirmed and sent to the president for his signature. In the haste surrounding the appointments, William Marbury's commission was overlooked. In December 1801 he applied to the Supreme Court for a *writ of mandamus* (an extraordinary court order compelling a public official to perform his or her duty), ordering James Madison, the outgoing secretary of state, to give him his commission as justice of the peace. Although the Court agreed to hear the controversial case, Congress enacted a law that stopped it from convening for fourteen months. In 1803 the Court finally heard the case of *Marbury v. Madison.*

Mary Ann Harrell and Burnett Anderson describe the quandary of the Court headed by Marshall:

> If the Court ordered Madison to produce that commission, he could simply ignore the order; President Jefferson would defend him. If the Court denied Marbury's right to his commission, Jefferson could claim a party victory. [Either decision would mean a significant loss of prestige for the Court.]
>
> Marshall found an escape from this dilemma. . . . Point by point he analyzed the case. Did Marbury have a legal right to his commission? Yes. Would a writ of mandamus enforce his right? Yes. Could the Court issue the writ? No.

Congress had said it could, in the Judiciary Act of 1789. It had given the Court original jurisdiction in such cases—power to try them for the first time. But, said Marshall, . . . the Constitution defined the Court's original jurisdiction and Congress could not change it by law. Therefore that section of the law was void. (1982: 25–26)

With this decision, one of the most important in the Court's history, John Marshall established the principle of *judicial review:* the power of the Supreme Court to determine the constitutionality of acts of Congress and actions of the president. Bernard Schwartz (1974: 32–33) states: "Had Marshall not confirmed review power at the outset in his original magisterial manner, it is entirely possible it would never have been insisted upon, for it was not until 1857 that the authority to invalidate a federal statute was next exercised by the Supreme Court."[3] But once the decision was made, the Court also claimed the right of judicial review over state legislation; the Marshall Court (1801–1835) overturned more than a dozen state laws on constitutional grounds (Carp and Stidham 1985).

Marshall also initiated a major change in the way opinions were presented by encouraging collective opinions in place of the usual seriatim (separate) opinions by each justice. He was responsible for the Supreme Court being the only one of our three branches of government that provides a written statement of its reasons whenever it renders a decision (Tribe 1985). G. Edward White (1976: 35) sums up Marshall's contribution: "Appointed to a court that could easily have become and nearly did become a resting place for minor political officials, Marshall gave to succeeding judges a national judiciary able to stand equal alongside the other two branches of the federal government."

State and Federal Courts

While the Supreme Court dominated constitutional issues, it was in the state courts that decisions were made affecting the day-to-day activities of most citizens. From the time of the ratification of the Constitution until the Civil War, the primacy of the state courts was not seriously questioned. The Judiciary Act of 1789 affirmed the primary role of the state courts and narrowly confined the jurisdiction of the federal trial courts. In 1793, however, the Supreme Court ruled in *Chisholm v. Georgia* that a citizen in one state could sue the government of another state in the Supreme Court. Laurence Tribe (1985: 55) notes that states "feared ruinous suits on Revolutionary War debts that they had not paid on Tory property that they had confiscated." As a result, the Eleventh Amendment was ratified in 1795 barring suits in federal court similar to the one sustained in *Chisholm.* In order to protect the independence of state courts—a practice known as *judicial comity*—the Eleventh Amendment provides that "the Judicial Power of the United States shall not be construed to extend to any suit in law or equity, commenced or prosecuted against one of the

United States by Citizens of another State, or by Citizens or Subjects of any Foreign State." It is of historical importance to note that the Bill of Rights—the first ten amendments to the Constitution—were intended to apply only to the federal government (although many states had similar clauses in their constitutions).

Slavery

The Constitution makes no direct mention of slavery, but as the result of a compromise to gain the support of Southern states, the document clearly recognizes that there could be property in people: Article I, Section 2, refers to "free persons" and "three-fifths of all other persons," and Article IV, Section 2, refers to a "person held to service or labor." In the years preceding the Civil War, issues of states' rights and slavery were paramount. In 1857, for the first time since *Marbury v. Madison,* the Court exercised the power of judicial review over a federal statute. In that year the Court decided the case of *Scott v. Sandford.* It involved the case of a black man, Dred Scott, who had filed a suit in a Missouri court in 1846. As a slave he had been taken into a frontier Army post in territory where the Missouri Compromise[4] banned slavery. He was subsequently taken back to Missouri where his master died. Scott, claiming his sojourn on free soil released him from slavery, brought suit, and in 1850 the state court declared him free.

The widow of Scott's master appealed, and the state's highest court ruled that, free on free soil or not, when Scott returned to Missouri he became a slave again. In an effort to make this a test case, Scott's lawyers arranged to have the widow pass title to her brother, John F. Sanford (misspelled in the records) of New York. This provided for the diversity of citizenship—Missouri and New York—necessary for bringing a federal appeal. Claiming Missouri citizenship, Scott sued for his freedom in St. Louis. In 1854 the Circuit Court of Appeals ruled that Scott could not be a citizen because he was a Negro. The case was certified to the Supreme Court that same year. Abolitionist feelings were running quite high; that year Congress passed the Kansas-Nebraska Act (which repealed the Missouri Compromise) opening up areas of the West to slavery, and fighting broke out in what became known as "Bloody Kansas."

In 1856 the Supreme Court heard the case of *Scott v. Sandford,* and early the following year a majority of the justices, each of whom rendered a separate opinion, voted to uphold the decision of the lower court: Scott was to remain a slave. In the language of Justice Peter Vivian Daniel, slaves were "*property*, in the strictest sense of the term." Furthermore, the Court ruled, the Missouri Compromise was unconstitutional; Congress had no right to limit the expansion of slavery. The scene was set for the most devastating war in America's history.

Reconstruction and the Expansion of Federal Authority

Following the Civil War, Southern states enacted the Black Codes, denying to blacks many of the basic rights secured to whites: freedom to move, to contract, to own property, to assemble, and to bear arms (Curtis 1986). The Republican-controlled Congress reacted with passage of the Fourteenth Amendment which was ratified in 1868. It reads in part: "No State shall make or enforce any law which shall abridge the privileges or immunities of citizens of the United States; nor shall any State deprive any person of life, liberty, or property, without due process of law; nor deny to any person within its jurisdiction the equal protection of the laws." Three years later, Congress passed the Civil Rights Law of 1871 providing federal courts with jurisdiction in equity—extraordinary authority to ensure fairness—to remedy state encroachments on individual civil rights. (Equity is examined in chapter 1.)

From the 1833 decision in *Barron v. Baltimore* until the ratification of the Fourteenth Amendment, the Supreme Court held that none of the rights in the Bill of Rights limited the states; and there is continuing controversy over whether or not the Fourteenth Amendment was meant to apply the Bill of Rights to the states. Michael Kent Curtis points out:

> From 1868 to 1925 [the Court] found very few of these liberties protected from state action. Those the states were free to flout (so far as federal limitations were concerned) seemed to include free speech, press, religion, the right to jury trial, freedom from self-incrimination, from infliction of cruel and unusual punishment, and more. State constitutions, with their own bills of rights, were available to protect the individual, but too often proved to be paper barriers. (1986:1)

Slowly, and over a long period of time, the Court began to apply these rights to the states; ironically, they served to protect conservative business interests against legislative enactments as in the *Lochner* case (discussed in chapter 1 and later in this chapter). In addition, Congress enacted legislation expanding the power of the federal judiciary with respect to federal laws in general and civil rights in particular. The Civil Rights Law of 1871 gave federal courts jurisdiction in equity to remedy state encroachments on individual civil rights.

Until 1885, however, the federal courts refused to sustain an action against a state official administering an unconstitutional law on the grounds that the Eleventh Amendment prohibited such suits. Between 1875 and 1885 state governments used this shield and passed unconstitutional legislation to nullify debt obligations, "which profoundly disturbed the conservative elements of the community" (Warren 1966: 942). The Supreme Court, conservatives argued, should be able to compel a state to pay its debts. In 1885, in *Poindexter v. Greenhow,* the Court, says Charles Warren (1966: 943), "made a clear distinction between a suit against a State or a State official to compel it or him to perform an obligation of the State, and a suit against a State official to recover damages for an act performed in carrying out an unconstitutional State law.'' The Court ruled that ''no official could claim an exemption from personal responsibility for acts committed under such an invalid law.''

In an extension of *Poindexter,* the Court ruled in 1909 (*Ex parte Young*) that the Eleventh Amendment does not bar a suit against a state official where a violation of constitutional rights is alleged and that the sovereign immunity enjoyed by state officials is nullified when ''under color of law'' they violate civil rights. These precedents have provided the basis for contemporary federal equity suits against public officials—ironically, suits often criticized by conservatives.

The increase in commerce and industry following the Civil War and fears of state-court parochialism (''home-town decisions'') lent support to increasing the role of the federal judiciary at the expense of state courts. In the immediate postwar years, there were important cases concerning currency laws and disputes between the states and the railroads. In what quickly became a trend, the Court ruled in favor of business and against organized labor. During the nineteenth century, until the time of the Civil War, the criminal conspiracy doctrine was used against unions. This approach was subsequently replaced by the use of equity in the form of an injunction restraining the civil, rather than the criminal, aspects of organized labor (Blumrosen 1962). The unions sought relief from Congress, but in 1908 the Supreme Court declared that Congress had no power with respect to union activities (*Adair v. United States*). It was not until the Great Depression that Congress stripped the federal courts of their power to issue injunctions in labor disputes (Norris-La Guardia Act), and in 1935 the Wagner (National Labor Relations) Act gave explicit protection to the rights of workers to organize and engage in collective bargaining.

Congress voted to impose a federal income tax, but the Court ruled it unconstitutional, resulting in the Sixteenth Amendment, which became part of the Constitution in 1913. In 1883 the Court again upheld the sanctity of property rights when it ruled that Congress, which enacted a statute in 1875 that granted blacks equal access with whites to inns, theaters, and public transportation, did not have the power to outlaw racial discrimination in private accommodations. As a result, eight states enacted legislation requiring railroads to maintain separate facilities for whites and blacks. In 1896, with only one dissenting vote, the Court ruled in *Plessy v. Ferguson* that these laws were reasonable; the doctrine of separate but equal received the blessing of the Supreme Court and remained the controlling decision in race relations until 1954.

The Early Twentieth Century

After the turn of the century, Court rulings supported the efforts of government in dealing with the giant trusts, such as the Rockefeller Standard Oil, which were undermining capitalism by restraining trade. The basic pro-business thrust of the Court continued, however, and in 1905 the *Lochner* case (ten-hour day for bakers) was decided.[5] In 1881 and 1922 the Court ruled that federal laws that prohibited child labor were unconstitutional; the right of young boys to continue working in coal mines and young girls in textile mills was upheld. Grant Gilmore (1977: 63) asks sardonically, ''If a ten-year-old child wants to work twelve hours a day in a textile mill, by what warrant is the legislature empowered to deprive the child's parents of their right to enter into such a contract on his behalf?'' It was not until 1941 that the Court reversed these child labor decisions.

Rogers Smith (1985: 75-76) states that the Court's willingness to support laissez-faire economic rights stemmed from a variety of political, legal, and intellectual influences of the late nineteenth century: ''Common law traditions, the legacy of Adam Smith's economic liberalism, and the social Darwinism of Herbert Spencer and William Graham Sumner were combined into a legal ideology that justified opposition to the extensive reform legislation of the Populist and Progressive eras on higher law grounds,'' which involved ''significant revisions in the natural law theories of the early liberals, but they appealed to those theories to justify their reading of the Constitution as intended to protect economic liberties.''

While the Court continued to provide protection for economic liberties, it had no difficulty in denying other forms of liberty. In a unanimous decision, the Court upheld the conviction of members of the Socialist party who, during World War I, had campaigned against the draft, and it supported convictions in similar anti-free-speech cases tried under the Sedition Act of 1918. The Court, however, began to expand the due process protections of criminal defendants: In cases that involved black sharecroppers, who in 1919, believing they had been cheated, rioted in Arkansas, the Court ruled for the defendants, declaring an obligation to ensure that criminal defendants received a fair trial in state courts. In the famous case of the Scottsboro Boys, the Court ruled that if a criminal defendant lacks an attorney and a fairly chosen jury, he or she cannot be convicted under law (*Powell v. Alabama,* 1932).

The Depression Years

In 1929 the stock market collapsed and the Great Depression quickly ensued. Millions of Americans were unemployed, farmers were forced off their lands, and the economy was in ruins. In 1932, Franklin D. Roosevelt was elected president and enjoyed an overwhelmingly Democrat Congress. With New Deal inspiration, Congress enacted a series of laws designed to provide emergency relief for farmers, coal miners, and the unemployed. The Court ruled these efforts unconstitutional. The depression was not limited to the United States; on its heels Mussolini had come to power in Italy and Hitler in Germany. Radicals of the right and the left were gaining considerable followings in the United States, but the Court's "nine old men," appealing to the principles of natural law, were supporting the status quo. In 1936 Roosevelt was reelected by a landslide, and Democrats won more than 75 percent of the seats in Congress; the Supreme Court, however, remained a bulwark against legislative efforts to respond to the Depression.

The Court was attacked by the judicial/legal realists, "who dismissed notions of natural law limits on governmental policies and methods as 'transcendental nonsense,' " notes Rogers Smith (1985: 78). Generally, the realists argued for a more utilitarian version of judicial lawmaking, although there was some disagreement over limitations that could be placed on government activity by the judiciary. However, it took a dramatic confrontation between the president and the Court to produce an agreement that the rights of property and contract were not absolute.

Court-Packing Plan

Since 1789 Congress had changed the number of justices several times: to seven in 1807, nine in 1837, ten in 1864, and back to nine in 1867. On February 5, 1937, Roosevelt asked Congress for the power to appoint an additional justice whenever a sitting member of the Court reached the age of seventy and did not resign, with the upper limit being fifteen members. In 1937 six justices were over seventy. In a speech before Congress (March 9, 1937), Roosevelt stated:

> I want—as all Americans want—an independent judiciary as proposed by the framers of the Constitution. That means a Supreme Court that will enforce the Constitution as written—that will refuse to amend the Constitution by the arbitrary exercise of judicial power—amendment by judicial say-so. It does not mean a judiciary so independent that it can deny the existence of facts universally recognized. . . .

Roosevelt argued that the Court had usurped the legislative function by "reading into the Constitution words and implications which are not there, and which were never intended to be there."[6] The president promised to appoint justices "who will act as justices and not as legislators."

The reaction to Roosevelt's "Court-packing" plan was overwhelmingly negative; even congressional opponents of the Court did not want to tinker with tradition. On April 12, the Court, in a reversal of a previous position, ruled an important piece of New Deal legislation, the Wagner Labor Relations Act, constitutional; shortly afterwards, a New Deal opponent announced that he was resigning from the Court. Without a change in the total number of justices, the president soon enjoyed a Supreme Court that upheld the constitutionality of his legislation. (By 1939, Roosevelt had appointed four justices to the Supreme Court.)

As war in Europe seemed imminent, the Supreme Court ruled that public school students who refused to salute the flag could be expelled; in 1943, it repudiated this decision. During the Second World War, in a unanimous decision, the Court upheld the internment of Americans of Japanese ancestry—persons with at least one-sixteenth "Japanese blood."

The Civil Rights Revolution

The Supreme Court, as the least democratic of our branches of government, has been able to render unpopular decisions: to support the interests of white people against the "natural rights" of persons of color, or the rights of employers against the interests of children, or the interests of business against the overwhelming wishes of Congress and the president. It can also insist that, no matter how strong the opposition, black persons have *all* of the rights of white persons.

But the Court has no powers of enforcement—Alexander Bickel (1962) refers to the Supreme Court as "the least dangerous branch"; it is totally dependent on the other branches, particularly the executive, to carry out its mandates. The president even appoints the U.S. marshals who are responsible for enforcing orders of the federal courts. This has been a problem on a number of occasions. President Andrew Jackson refused to enforce a decision of the Court that was designed to protect the treaty rights of Native Americans against their violation by the state of Georgia. In a Maryland case, President Lincoln defied the Court's writ of habeas corpus on the eve of the Civil War. Gregory Caldeira notes that:

> The lack of any formal connection to the electorate and its rather demonstrable vulnerability before the president and Congress mean that the United States Supreme Court must depend to an extraordinary extent on the confidence, or at least the acquiescence, of the public. (1986: 1209)

Brown v. Board of Education

Linda Carol Brown, eight years of age, had to cross a railroad yard in Topeka, Kansas, to reach a bus that would take her to a school twenty-one blocks away; there was another school five blocks away from her home, but it admitted only white children. Her father appealed to the federal courts, which, in accord with *stare decisis,* ruled against him; the doctrine of separate but equal had been upheld by the Supreme Court in *Plessy v. Ferguson.* When the case (and three others from Delaware, South Carolina, and Virginia) reached the Supreme Court, a unanimous 1954 decision (*Brown v. Board of Education of Topeka, Kansas*) resulted.

The Court found that equity required the abrogation of school segregation. Without rejecting the precedent of separate but equal established in *Plessy,* the Court, using controversial sociological and psychological evidence, held that "separate educational facilities are inherently unequal." Instead of ordering immediate desegregation of all public schools, however, the Court used the phrase "with all deliberate speed," which served to encourage the South to respond with resistance and delay. In the years that followed, however, the Court summarily invalidated a host of other laws requiring segregation in public facilities and interstate commerce.

While the Court was considering *Brown*, President Dwight D. Eisenhower attempted to influence the outcome by inviting Chief Justice Earl Warren and South Carolina school board counsel John W. Davis, a former president of the American Bar Association, to the White House. According to Warren's recollections (1977: 291–92), the president assured the chief justice that Southerners were not bad people: "All they are concerned about is to see that their sweet little girls are not required to sit in school alongside some big overgrown Negroes." In 1957, Governor Orval Faubus of Arkansas defied a federal district court order based on *Brown* and called out the National Guard to prevent black students from entering Little Rock High School. An angry mob of whites surrounded the school. After several days of indecision, President Eisenhower ordered U.S. Army paratroopers into Little Rock—however reluctantly, the decisions of the Supreme Court would be upheld.

Other Warren Court Decisions

State legislatures had been dominated by rural voters (in the North that meant Republicans) by a practice known as *gerrymandering*. Legislative districts were drawn in such a fashion that less populated rural areas had more legislators than heavily populated urban districts. In 1962 and 1964 the Court initiated a legislative revolution in the United States when it determined in *Baker v. Carr* that legislative and congressional districts had to have populations that are roughly equal—"one man, one vote." Rural domination ceased and Democrats took control of many legislatures in populous states that had heretofore always been Republican.

In 1962 and 1963 the Court ruled that prescribed religious ceremonies in public schools were unconstitutional.

Due Process Decisions

During the 1960s the Court handed down a series of landmark (and highly controversial) due-process decisions. In 1914 the Court (in *Weeks v. United States*) had ruled that evidence obtained in violation of the Fourth Amendment's prohibition against illegal search and seizure was not admissible in federal criminal cases. This decision established the *exclusionary rule*, and in 1961 (in *Mapp v. Ohio*) the Court, citing the Fourteenth Amendment, extended the rule to state criminal cases. The Court recognized that the exclusionary rule would sometimes have the effect, as Supreme Court Justice Benjamin Cardozo had noted generations earlier, of permitting the criminal to go free because the constable has blundered. However, the Court also recognized the potential for a greater evil: unbridled police powers.

In the *Mapp* decision the justices said, "we can no longer permit it [the due-process clause] to be revocable at the whim of any police officer who, in the name of law enforcement chooses to suspend its enjoyment." In 1963 the Court ruled in *Gideon v. Wainwright* that the states must provide counsel for all indigents in felony cases, and in 1966 the Court determined in *Miranda v. Arizona* that prior to any questioning, the police must warn a suspect of the right to remain silent. (Due process in criminal cases is discussed in chapter 6.)

The Burger Court

The chief justice stepped down, and the era of the Warren Court (1953–1969) was over. President Richard Nixon chose in his place Warren Burger (1969–1986). In 1972 the Burger Court found that the capital punishment laws were in violation of the Eighth Amendment's guarantee against "cruel and unusual punishment." The decision in *Furman v. Georgia* stopped executions until 1976, when the Court ruled that statutes imposing capital punishment, if drafted in a certain manner, were constitutional. In 1973 the Court decided (*Roe v. Wade*) that state laws prohibiting abortion unconstitutionally restricted personal liberty and the right to privacy guaranteed by the Fourteenth Amendment. The Court also began trimming some of the decisions of the Warren Court that had provided extensive due-process rights to criminal suspects and prison inmates. (See chapter 6 for further discussion.) Associate Justice William J. Brennan, Jr., recalled (1986) that in 1963 the Warren Court sustained 86 percent of the cases involving constitutional issues, while in 1983, the Burger Court sustained them in only 19 percent of the cases. In 1986 Chief Justice Burger stepped down, and President Reagan appointed Associate Justice William Rehnquist to head the Court.

Strict Constructionism, Equity, and Original Intent

The Supreme Court remains the most controversial of our three branches of government. Much of the controversy involves weighing the principle of equity—"let justice be done"—against the position of the *strict constructionists* who, Laurence Tribe (1985: 42) notes, argue that the justices

must take the Constitution as they find it, and not make things up as they go along. Even if the Justices are appalled by the results this method produces, or believe that the Constitution's literal commands are severely out of step with the times, it

> is not their job to rewrite it. That prerogative belongs to the Congress and the President—and ultimately to the people, who retain the power to *amend* the Constitution. (Emphasis in original)

Words, however, often lack clarity and can be given more than one interpretation. Tribe (1985: 42) states that nearly all of the Constitution's most important phrases—such as "unreasonable searches" and "due process of law"—"are deliberate models of ambiguity."

When there is ambiguity in applying a constitutional provision to specific cases, strict constructionists argue that the justices should utilize the concept of *original intent* (Polin 1986). Ronald Dworkin describes two basic schools of thought:

> One side argues that in spite of the difficulties every effort must be made, with the resources of history and analysis, to discover what the collective intention of the constitutional framers was on disputed matters of interpretation. They believe that dogged historical study will reveal important and relevant original intentions. . . . The other side argues that any effort to discover the original collective intention of the Framers will turn out to be fruitless, or even perverse. It will end in the discovery that there are no, or very few, relevant collective intentions, or perhaps only collective intentions that are indeterminate rather than decisive one way or another, or perhaps intentions so contrary to our present sense of justice that they must in the end be rejected as a guide to the present Constitution. (1985: 38–39)

Attorney General Edwin Meese has stated that it was Ronald Reagan's intention during his presidency to appoint to the federal courts persons who have a traditional approach to the judiciary; that is, persons whose deliberations and decisions will be in accord with what was intended by the framers of the Constitution:

> Where the language of the Constitution is specific, it must be obeyed. Where there is a demonstrable consensus among the framers and ratifiers as to a principle stated or implied by the Constitution, it should be followed. Where there is ambiguity as to the precise meaning or reach of a constitutional provision, it should be interpreted and applied in a manner so as to at least not contradict the test of the Constitution itself. (1986: 38)

Federal appellate judge Irving R. Kaufman (1986) states, however, that there is a paucity of material on which to make a determination of original intent. The minutes of the Constitutional Convention and James Madison's notes of the proceedings (published in 1840) are very cursory, particularly with respect to the role of the judicial branch. In addition, since the Constitution required ratification by the state legislatures, does their intent also need to be considered? In fact, argues Judge Kaufman, many provisions in the Constitution were left deliberately vague; when the framers had a clear intent, they were explicit: "Article II, for example, specifies a minimum Presidential age of

thirty-five years instead of merely requiring 'maturity' or 'adequate age' ''
(Kaufman 1986: 59).

Attorney General Meese (1986) responds by arguing that the period of the
creation of the Constitution was alive with pamphlets, newspapers, and books
on the great issues of the day. Furthermore, he says that ''the disputes and com-
promises of the Constitutional Convention were carefully recorded. The minutes of the Convention are a matter of public record.'' Edward Levi (1955: 41),
a former U.S. attorney general, states that when it comes to a constitution, a
change of mind from time to time is inevitable: ''There can be no authoritative
interpretation of the Constitution. The Constitution in its general provisions
embodies the conflicting ideals of the community.''[7]

A 1986 poll by CBS News and the *New York Times* (Clymer 1986) revealed that the public is closely divided on whether the Supreme Court is doing
a good job. Forty-six percent of those who responded gave the Court a rating of
''excellent'' (7 percent) or ''good'' (39 percent), while 48 percent gave it a
rating of ''fair'' (41 percent) or ''poor'' (7 percent). However, this was an improvement over ratings given in 1973 (37 percent positive, 51 percent negative). Adam Clymer (1986: 11) notes that ''in two key areas, abortion and the
rights of people accused of crime, the public sided with the High Court against
its critics.'' Only one-third of those polled said that the Court was too soft on
people accused of crimes. A modest plurality, 49 to 43 percent, said that they
favored the Court's decisions on abortion. (For an examination of the ebb and
flow of public esteem for the Supreme Court, see Caldeira 1986.)

Now that we have looked at the definitions of law and its history in the
United States, in the next chapter we will look at the history of the legal profession and legal education, and at the practice of law in contemporary America.

Notes

1. Grant Gilmore (1977: 1) notes that ''in most societies at most periods the legal
profession has been heartily disliked by all non-lawyers: a recurrent dream of social
reformers has been the law should be (and can be) simplified and purified in such a way
that the class of lawyers can be done away with. The dream has never withstood the cold
light of waking reality.''

2. The support given to lynching by the law enforcement and legal community,
however, was not simply a phenomenon of the nineteenth century. For a graphic examination of a 1959 case, see Smead (1987).

3. David Currie (1985) states that the Court ruled acts of Congress unconstitutional prior to *Marbury,* but the Court had failed to justify the decisions by invoking the
power of *judicial review.*

4. The Missouri Compromise involved statutes passed by Congress in 1820 and
1821 to deal with the issue of extending slavery. Under the compromise, Maine was

admitted as a free state, Missouri as a slave state, and slavery was banned in much of the Louisiana Purchase.

5. In 1917 *Lochner* was overturned and the constitutionality of the ten-hour law upheld in *Bunting v. Oregon.*

6. Similar sentiments have been voiced by contemporary critics on the right, particularly Attorney General Edwin Meese and President Ronald Reagan.

7. In celebration of the bicentennial year of the Constitutional Convention numerous works have been published lending insight to this ongoing debate. In particular, Kurland and Lerner 1987; Peters 1987; and the republished *Notes of Debates in the Federal Convention of 1787* by James Madison.

3

Legal Education and the Practice of Law

Legal education and the practice of law are closely intertwined with the social, economic, and political changes of American history. In this chapter we will review that history from colonial times to the present state of legal education and the practice of law in the United States.

Legal Education

Only a small number of attorneys in the American colonies were trained in England, and some aspiring American lawyers traveled to England to attend the Inns of Court in London. Most American attorneys, however, including such notables as Thomas Jefferson, Alexander Hamilton, and Abraham Lincoln, gained a legal education through the system of clerkship, serving as an apprentice to an established attorney. The law clerk studied the common law as set down by Sir Edward Coke (1551–1634) and, most importantly, William Blackstone. He read the statutes, copied legal documents, and watched his tutor practice law.

The first law schools evolved out of this system as some attorneys found the teaching of law more rewarding than the practice of law. The earliest law office-school was established in Litchfield, Connecticut, in 1784, although at the time there were also law professorships at a number of universities. The first law professorship was established at William and Mary in 1779 by then-governor Thomas Jefferson, to which he appointed George Wythe, a signer of the Declaration of Independence.[1] Yale, Columbia, the University of Pennsylvania, the University of Maryland, and the University of Virginia all established law professorships by the early part of the nineteenth century. As noted in the last chapter, the early efforts of colleges to establish law as a scholarly study were not a success, and it was not until 1817 that the first university law school was established at Harvard.

Harvard Law School

Isaac Royall, a loyalist, fled to England during the Revolution and died there in 1781. His will bequeathed an endowed chair to Harvard University for a "Professor of Physick and Anatomy" or a professor of law. The school chose the latter. Harvard had a great deal of difficulty securing the lands Royall left to the university, since there was hostility toward even dead loyalists who had fled during the war. In addition, the idea of law as a course of study at an institution of higher learning was not universally accepted. Critics argued that if legal education was to be practical, it would not be academically respectable; on the other hand, if it were to be respectably academic, it would be professionally unprofitable (Sutherland 1967). It was not until 1815 that the Harvard Corporation chose the chief justice of Massachusetts, Isaac Parker, as its first professor of law.

Legal education at Harvard was hardly disciplined scholarship; no readings were assigned and there were no examinations. The school offered the degree of Bachelor of Laws to students who completed the prescribed eighteen months of academic requirements. The degree could be earned by those who had already completed an apprenticeship in the law office of an attorney; a college degree was not necessary to attend law school. Blackstone's *Commentaries* and moot courts were the cornerstone of legal education at Harvard. Professors spent their time preparing cases for argument and classroom questions for their students (Sutherland 1967).

In the early 1820s colleges began to incorporate private law schools that were interested in the prestige of such an affiliation, because in most states only universities were empowered to give degrees. Yale absorbed a local law school in 1824, and in 1829 Harvard reorganized its law offerings and brought in a professor from the Northampton Law School (Stevens 1971). The college in general, and the law school in particular, however, suffered a series of reverses and a declining student population. By the 1830s Harvard was making a comeback, and there was an increasing study of judicial decisions—case law. The school began to attract students from throughout the country. "By 1844, the school had 163 students—a remarkable number for the period," notes Robert Stevens (1971: 418). Declining standards for admission to the bar, however, led to a lowering of standards for admission to the Harvard Law School, and students not qualified for admission to Harvard College were allowed into the law school (Stevens 1971).

Other university law schools were established, and by 1840 there were nine university-affiliated law schools. By 1850 there were fifteen law schools in twelve states (but none in the remaining nineteen). In the years following the Civil War, there was a dramatic growth in formal legal education, "a revival of law teaching in the East (including Columbia, New York University, and the University of Pennsylvania) with the result that, by 1860, there were twenty-one law schools in existence'' (Stevens 1971: 425). By 1870 there were thirty-one law schools (Friedman 1973), and in that year Christopher Columbus Langdell became Dean of the Harvard Law School.

Langdell and the Case Method

Langdell was born in New Hampshire in 1826, attended Exeter and Harvard, but left before finishing his degree requirements. He clerked in a law office for one and a half years, and returned to Harvard where he supported himself as the school librarian. It took him three years, but Langdell finally earned his LLB in 1853. For the next sixteen years he practiced law in New York. A poor trial lawyer, Langdell specialized in research for other attorneys (Sutherland 1967). He was appointed a professor of law at Harvard, and in 1870 was elected dean of the three-member law faculty, a position he held until his resignation in 1895 (Feldstein and Presser 1984).

Admission standards were raised; only those who already showed intellect and possessed a Bachelor of Arts degree, or passed a strenuous entrance examination, could enter the law school. (In 1909 the examination alternative was discontinued.) Langdell required proficiency in French or Latin, although in some cases another language could be substituted. In 1871, the course of study for the LLB was lengthened from eighteen months to two years. In 1872 there were prescribed examinations required at the end of the first year as a condition of admission to the second year of study. In 1899, the curriculum was extended to three years of residence, and examinations had to be passed at the end of each year (Sutherland 1967). As important as these changes were, it was the method of instruction at Harvard that revolutionized the study of law in the United States. Grant Gilmore (1977: 42) refers to Langdell as ''an essentially stupid man'' who early in his life hit on one great idea—the case method—''to which, thereafter, he clung with all the tenacity of genius.''

Langdell introduced the *case method* as the basic pedagogical tool for educating lawyers at Harvard. Textbooks were abandoned in favor of casebooks containing appellate-court decisions. By reading and analyzing the opinions of appellate judges, the law student would learn how to spot similar issues in factually different situations and gain an understanding of judicial thinking. David Margolick reports that Langdell

> argued that the law was a science that could be reduced to a finite number of principles embedded in court decisions. Speculation into jurisprudence [the system of justice] and other, loftier disciplines [sociology, political science, psychology, economics] was banished from Dean Langdell's world. Cases, he maintained, were the lawyers' specimens, and law libraries were for them what

laboratories . . . are to the chemists and physicists, the museum of natural history to the zoologists, the botanical gardens to the botanists. (1983a: 22)

The case method teaches students the skill of legal reasoning through cases
that are carefully selected. According to Langdell, "the vast majority [of
cases] are useless, worse than useless, for any purpose of systematic study"
(Gilmore 1977: 47). In his pioneering casebook on contracts, Langdell relied
almost entirely on sequences of English cases arranged chronologically,
abridged, and organized in a systematic manner in a law casebook. Typically,
the casebook does not explicitly state the basis for the selection and organization of the cases. Instead, guided by questions in the casebook or from the instructor, the student learns how to dissect an appellate decision and analyze its
constituent parts. The student

> learns to relate one case to another, to harmonize the outcomes of seemingly in-
> consistent cases so that they are made to stand together. By taking and putting
> together different cases, the student acquires a way of thinking and working with
> cases that constitutes the fundamentals of legal reasoning, as well as knowledge
> of doctrinal rules presented by these cases. (Loh 1984: 15)

The burden is on the student to make sense of the decisions. "There is no
single correct way of analyzing or synthesizing opinions," says Wallace Loh
(1984: 16). "In the case method of study, it is the process, not the outcome that
counts." Each case has to be read several times to make sure nothing of importance has been missed, and students must come to each class prepared to discuss and analyze a group of actual appellate decisions. The role of the law professor is to goad and stimulate, asking questions in a Socratic method to explore
the facts of the case, to determine the legal principles applied in reaching the
result, and to analyze the method of reasoning used. He or she will often play
the devil's advocate, challenging students to defend their reasoning (*Prelaw
Handbook* 1983).

Absent from Langdell's curriculum was any discussion of statutes, and his
casebooks were devoid of explanatory notes or comments—there was nothing
to aid the student. Classroom lectures bewildered students as every possible
legal principle was extracted from each case. Says Arthur Sutherland:

> Langdell would first ask a man to "state a case"—tell what the facts were, how
> the litigation developed, what point was at issue, what the court had decided, and
> the court's reasoning. Then he would ask whether the student agreed with the
> result, and why; whether the case followed others which the class had read, or
> was inconsistent; whether it could be "distinguished"; and so on." (Sutherland
> 1967: 179)

By the end of Langdell's first year as dean, class attendance had dropped considerably as had student enrollments. In 1872, nearby Boston University

opened a law school for students who were not happy with the innovations at Harvard.

Contrary to the expectations of his critics, however, by 1874 enrollments were increasing as Langdell's case method began to gain adherents. "Gradually," notes Joel Seligman (1978: 41), "the advantage of Langdell's technique became appreciated. By teaching students law from court decisions, an original source, Langdell taught legal reasoning more effectively than did the textbook professors." By 1895, the year he stepped down as dean (he continued to teach until his death in 1905), it was clear that Langdell's reforms had brought a large and able student body to Harvard. Enrollments soared and standards were raised; in 1896 law at Harvard became a graduate education requiring three years of study with vigorous examinations at the end of each year. By 1895 the Harvard Law School had ten professors and over four hundred students; by 1907 there were fourteen professors and more than seven hundred students (Stevens 1971).

Harvard became the model for other university law schools, and the use of the case method spread rapidly; many hired Harvard professors and law graduates to help them convert to the new system of teaching law. By 1908 there were more than thirty law schools using the case method (Seligman 1978). What started as innovation at Harvard led to a revolution that eventually became the norm for legal education in the United States. The other schools even copied the Harvard approach of required courses (adhering to the case method) during the first year of study, with electives for the next two years. In "fifty years one school had, intellectually, socially, and numerically overwhelmed all others" (Stevens 1971: 434–35).

The case method also had economics in its favor, allowing for one professor to educate classes of as many as 150. Langdell "proved to the presidents of universities all over America that they too could make money by opening a law school and hiring just a few people to teach" (Turow, 1978: 122).

The case method resulted in a new profession: law professor. Prior to 1870 it was the practicing lawyer who became the teacher, often on a part-time basis. The case method, however, made stringent demands on time and intellect; part-timers could not devote the time necessary for preparation, and those practitioners with leisure time "lacked the intellectual flexibility to cope with the analytical, inductive process that comprised the core of the case method" (Auerbach 1971: 552). Case-method law professors were frequently recruited right out of school without any practical experience in law. The teachers of law at the major schools came to comprise an influential elite that would affect the legal and political life of the United States.

In spite of the rigors of the case method, it still predominates legal education today. The *1986–88 Columbia University School of Law Bulletin* describes how the case method works in the modern law school:

> The student may be called upon to summarize orally an assigned case, with the teacher then asking the student questions about it or about a hypothetical set of facts similar but not identical to those of the case. The objective is to lead students to think for themselves by bringing out arguments for or against the particular legal rule, and in so doing to get each student to focus upon the facts of the case. (P. 50)

Scott Turow (1978: 61) recorded his frustrations as a contemporary first-year student at Harvard Law School under the Langdell method: "I keep waiting for things to relent somehow. I'm blown out. I've never experienced mental exhaustion like what I felt by the end of each day this week. The ceaseless concentration on books and professors . . . left me absolutely blithering when I got home each evening."

Criticisms of and Challenges to the Case Method

Langdell's career at Harvard coincided with an era of unbridled growth for American capitalism. The wheels of industry were greased with the labor of waves of immigrants—men, women, and children whose welfare was barely a governmental concern. Positivism and social Darwinism were popular among the educated classes, and the theories of Herbert Spencer provided an aura of science to doctrines that were inimical to the interests of the "huddled masses yearning to breathe free." Like biological evolution, case law was a slow evolutionary process that placed brakes on legislatures' statutory interventions into natural legal processes. The preoccupation with judicial decisions and opinions of the past meant that this legal science would be distinctly conservative, and it was bitterly criticized by judicial and legal realists.

The model of education at Harvard was uncritical—it was law devoid of any political or social context. The lawyer qua scientist was to be rigorously educated to serve the interests of clients without regard to political beliefs or issues. But who could afford the price of such talented scientists, who had an undergraduate degree and three years of intensive graduate education? It was apparent that the Harvards of America were preparing lawyers to serve corporate America. Joel Seligman describes the growth of this trend:

> At about the turn of the century, a number of the new corporate partnerships became convinced that Harvard Law School provided the most effective preparation for their type of practice. As a result, Harvard Law graduates initially received higher salaries than graduates of other law schools. In an unashamedly acquisitive age, such a reputation was no small matter. Harvard Law School could brag that it attracted students from every state of the Union. Law schools desirous of preparing their graduates to serve in the best-paying firms were inclined to follow Harvard's lead. (1978: 44)

The judicial and legal realism and sociological jurisprudence of the 1920s and 1930s challenged the case method and its narrowness of focus. Their advocates also questioned the purpose of legal education. A group of legal scholars, particularly those associated with Columbia and Yale, argued for the inclusion of a broad spectrum of courses as part of legal education. There was a clash between those who wanted the law school to be a place of scholarship, and those who insisted on legal education remaining professional, that is, dedicated to the goal of educating and training practitioners. While they were not successful in changing the goals of legal education, the realists killed the idea of law as an exact science: "Legal rules could no longer be assumed to be value-free," and the predictive value of these rules was seriously questioned (Stevens 1971: 480).

The *1985–1986 Yale Law Bulletin* (YLB) notes that in some areas "the appellate opinion as the exclusive source of 'case' material was found to be too limited a vehicle for learning about legal rules, much less about the legal system." The realists sought to make the "science" of law more useful "by infusing it with the social sciences, locating law and legal institutions in the context of the entire social process, with attention not only to courts but also to legislatures, administrators, and the consumers of law—the people" (YLB: 16). An American Bar Association publication on law schools also describes the realists' challenge to the case-method approach:

> The movement infused certain law schools with intellectual excitement. At Yale and Columbia, particularly, inquiring and challenging minds were busy comprehending the function of law and evaluating its effects. The Columbia law faculty, reflecting the pragmatic, technological orientation of this era undertook the Herculean task of reorganizing its entire curriculum along functional lines with the goal of teaching law as an integral part of the social sciences. (1980: 7)

"Since World War II," notes the *Yale Law Bulletin* (1985–86: 16) "there has been a development of casebooks made up of 'cases and materials' where once there were only appellate opinions. There have been efforts to blend sociological and realist views, to move them on to 'policy science,' or to portray law in terms of context and process." In addition there has been an expansion of the law-school curriculum, adding social-science faculty and courses on jurisprudence, legal history, and legal philosophy, although curricula remains slanted toward the needs of business. Criticism of contemporary legal education has centered on the narrowness of focus and the ideological implications of an education that prepares students for corporate practice. A leader in the Critical Legal Studies movement, Duncan Kennedy (1982: 40) of the Harvard Law School, refers to legal education as "ideological training for willing service in the hierarchies of the corporate welfare state." Legal principles, CLS adherents argue, are not neutral,

> but biased in favor of certain economic and social arrangements that are themselves neither inevitable nor just. What's more, the law is not consistent, but radi-

cally indeterminate, capable of producing opposite results in similar cases depending on the outcome the judge desires or the system requires. Finally, the law
is not apolitical, but in fact the instrument and enforcer of a specific political
ideology—the ideology of liberal capitalism. (Menand 1986: 21)

Contemporary Legal Education

Robert Stevens (1971: 505) summarizes the relationship between legal education and the American Bar Association's (ABA) campaign to restrict the
practice of law (discussed later in this chapter):

> It had begun in the 1870's as a requirement for some period of law study followed
> by a bar exam. The second stage was recognition of law school as an alternative
> to apprenticeship. The third stage was the requirement of law school without the
> alternative of office study; and the fourth was recognition only of A.B.A.-
> approved law schools.

As a result of ABA accreditation and the influence of the Association of American Law Schools (AALS), legal education in the United States has become rather
standardized. In fact, the first-year education of law students is rather uniform
across schools, with each student required to take most or all of the following
courses:

1. Civil Procedure
2. Constitutional Law
3. Contracts
4. Criminal Law
5. Property Law
6. Torts
7. Legal Research and Writing

These courses are briefly described in the box "First-Year Courses at the Columbia University School of Law."

Duncan Kennedy offers a critical description of the lessons of today's law
school, where students

> learn to retain large numbers of rules organized into categorical systems (requisites
> for a contract, rules about breach, etc.). They learn "issue spotting," which means
> identifying the ways in which the rules are ambiguous, in conflict, or have a gap
> when applied to particular fact situations. They learn elementary case analysis,
> meaning the art of generating broad holdings for cases so they will apply beyond
> their intuitive scope, and narrow holdings for cases so that they won't apply where
> it at first seemed they would. And they learn a list of balanced, formulaic, pro/con
> policy arguments that lawyers use in arguing that a given rule should apply to a
> situation despite a gap, conflict, or ambiguity, or that a given case should be ex-
> tended or narrowed. These are arguments like "the need for certainty," and "the
> need for flexibility," "the need to promote competition," and "the need to encour-
> age production by letting producers keep the rewards of their labor." (1982: 45)

First-Year Courses at the Columbia University School of Law

Civil Procedure A
Civil procedure as one mode of resolving legal disputes. The conduct of civil litigation: the relationship of procedure to substantive law; remedies; the reach of judicial authority; pleadings and amendments. The purposes and characteristics of procedural rules analyzed in the light of proposed reforms.

Civil Procedure B
A continuation of *Civil Procedure A*. Major emphasis on pretrial discovery, the right to a jury trial and appellate procedure, judgments and former adjudication, and alternatives to courts in resolving disputes. Contemporary problems of judicial administration are considered.

Constitutional Law A
This is the first term of an integrated two-term offering, of at least 6 points, which deals with the constitutional system of the United States in terms of the judicial function in constitutional cases, federalism and the respective powers of the federal and state governments, a separation of powers among the three branches of the federal government, and the limitations imposed upon the powers of both federal and state governments for the protection of individual rights. The emphasis of the first-year portion of the course is on all issues but the last; the second term course (which is taken in the second or third year), in which individual rights are dealt with, is required.

Contracts A
An introduction to the law of contracts: bargained-for exchange and other bases for enforcement, the bargaining process, policing the bargain; and the requirement of a writing. Included are problems relating to consideration and its equivalents, offer and acceptance, and the Statute of Frauds.

Contracts B
A continuation of *Contracts A*. Remedies, interpretation, performance and breach, impossibility and frustration, third-party beneficiaries, and assignment and delegation.

Criminal Law
The exploration of major problems of the criminal law and of its administration, viewed as a device for controlling socially undesirable behavior. Emphasis on the issues that necessarily arise in the formation and application of a satisfactory penal code.

Legal Methods
An introduction to legal institutions and processes; the skills necessary in the professional use of case law and legislation. The sources and forms of Anglo-American law, the analysis and synthesis of judicial precedents, the interpretation of statutes, the coordination of judge-made and statute law, and the uses of legal reasoning.

Legal Method: Tutorial Seminar
Intensive training in the analysis of legal problems and use of legal material, through seminar discussion, written assignments, and personal conferences.

Moot Court
Each student is required to write a brief and argue the case orally.

Property
Property as an institution in the late 20th century, with major stress on the legal devices for allocating and developing land resources. The nature of property; interests created by private arrangement or operation of law, including landlord and tenant, adverse possession, and marital interests; planning and zoning.

Torts
An introduction to the different bases of tort liability and the various functions of tort law. The relationship of tort law to other legal areas. Negligence, strict liability, intentional torts, defamation, and the right of privacy.

The ABA Task Force on Lawyer Competency and the Role of the Law Schools reports that

> The traditional "socratic method" of legal instruction continues to be used in first-year law classes as an extremely effective technique for developing analytical skills, but is less dominant today in the upperclass years. It is supplemented by a diversity of teaching methods that, like the "socratic method," are designed to foster fundamental skills and require students to make use of legal materials in performing lawyer-like functions. (1979: 13)

Second- and third-year courses are often taught in seminar style, rather than the confrontational (between instructor and student) manner of the Socratic method. Seminar courses may only be one-third as large as typical first-year case-method courses.

Besides an ABA-mandated course in Professional Responsibility and usually participation in a moot court and/or clinical experience, there are no additional course requirements common to all law schools. Many have broadened their required course offerings. The University of Virginia requires Agency and Partnership, Family Law, Introduction to International Law, and Law and Economics. Cornell requires Legal Process, and two courses in Practice Training. Harvard requires Problems in Legal Practice and Methods. The University of California at Los Angeles requires Facts, Clients and Lawyers (product-liability and fact investigation). The University of Chicago requires Elements of the Law (legal reasoning, and the relationship between law, social, economic, and political issues). The University of Pennsylvania requires Labor Law and offers the student the choice of one of four courses: American Legal History, Economics of Law, Income Security (welfare, Social Security), or

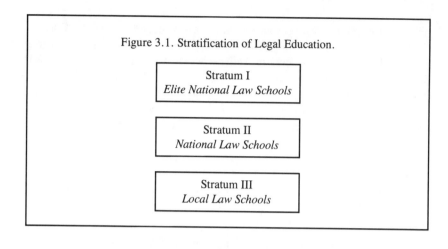

Figure 3.1. Stratification of Legal Education.

Stratum I
Elite National Law Schools

Stratum II
National Law Schools

Stratum III
Local Law Schools

Legal Philosophy. Students at the State University of New York at Buffalo are required to take Federal Income Taxation.

University law schools frequently draw upon faculty from other disciplines—economics, business, sociology, psychology—to present separate courses or to team teach such courses as family law, antitrust law, criminal law. Some observers see this as obeisance to scholarly traditions rather than a genuine liberal-arts commitment on the part of law schools. The stress is clearly on professional training rather than scholarship and is reflected by greater student interest in courses that promote career preparation than in scholarly pursuits.

One important innovation in the direction of scholarship and the broadening of legal education is the joint-degree programs offered at a number of universities. These combine law with a second discipline. For example, Columbia University offers joint-degree programs leading to a JD/MBA (Master of Business Administration), JD/MS-Journalism, JD/MPA (Master of Public Administration), JD/MFA (Master of Fine Arts), JD/MS-Social Work, JD/MS-Urban Planning. A number of universities combine a law degree with a doctorate in these and additional disciplines for a JD/PhD.

The similarity of required courses does not mean that all schools are equal. In fact, there is a great deal of stratification in legal education and it reflects, and is reflected back, by the stratification in the legal profession. Of the 175 accredited law schools, less than twenty are consistently referred to as the most prestigious law schools in the United States. It is largely irrelevant whether these schools actually provide a superior education; what matters is that they are perceived by those who employ law school graduates, particularly national law firms, corporations, and investment banks, as being superior—in this case perception creates its own reality. Most of these schools are private institutions that are part of equally prestigious universities—Chicago, Columbia, Cornell, Duke, Harvard, New York, Northwestern, Stanford, Yale—but state universities are also prominent on any list of elite schools—California at Berkeley, California at Los Angeles, Michigan, Virginia, Texas at San Antonio, and some include the Universities of Illinois, Minnesota, North Carolina, Washington, and Wisconsin. There is a certain amount of homogeneity among elite schools, since their faculty are generally graduates of elite law schools (American Bar Association 1980).

Entry into these institutions requires exceptionally high college grades and scores on the Law School Aptitude Test (LSAT). Harvard, for example, receives about 6,000 applications each year for a class of 550; Yale and Stanford more than 3,000 for about 175 spaces each; Columbia about 5,500 for approximately 300 spaces. Scott Turow reports:

> Because of variations from college to college in academic standards, law schools tend to favor applicants from undergraduate schools whose marks have proved reliable in the past. At law schools like Harvard, that means a continued influx from the Ivy League colleges, with smaller and lesser-known schools at a disadvantage. The sole leveler is the LSAT—the only measure common to all applicants. . . . The test is administered in a session which lasts only four hours, and . . . a grade below the median of 500 makes it difficult to get in at most American law schools. (1978: 28)[2]

At the middle of the stratification system are other law schools that are part of state or private universities, and a number of them are church-affiliated, for example, Notre Dame, St. John's, and Loyola. Top graduates of these institutions, particularly those who have served on the law review, may be found in national law firms. (Law review refers to a student-run journal containing articles by noted legal scholars—professors, jurists, and attorneys—as well as case summaries prepared by the students. Participation in law review is an honor that has traditionally been reserved for the top students.) At the bottom of the stratification system are the law schools that are not part of a larger university, the commuter schools that tend to educate local students for a local practice. Graduates of these schools are overrepresented in the ranks of solo practitioners and local government. There are also law schools that have not been accredited by the ABA but whose graduates can be admitted to the practice of law in a number of states if they pass the bar examination. California, for example, has experienced a growth industry in such schools since it has a very liberal policy with respect to qualifications for taking the bar examination.

Criticism of Today's Legal Education

Legal education in the United States has been subjected to severe criticism. The elite institutions, in particular, have been criticized for turning out narrowly educated technocrats dedicated to the perpetuation of corporate interests at the expense of the urban and rural poor, farmers, consumers, the environment. . . . As David Margolick (1983a: 21) points out: "For many students, law school has become more a conduit to lucrative positions in large law firms than an opportunity to ponder the larger questions about law and justice." The overwhelming preference among top law graduates for such positions represents what Harvard President Derek Bok, himself a lawyer, in a widely reported speech refers to as "a massive diversion of exceptional talent into pursuits that often add little to the growth of the economy, the pursuit of culture or the enhancement of the human spirit." As noted earlier, many law schools are offering courses designed to broaden the education of their students, and there are law clinics through which students receive a more realistic legal experience and sometimes have the opportunity to serve the interests of the poor. However, the bulk of legal education is narrowly focused to meet the needs of business, not the public interest, and the heavy recruitment at the elite schools by national law firms tends to provide reinforcement for the status quo.

Beginning in 1983, law schools began to experience a significant drop in applications and enrollments. Edward Fiske (1986: 1) notes that "legal educators attribute the decline to various causes, including what is perceived as a glut of lawyers as well as growing student interest in fields like computer science and business and a declining image of the profession." (Medical, dental, and veterinary schools have also experienced a decline in applications.)

Bar Associations and the Practice of Law

In colonial times each colony set its own standards for admission to the bar, which usually involved a long period of apprenticeship. In the years following the Revolution and particularly during the era of Jacksonian Democracy (1828–36), lawyers were extremely unpopular. Strong feelings of democracy and concomitant opposition to the monopolization of legal practice led to the demise of standards for entry into legal practice. Roscoe Pound (1953) notes that during the first third of the nineteenth century there was a legislative breaking down of educational and training requirements for admission to the practice of law. In 1800 a definite period of preparation for admission to the bar was prescribed in fourteen of the nineteen states or organized territories that then made up the Union.

By 1840 it was required in only eleven out of thirty jurisdictions. In New Hampshire in 1842, Maine in 1843, Wisconsin in 1849, and Indiana in 1851, any citizen and voter could enter into the practice of law upon no other evidence than that of good character. By the eve of the Civil War, only nine of thirty-nine jurisdictions had standards, and in those states they were usually quite low.

Pound (1953:230) notes that ''good-natured lawyers gave certificates of 'regular and attentive study' liberally to the asker with little or no inquiry,'' thus qualifying the person for admittance to the bar.

Standards remained quite lax in most states during the nineteenth century, and not at all uniform from state to state; government control of all occupations, in fact, remained quite weak. An open-ended bar attracted ambitious, if not talented, persons, and by 1850 there were more than 20,000 lawyers in the United States, about 64,000 in 1878, and more than 100,000 by 1900. In some areas, lawyers formed guilds (bar associations) to restrict the entry of new practitioners by holding down the number of apprenticeships.

While there was a variety of bar associations by the early part of the nineteenth century, these groups were not very effective, and they failed to exert any real control over who was admitted to the practice of law. After 1870, however, bar associations became vigorous in their fight to limit entry into the practice of law, primarily by raising standards. The bar-association movement to limit entry coincided with the appointment of Langdell at Harvard and the rise of the case method in legal education. ''The two movements went hand in glove,'' says Lawrence Friedman (1973: 536). The case method served to define the practice of law as a distinct and scientific discipline that required extensive education and training; there was now justification for a monopoly of practice.

The bar association movement was characteristic of many professions at the turn of the century. Lawyers, like doctors, ''flocked into professional associations whose growth—the number of bar associations jumped from 16 in 1880 to more than 600 by 1916—expressed the impulse for professional cohesion in a fragmented society undergoing rapid change'' (Auerbach 1976: 62–63). In some cities, such as New York, bar associations were a response to rampant judicial corruption. As bar associations became more effective, standards for practice were raised. By 1890 nearly half of the states required some minimum preparation for practice, and subsequently a growing number of states began requiring stringent minimum levels of education as well.

There was some conflict between the bar associations and law schools over the ''diploma privilege.'' Beginning with Virginia in the 1840s, states agreed to admit the graduates of leading law schools to the bar without further examination. By 1870 nine schools in seven states had this privilege. The bar associations were successful in their efforts against the diploma privilege, however, and very slowly statewide boards of examiners became the norm.

Standards for admission to the bar are still regulated by each state and differ accordingly. Most states require candidates to have graduated from an accredited law school, show evidence of ''sound character,'' and pass an examination testing their knowledge of the law and skill in legal reasoning. The typical bar examination consists of twenty to thirty questions requiring the candidate to analyze hypothetical cases and set forth proposed solutions and the applicable laws. The exam usually lasts two or three days. Once admitted, a lawyer may practice only in the state where he or she is a member of the bar, although many states have reciprocal agreements and will admit lawyers from other jurisdictions who have practiced law for a certain number of years.

In 1913, Herbert Harley founded the American Judicature Society as a vehicle for judicial reform, including compulsory membership in bar associations. In labor-management relations, this is referred to as the ''closed shop,'' but Harley chose the more positive-sounding term *integrated bar* (McKean 1963). More than thirty states have an integrated bar, compulsory membership being mandated by the legislature or that state's highest court, and all lawyers must pay dues and subject themselves to its rules or forfeit the right to practice law in that state. Exemplifying the bar association's influence over admission to state bars is the ''Attorney's Oath of Admission'' provided by the American Bar Association (see box).

Attorney's Oath of Admission

I do solemnly swear:

I will support the Constitution of the United States and the Constitution of my State;

I will maintain the respect due to courts of justice and judicial officers;

I will not counsel or maintain any suit or proceeding which shall appear to me to be unjust, nor any defense except such as I believe to be honestly debatable under the law of the land;

I will employ for the purpose of maintaining the causes confided to me such means only as are consistent with truth and honor and will never seek to mislead the judges or jury by any artifice or false statement of fact or law;

I will maintain the confidence and preserve inviolate the secrets of my client, and will accept no compensation in connection with his business except from him or with his knowledge and approval;

I will abstain from all offensive personality, and advance no fact prejudicial to the honor or reputation of a party or witness unless required by the justice of the cause with which I am charged;

I will never reject, from any considerations personal to myself, the cause of the defenseless or oppressed, or delay any man's cause for lucre or malice, so help me God.

Note: The American Bar Association commends this form of oath for adoption by the proper authorities in all the States and Territories.

For most of their history, bar associations typically represented a distinct part of the legal profession—exclusively white, male, mostly Protestant, and devoid of the immigrant class. Around the time of the Great Depression in

1929, this actually led, in some urban areas, to the formation of competing bar associations: those composed of solo practitioners and members of small firms and those whose members represented banks and corporate clients (Glick 1983).

The American Bar Association (ABA)

The idea of a national association of lawyers originated in 1878 at a meeting of the Connecticut Bar Association with a motion to have a committee consider the establishment of an association of American lawyers. The committee of prominent members of the Connecticut bar subsequently reported in favor of the idea, and a circular signed by prominent attorneys from throughout the United States called for a meeting on August 21, 1878, in Saratoga Springs, a vacation spa just north of Albany, New York, famous for its mineral water and gambling. Although the summons for the gathering had been signed by 607 lawyers in forty-one states, territories, and the District of Columbia, only seventy-five persons from twenty-one states and the District of Columbia attended (Carson 1978). The South was well represented—many lawyers apparently saw the meeting as an opportunity to escape the southern heat—and the American Bar Association (ABA) chose as its first president James O. Broadhead, a Virginian who had moved to Missouri, where he sided with the Union. The delegates met during Reconstruction and the scandals of Ulysses S. Grant's second term as president.

Within a year the ABA had 284 members in twenty-one states. From 1878 to 1889 it met annually or every other year in Saratoga Springs and then, until 1902, alternated between Saratoga Springs and other cities. By 1909 the ABA had 3,716 members; by 1924 it had 22,024 members. The increase was due to a reorganization that established state directors and eleven district directors to tie local associations closer to the national. In 1936 the ABA adopted a federalized system of governance, with the ruling body being the House of Delegates, whose membership is selected by state and local bar associations. The ABA is now headquartered in Chicago.

Throughout its history, the ABA commissioned studies on a variety of matters important to the legal profession and recommended reforms on various issues such as uniform state laws, reciprocity for attorneys in one state to practice in others, maritime law, criminal law and procedure, patents and trademarks.

In 1917 the ABA passed a unanimous resolution condemning all attempts "to hinder and embarrass the government" as being pro-German "and in effect giving aid and comfort to the enemy" (quoted in Auerbach 1971: 582). There was also a Committee on American Citizenship established in 1922 "in an earnest effort to stem the tide of radical, and often treasonable, attacks on our Constitution, our laws, our courts, our law-making bodies, our executives and our flag'' (Sunderland 1953: 108). Professionalism was equated with patriotism.

Absent from the ABA agenda was any interest in issues important to working men, women, and children, or segregated blacks in the ''land of the free.'' In 1912 the executive committee of the ABA unknowingly admitted three black lawyers. A past president of the bar association, Moorfield Storey (a white lawyer from Boston, who was also the first president of the National Association for the Advancement of Colored People), protested the rescinding of their membership. A compromise was reached: the three blacks were allowed to maintain their membership, but all future applicants were required to identify themselves by race, and no additional blacks were admitted for the next half century.

In 1916, President Woodrow Wilson nominated a brilliant graduate of the Harvard Law School, an outstanding corporate attorney—but a Jew—to the Supreme Court. The appointment of Louis D. Brandeis was vigorously opposed by Elihu Root, the ABA president, and six former ABA presidents, including Moorfield Storey (Auerbach 1976). In 1916, at an ABA dinner held in his honor, Root expressed his dismay that 15 percent of New York lawyers were foreign born, while an additional third of the lawyers in the metropolitan bar had foreign-born parents. He urged that alien influences be ''expelled by the spirit of American institutions'' (quoted in Auerbach 1971: 572). The ABA's quest for higher standards was often a thinly disguised effort to prevent ''foreign elements'' from pursuing a career in law. These efforts were opposed by the ''foreign elements,'' night-law-school graduates, many of whom became legislators and judges.

In 1900, the ABA's Section on Legal Education organized a meeting of law school delegates in Saratoga Springs. At this meeting the Association of American Law Schools (AALS) was established for ''the improvement of legal education in America, especially in the Law Schools'' (Sunderland 1953: 47). To be eligible for membership in the AALS, law schools had to comply with requirements for admission and length of study (not less than two years prior to 1905, and three years thereafter). Schools that failed to maintain the requirements were dropped from the AALS. There was friction between the teachers of law and the practitioners. ''To generalize,'' says Jerold Auerbach (1971: 570), ''teachers tended to view law as an instrument of social change; practitioners saw it as a means of social control.'' In 1914, after the ABA shifted its annual meeting from August to October, an inconvenient time for teachers, the AALS ceased to have any organizational connection to the ABA. The accreditation of law schools, however, is the responsibility of the Council of the Section on Legal Education and Admissions to the Bar of the ABA, and a few law schools that are not members of AALS are among the more than 170 law schools accredited by the ABA. Accredited law schools require three years of full-time study and the passage of examinations in order to qualify for an LLB or JD (the two degrees are equivalent).

Stratification of the Legal Profession

Before the Civil War the most prominent lawyers made their reputations in courtrooms and often went into politics—they were the great litigators and orators. By the close of the nineteenth century, while most lawyers still went to court, "the Wall Street lawyer, who perhaps never spoke to a judge except socially, made more money and had more prestige than any other lawyer" (Friedman 1973: 549). At the time of the founding of the ABA, according to Gerald Carson (1978: 11–12), the "legal profession was changing rapidly with the railroad lawyer and the businessman-lawyer emerging as the dominant type, keeping step with the emerging interpretation of the due process clause of the Fourteenth Amendment" in support of business (as in the *Lochner* decision, discussed in Chapter 1), "and the needs of the corporate form of organization in the new industrial age." By the turn of the century, the ABA was headed by railroad and corporate attorneys and a pattern of stratification was emerging, a situation strengthened by the advent of the *Craveth system.*

National Law Firms

In 1906, Paul D. Craveth (1861–1940), who graduated at the top of his class at Columbia Law School, became the head of a Wall Street law firm that had been founded in 1819. He recruited associates right out of law school, thus avoiding experienced lawyers who had developed "bad habits"; the ideal candidate was a Phi Beta Kappa and editor of the law review from Harvard, Columbia, or Yale. The Craveth system provided an internship for new recruits that was designed to supplement Ivy League law-school study with a kind of practical postgraduate induction into the world of corporate law and lawyering (Smigel 1964). Long hours and hard work were demanded, and the Craveth lawyer was expected to be wholly devoted and loyal to the clients. Those unable to meet the Craveth standard were not retained.

Each lawyer-intern did general work for several years, usually for a number of the firm's partners, before being placed in an area of specialization. Responsibilities increased with improved competence, and before the tenth year, the question of partnership arose, and a lawyer either became a partner or left for other work. However, Craveth-trained attorneys were in such demand that finding other work was not at all difficult. In fact, as Erwin Smigel (1964) notes, a firm such as Craveth, Swaine and Moore is so well established that it can afford to assist its associates in setting up a practice elsewhere and will

Figure 3.2. Stratification of the Legal Profession.

Stratum I: Elite Law Firms
Wall Street Law Firms
Large National Law Firms

Stratum II: Corporate Attorneys
Fortune 500 Firms
Large Corporations

Stratum III: Lawyers
Solo Practitioners
Small Law Firms
Attorneys for Small Corporations
Government Attorneys

often refer cases to them. With the firm's blessing, lawyers who leave are often permitted to take with them cases on which they have been working. In 1986, Craveth had about 250 lawyers, 58 of them partners (Reich 1986).

The pattern set by Craveth was soon followed by other law firms, and collectively they became known as the *Wall Street lawyers,* attorneys who are totally dedicated to the interests of their clients and who will expend an unlimited amount of time and effort on the client's behalf. The attorneys of these law firms generally provide counseling, as opposed to trial advocacy. In fact, for the Wall Street law firm, litigation generally represents failure; these firms practice preventive law whose goal is to avoid the uncertainty of trial courts. While Paul Hoffman (1982) once noted that Wall Street law firms were often forced to recruit expert litigators from outside their traditional sources—from government service, for example—to handle trials, this appears to be changing. Cary Reich (1986: 24) writes that about one-third of the Craveth work now involves litigation: "The winds of change that have swirled through corporate America in recent years—the mega-takeovers, the class-action suits, the rise of leveraged buy-outs and other complex financial transactions—have placed corporate litigators more and more in positions of power." At Craveth the top litigator had a 1986 income of about $1 million.

The clients of such firms, of course, must be able to pay for dedication—the Wall Street Lawyer represents corporate America and provides a model for large national law firms that counsel corporations, not individuals. These firms recruit graduates with good grades from the elite law schools. Traditionally, qualifications included lineage—the "right" social background—which had the effect of keeping out many Catholics and Jews and virtually all blacks, few of whom graduated from prestigious law schools. This has changed with the times, although the law firms representing "blue-chip" corporations remain about 95 percent white (Margolick 1983b) and predominantly male. Although only a small percentage of partners in national law firms are female, an increasing number of women are being hired as associates (Press 1984).[3]

At most big firms there are associates and partners, the former work for the latter; in fact, the partners earn profits largely on hourly billings of the salaried associates, and the more associates, the greater the profits. The profits of the firm are typically shared by the partners in proportion to their seniority and the amount of work brought in. Most large firms have two or three associates per partner, and an associate should bring in three times his or her salary: one-third to the associate, one-third for overhead, and one-third for the firm (Lewin 1983). In competition for students from elite law schools, some New York firms provide summer internships for third-year students at salaries of about $1,000 a week. The starting salary for a student right out of law school hired as an associate from the class of 1987 is as high as $80,000. A number of prestigious law firms have begun employing staff attorneys at salaries considerably lower than that commanded by associates. The staff attorney is typically a graduate of a less prestigious law school, or an elite law school graduate with mediocre grades, who will handle much of the mundane work of the firm for which the billing will be considerably less than legal work handled by an associate or partner (Lewin 1987a). Systemized recruitment patterns channel legal talent into corporate firms that provide comprehensive services to a restricted clientele (Auerbach 1976).

While there is not a simple one-to-one relationship between size and prestige, the most prestigious law firms each have over two hundred lawyers. There are about fifty firms in the United States with more than two hundred lawyers, the largest having more than seven hundred lawyers (Lewin 1987a) and hundreds of support staff, including paralegals, administrators, and librarians. While most of the largest firms in the United States are in New York, some can also be found in Chicago, Cleveland, Houston, Los Angeles, Philadelphia, and San Francisco. Many New York law firms have offices in Washington, D.C.,[4] and they have been "streaming into Los Angeles these days, snatching away partners and associates from local firms with juicy wage hikes" (Kristof 1986a: F14)—Los Angeles is a gateway to the Orient and in many respects the nation's second city in commerce and finance.

These national law firms represent the corporate elite, companies found on the *Fortune* (Magazine) "500" list; for example, Exxon is represented by Baker and Botts of Houston; General Motors is represented by Well, Gotshal and Manges of New York; Craveth, Swaine and Moore represents IBM, Texaco, and CBS. As James Stewart (1984: 14) points out, "only such clients can afford the elite corporate law firms and the kind of practice for which the firms pride themselves—one in which no stone is left unturned, no matter how seemingly insignificant, and with virtually no regard for time or money."

Keenly aware of the criticism leveled at them, national law firms typically provide free, or *pro bono,* legal services. As part of their apprenticeship period, associates are often required to serve public-interest groups such as those involved in civil liberties, civil rights, and consumer and environmental issues. During the politically volatile 1960s, in order to recruit desirable law-school graduates, prestigious law firms often found it necessary to promise prospective associates that they could work on public-interest issues on company time. Partners in national law firms are sometimes called on for government service, usually at the federal level. This temporary financial loss can frequently be more than offset by the contacts and exposure resulting from a highly visible cabinet position.

A more recent development among elite law firms has been the establishment of subsidiaries handling nonlegal business such as real estate, banking, insurance, lobbying, health care and environmental consulting, and economic research. This raises the possibility of a conflict of interest between the subsidiary providing business advice and the law firm providing legal advice; for example, in the event of bad financial advice, will the law firm recommend that the client sue the law firm's subsidiary? "Because lawyers have always been prohibited from splitting their fees with nonlawyers," Tamar Levin (1987b: 29) points out, "law firms that want to engage in outside business have had to establish them as separate entities." Some states and the District of Columbia, she notes, are considering legislation to end the ban, making it possible "for law firms to have partners who are not lawyers at all." She (1986) also reports that an increasing number of law graduates who might otherwise join corporate law firms are seeking careers in investment banking and management consulting.

Corporate Attorneys

In addition to retaining national law firms as *outside counsel,* large corporations employ salaried attorneys, often persons recruited away from national law firms, as *in-house counsel.* Abram and Antonia Chayes (1984) point out that over the last decade there has been a rapid growth in both the importance and the size of corporate legal offices. Paul Hoffman (1982: 28) notes that the size of corporate legal staffs exceeds that of many national law firms: "Now they have grown so big that they can train their own lawyers and compete with the firms in recruiting from law schools." The American Corporate Counsel Association has more than 4,200 members (Chayes and Chayes 1984).

The legal division of major corporations is headed by a senior management official, the general counsel. The office of the general counsel does not represent the employer; rather, in-house counsel is involved with the myriad of legal concerns that are part of modern corporate activity:

1. assisting with strategic planning whenever there are important legal implications; providing a legal analysis to the board of directors and an evaluation of available options;
2. monitoring business activities to ensure compliance with statutory and regulatory requirements, for example, securities, civil rights, and employee health and safety regulations;
3. providing continuing in-service education to ensure that corporate personnel understand compliance requirements;
4. serving as the corporation's liaison to the national law firm on retainer to the corporation.

If litigation is necessary, however, outside counsel will usually represent the corporation in court.

Stratum III Lawyers

The legal profession can be conceived of as having three strata. *Stratum I* attorneys are partners and associates in the national law firms; *Stratum II* are corporate attorneys. In this section we will discuss the rest—*Stratum III* attorneys.

There are about 700,000 attorneys in the United States. Since 1950 the number of attorneys has grown twice as fast as the population; by 1984 one in every 364 persons was a lawyer (Curran 1986), three times the ratio in England, and more than nine times the ratio in France. Japan, which has a little more than half the population of the United States, has about 11,000 attorneys. Derek Bok (1983), president of Harvard University and former law school dean, has been critical of the apparent overproduction of lawyers in the United States: "A nation's values and problems are mirrored in the ways in which it uses its ablest people. In Japan, a country only half our size, 30 percent more engineers graduate each year than in all the United States. But Japan boasts a total of less than 15,000 lawyers, while American universities graduate 35,000 every year. It would be hard to claim that these differences have no practical consequences. As the Japanese put it, engineers make the pie grow larger, lawyers only decide how to carve it up."[5] According to the American Bar Association, Washington, D.C. has the highest ratio of lawyers to population: one for every 25 persons. Wilmington, Delaware, where most major corporations are incorporated, has one for every 64 persons; the ratio in New York City is one for 177, below those of Harrisburg, Pennsylvania (1:57), and Olympia, Washington (1:65).

About half of the attorneys who practice law (about 30 percent of those who have been admitted to the bar have non-law related jobs) are in one- or two-lawyer firms or in solo practice. Lawyers in firms of four to ten lawyers account for about 20 percent of the lawyers in practice, and those in firms of eleven or more attorneys account for the remaining private practitioners. About 10 percent of all practicing attorneys are employed by government agencies on the federal, state, county, or municipal level (based on Curran 1983). A study commissioned by the ABA (Blodgett 1986) found that the "typical" lawyer is male (85 percent of all practicing lawyers are men), thirty-nine years of age, specializes in personal-injury, products-liability, and business law, and earns between $75,000 and $100,000 a year.

While the prestige of Stratum III attorneys is considerably less than that of their Strata I and II colleagues, income is not the decisive factor. In fact, there are some Stratum III attorneys whose income surpasses that of most of those in Strata I and II. This is due to the contingency fee, a controversial outgrowth of two interrelated realities: the inability of urban working poor to secure legal representation and the growth of night law schools.

Night Law Schools

As the requirements for entry into the practice of law increased, so did the costs associated with becoming an attorney; correspondingly, the number of persons able to afford legal representation declined. During the peak years of American immigration, 1905–1914, ambitious young men saw the interrelated areas of politics and law as the quickest way to an acceptable level of economic and social success. Immigrant and first-generation Jewish and Catholic young men, however, were shut out of university law schools by economics and prejudice. University law schools and the bar associations were the bastions of Protestant America, which mistrusted the urban Catholics and Jews as alien influences intruding on American traditions. The night law school was a result of these dynamics.

Most night law schools were established around the turn of the century. These proprietary institutions provided a relatively inexpensive legal education for urban young men who worked during the day. Their libraries were deficient, they utilized part-time instructors, and the lecture—not the case—method was the norm. During the 1920s the part-time and evening law schools were growing more quickly than the full-time schools. In 1923–1924 the number of students attending part-time schools exceeded those at the full-time law schools (Stevens 1971). Thomas Koenig and Michael Rustad (1985: 190) report that "the battles between the high-status, university-affiliated law schools and those which were run for profit in the evening was front-page news during the 1920s.'' The ABA and the AALS began to cooperate in opposing these new entities, to keep the night law school out of the world of academic respectability (Auerbach 1976), and to prevent its graduates from entering the bar. This proved to be no easy task, because the graduates of night law schools often did better on bar examinations than their more prestigious counterparts. For example, while Harvard employed the case method designed to teach the student to "think like a lawyer," graduates of the nearby Suffolk Law School could outscore many of the Harvard men because their courses had been explicitly designed to get them through the bar examination (Koenig and Rustad 1985). Also in the favor of the night law schools was the clout of urban political machines, which had close ties to low-status law schools.

Intertwined with the ABA and AALS efforts against night law schools were anti-urban attitudes, as well as significant amounts of nativism, anti-Semitism, and anti-Catholicism. These found expression in ABA canons prohibiting advertising—law firms or rural practitioners with social contacts did not need to advertise—and the soliciting of clients. These canons penalized the urban lawyer and his potential clients "who might not know whether they had a valid legal claim or where, if they did, to obtain legal assistance" (Auerbach 1976: 43). Those who violated the canons by soliciting personal-injury clients were referred to as "ambulance chasers." Not only did the precedent of case law mitigate against workers recovering for damages without the help of a lawyer, but they were also denied access to legal counsel.

Contingency Fee

The *contingency fee* provided a partial answer to some of these problems. A plaintiff's attorney in a personal-injury case receives no retainer (compensation paid in advance); if the case is lost, the lawyer receives no payment; if the lawyer is successful, the plaintiff shares a percentage of the compensation with his or her attorney. While this practice had been declared legal by the Supreme Court in 1877 (*Stanton v. Embry*), the American Bar Association challenged it on grounds of propriety and recommended that contingency fees be supervised by the judiciary—fees received by law firms from corporate interests would, of course, remain free of any scrutiny. Corporation lawyers argued that because contingency fees would cause spurious lawsuits instigated by shyster lawyers, contingency contracts required supervision. These same lawyers who argued that legislation providing a minimum wage or maximum hours of employment (e.g., a forty-hour workweek) were infringements on the freedom of contract found no contradiction with their stand on contingency contracts. Of no small historical interest is the current controversy pitting trial lawyers and the contingency fee against the insurance industry and its clients.

The United States is a litigious society. According to the Insurance Information Institute, in 1985 there were approximately 16 million civil suits filed in state and federal courts—about one for every fifteen Americans. In 1986, insurance companies instituted a vigorous lobbying campaign for a statutory cap on tort judgments.[6] They have received support from local governments and doctors, as well as a variety of business and charitable organizations, all of whom have had to pay increasingly high insurance premiums. In a protest against insurance rates and tort judgments, some obstetricians in Massachusetts went "on strike" briefly in 1986 (Cavalier 1986). In some instances, local governments have dropped their insurance coverage (and, correspondingly, public services). Insurance companies claim that the increase in rates is the result of defending against lawsuits and, most importantly, against judgments that are out of step with the tort concepts of fault and wrongdoing. They claim that judges and juries often hold "deep-pocket" defendants liable simply because they have the resources to compensate plaintiff victims. Trial lawyers argue, however, that the increase in tort litigation has been proportionate to the increase in population. "Sue the bastards" is apparently an old American tradition, and there are more lawyers than ever apparently eager to carry the tradition forward.

An additional element in this controversy is the mass tort or *class action lawsuit:* "In a class action there are a few nominal plaintiffs who are members of the class, but the suit is usually the entrepreneurial undertaking of a law firm for a contingent fee. In class action cases the most important decision the court must make is whether the alleged claims can be combined into one lawsuit. A decision that the claims cannot be combined will inevitably cause the whole matter to go away because no one plaintiff has enough at stake to justify bringing the suit. Certification of the class, on the other hand, may allow the aggregation of small claims to the tune of millions of dollars—and a 30 percent contingent fee interest in an award of that size definitely justifies some real care and attention by the plaintiffs' law firm" (Neely 1985: 45). While Scott Baldwin (1984), president of the Association of Trial Lawyers of America, argues that the contingency fee is the only sure way to protect the "little guy," Stephen Case (1984) of the Wall Street firm of David Polk and Wardell argues that in mass torts or class action suits, attorneys are grossly overcompensated. Case notes that in every tort case two issues must be resolved: (1) Did the defendant commit a wrong—market an unsafe product, for example? and (2) How much money should the claimant receive? In mass torts there can be dozens, and sometimes hundreds or thousands of claimants represented by a single attorney or small law firm. Contingency fees in such cases can range in the millions, although the work involved is not significantly more complex than in single-plaintiff cases.

Baldwin counters that references to the mass tort by attorneys representing corporate interests are merely a smoke screen to divert attention away from the very real damages, pain, and suffering inflicted upon real persons who, without the contingency fee, would not have the funds needed to deal with the legal resources of corporate law firms. In fact, trial lawyers involved in class action lawsuits must often expend considerable resources over many years in a venture that may yield no profits. In cases such as those involving the Dalkon Shield, asbestos, and Rely tampons, there were thousands of clients and complex scientific questions that had to be dealt with. In some cases they required an investment by the lawyers of several million dollars. For example, in the Agent Orange case, five lawyers contributed a minimum of $250,000 each to a common defense fund (Wagner 1986). A cap on judgments would make such cases not worth the gamble, leaving the injured parties without legal representation—and it would reduce the incentive to deal with the negligence that is at the root of personal injury judgments.

Some states, however, have enacted legislation limiting pain-and-suffering awards. The cases of Harry Jordan and of Agnes Mae Whitaker exemplify the difference that such legislation makes. Harry Jordan was a Californian with a malignant kidney. His Los Angeles surgeons accidentally removed the healthy one, relegating him to a short and painful life. The victim's award was reduced to $256,000 as the result of a California statute that limits pain-and-suffering awards (Quinn 1986). On the other hand, a jury in New York awarded Agnes Mae Whitaker, a victim of medical malpractice, a compensatory award of $7 million. Doctors at Lincoln Hospital had failed to diagnose an intestinal constriction that caused an infection that required the removal of most of her small intestine. The jury also awarded Ms. Whitaker an additional $58 million dollars for pain and suffering (*New York Times,* editorial, July 24, 1986: 22). In 1987, the American Bar Association endorsed a controversial plan that would place some limits on the rights of injured parties to sue and recover damages, and the association endorsed greater discretion for trial judges to reduce awards they consider excessive.

Because tort judgments can be quite substantial, Stratum III attorneys who practice personal injury law on a contingency basis can earn incomes well in excess of those earned by most Stratum I attorneys. Indeed, there is an organization of attorneys, the Circle of Advocates, whose members have all won at least one one-million-dollar judgment. In 1983, one such attorney earned $1 million, nearly five times the average for partners in the largest national law firms in that year. A graduate of the University of Illinois, a state school, this attorney practices law in the impoverished city of East St. Louis, Illinois, and gets one-third of each award plus expenses (Jenkins 1984).

The solo attorney, who predominates in Stratum III, is typically identified by his lack of a prestigious legal education and a social background that has kept him or her out of the circles of power and wealth that lawyers from the national law firms routinely frequent. The solo practitioner does not have the readily available research and investigative resources of a large law firm. By default most solo lawyers end up doing the "dirty work" of the bar (Ladinsky 1963). Instead of depending on contacts with the world of big business, the solo practitioner depends on family, neighborhood, ethnic group, and local political contacts for clientele. He or she generally works for individuals, and the nature of the work may be distasteful. As John Heinz and Edward Laumann (1982: 93) note: "Divorce work involves emotionally charged, embarrassing personal situations . . . ; personal injury work deals with grisly facts and with claimants who are badly maimed; and criminal work often requires the lawyer to associate with persons who are less than pleasant."

Heinz and Laumann (1982: 331) also observe that while there is not a strong relationship between the prestige of a particular field of law and a lawyer's income, there is a high correlation with the prestige of clients: "Fields that serve corporate, wealthier, more 'establishment' clients are accorded more deference within the profession than are those that serve individual, poorer clients." The authors also identify types of law practice whose prestige ranking is somewhat ambivalent.

> For example, the practice of labor law (both for unions and management) involves considerable financial stakes, but it also involves association with blue-collar workers and their representatives. Similarly, the lawyers who represent defendants in personal injury cases usually work for high status clients, since those defendants are typically insurance companies, but their work also involves unsavory fact situations. (1982: 93)

A more recent phenomenon in the private practice of law is the storefront law office that offers "no-frills" or "discount" legal assistance. Some law firms have more than a hundred such offices throughout the country and promote their services by heavy advertising. Prior to 1977, attorneys were not permitted to advertise. A Supreme court ruling in that year reversed the prohibition, and since 1977 there has been extensive use of advertising by lawyers, especially on radio and television. These firms earn their profits by handling a large volume of relatively uncomplicated cases, such as uncontested divorces, simple wills, and bankruptcies or personal injury claims where the total dollar amount is relatively small. On the fees that they typically charge, these firms cannot easily engage in full-scale litigation, and they have been criticized for "settling too quickly for too little" (Gould 1986: F15). There is a great deal of lawyer turnover in these firms, and this can affect continuity of service in more complex cases, such as contested divorces, which can take several years to complete.

In any event, as Lief Carter points out:

> Contrary to the impression that television drama gives, with its emphasis on courtroom battles, most lawyers generally practice "preventive law." They help people discover ways to reduce their taxes or write valid wills and contracts.

They study complex insurance policies and bank loan agreements. Such efforts reduce the probability of conflict. Most lawyers usually play a planning role. They help people create their own "private laws," laws governing their personal affairs and no more. (1984: 4)

Now that we have seen how legal education and the practice of law developed in the United States, in the next chapter we will examine the places most attorneys do their lawyering—the federal and state courts.

Notes

1. Wythe was poisoned in 1806 by his grandnephew in a dispute over Wythe's will. The only witnesses were two former slaves freed by Wythe. Under Virginia law blacks were not permitted to testify against whites and the murderer went free (Noonan 1976).

2. Typically, a law school will use a formula that combines the LSAT score and the applicant's grade-point average (GPA). For example, the four-point GPA is multiplied by ten, making it a forty-point scale, which is the range of the LSAT. The GPA is then added to the LSAT score, yielding an index score. Thus, a GPA of 3.5 and an LSAT score of 37 would result in an index of 72 ($3.5 \times 10 + 37$). Law schools frequently use a minimum index score as a screening device. Those below the minimum will not ordinarily receive further consideration. Those meeting or surpassing the minimum are then judged by an admissions committee, which, in addition to the index score, will consider extracurricular activities and a host of nonacademic variables. Most law schools require applicants to submit personal statements, the specifications of which vary from school to school.

3. For an historical examination of discrimination against women in the practice of law, see Morello 1986.

4. Many Washington law firms practice "influence" rather than law. Thus, prestigious firms operating in the District of Columbia frequently have former senators, congressmen, cabinet officials, and White House staff as partners because of the access these persons presumably have with government decision-makers.

5. Charles Stevens (1985) points out, however, that in Japan thousands of additional professionals who do not necessarily correspond exactly to the American lawyer perform important legal services. He estimates that while the lawyer-to-population ratio in the United States is about 1:500, in Japan it is actually about 1:1000.

6. The basis for a tort is the claim that a specific injury was caused by negligence. It is the responsibility of a jury to determine whether an injury occurred; whether the pain, suffering, and/or loss of income are great enough to justify compensation; whether negligence caused or contributed to the injury; and, if so, how great the compensation should be.

4

The Judicial Branch: State and Federal Courts

A court is a public body for resolving disputes in accordance with law, either by finding or making law. In every case the court must determine the facts and their legal significance. If the court determines their legal significance by applying an existing rule of law unchanged (finding law), it is engaged in pure dispute resolution. "But if to resolve the dispute the court must create a new rule or modify an old one, that is law creation," says Richard Posner (1985: 3). Both activities involve the courts in policy-making.

The Courts and Policy-Making

The decisions of the judicial branch of government affect virtually all areas of life in the United States. Donald Horowitz (1977: 12) points out that the American "proclivity to think of social problems in legal terms and to judicialize everything from wage claims to community conflicts and the allocation of airline routes makes it only natural to accord judges a major share in the making of social policy." In more recent years, he notes, the courts have been called upon to deal with a variety of issues that heretofore were the province (attended or unattended) of the legislative and executive branches. The Supreme Court has revolutionized race relations, altered forever the manner in which legislative districts are drawn, overhauled the procedures of the juvenile court, dramatically increased the rights of accused criminals, prohibited prayer in public school, and struck down laws prohibiting abortion. State and federal courts have struck down minimum residency-requirement laws for welfare recipients and expanded welfare eligibility, causing states to increase their welfare budgets. They have established elaborate standards for all aspects of prison life and have ordered some prisons closed, and they have done the same for mental institutions. The courts have ordered the equalization of school expenditures and established procedures for the handling of school discipline. Using the powers of equity, they have enjoined the construction of roads and bridges as damaging to the environment and have ordered the Forest Service to stop the clearing of timber. They have ordered the Army's Corps of Engineers to maintain America's nonnavigable waterways, and have eliminated the requirement of a high school diploma for a firefighter's job. They have taken over the operation of the entire state prison system in Alabama and of South Boston High School in Massachusetts.

Implementation of Judicial Decisions

As Charles Johnson and Bradley Canon (1984) point out, however, judicial decisions are not self-implementing. While responses by the lower courts to most controversial Court decisions have been immediate and the implementation by other government agencies almost complete (for example, the 1973 abortion decision in *Roe v. Wade*), compliance was not forthcoming in the 1954 desegregation decision of *Brown v. Board of Education of Topeka, Kansas,* and the 1963 decision prohibiting prayer in public schools (*Abington School District v. Schempp*) was implemented to varying degrees across the country. It is sometimes necessary for judges to retain jurisdiction after immediate legal issues have been settled, in order to monitor the implementation of a court decree (Lieberman 1981: 30). For example, in 1987 the federal district judge, monitoring a 1981 settlement of a lawsuit against the Texas prison system, held the state in contempt of court for failing to carry out court-ordered reforms. On the same day, a judge of the Massachusetts Superior Court ruled that the state welfare department had ignored his order to provide a standard of assistance that would allow welfare recipients to rear their children at home. Accordingly, he ordered a 30 percent increase in welfare benefits (*New York Times,* January 6: 7).

While some judicial decisions simply lack the clarity necessary for easy implementation, for example, attempts to define pornography, others have been subjected to one of three forms of opposition: defiance, avoidance, or limited application (Johnson and Canon 1984).

1. Defiance. Overt defiance, a relatively rare and highly unprofessional response in which a lower-court judge refuses to follow the decisions of a higher court. Examples of defiance were seen in the South when some judges refused to uphold and implement the decision in *Brown*. Defiance may also take the form of simply ignoring the higher court's policy. This is more easily done by a trial court, since appellate tribunals promulgate written decisions that are available to the public.

2. Avoidance. Procedural or technical considerations can be used in order to avoid having to implement unacceptable higher court policy. A judge may also separate out the repugnant language of a decision as dicta, or commentary outside of the *ratio decedendi*. Such tactics serve merely to delay implementing judicial policy.

3. Limited application. Since this is a normal response to many judicial decisions, a judge can *distinguish away* the precedent from the case at issue.

Some judicial decisions lack the degree of clarity and specificity necessary to implement them. Vague decisions, such as those concerning obscenity or de facto segregation, often result in numerous interpretations, which may encourage lower-court judges who oppose the decisions to resort to avoidance or limited application. Confusion over what is required by a decision may also result in multiple interpretations throughout a state, a federal circuit, or, in the case of the Supreme Court, the country.

Jurisdiction

Jurisdiction is basic to understanding the organization of a court system; it is the geographic area, subject matter, or persons over which a court can exercise authority. The area of geographic jurisdiction is referred to as *venue*, and it can be limited to a particular district, city, or county.[1] The jurisdiction of a state court never extends beyond the state's borders. However, various states have *long-arm statutes* that provide for jurisdiction over nonresident persons or corporations if they have ties to that state by virtue of business transactions such as the supplying of goods or services. These statutes are used to exercise jurisdiction over nonresident motorists who are involved in motor vehicle accidents.[2] *Subject jurisdiction* refers to the category of cases the court is authorized to consider, for example, misdemeanors, felonies, or civil matters. *Person jurisdiction* refers to the authority to hear cases involving adults or juveniles—the latter usually come under the jurisdiction of a special juvenile court (which will be discussed in chapter 7).

Original jurisdiction refers to the authority to hear or act upon a case from the beginning to its conclusion. *Appellate jurisdiction* refers to the authority to review decisions made by a lower court, to hear cases on appeal. *Limited jurisdiction* means that the court has original jurisdiction in only a limited number of narrowly defined cases, for example, only misdemeanors or civil cases where the money in dispute is below a specified sum, or only traffic cases. *General jurisdiction* refers to the authority of a court to hear any type of case, civil or criminal, misdemeanor or felony, those involving small amounts of money and those involving unlimited amounts.

In only one case is the jurisdiction of a court established by the United States Constitution. Article III says, "The judicial power of the United States shall be vested in one supreme court, and in such inferior courts as the congress may from time to time ordain and establish." Similarly, state courts derive their authority from state constitutions and legislative enactments.

While there are systems of trial and appellate courts in each state, most are not at all systematic. The reason is that the history that shaped our judicial system has mitigated against uniformity. Consequently, it is difficult to generalize about state courts. Some states, such as Illinois, have created unitary court systems whose structure is relatively simple (figure 4.1). Other states, such as New York, have a confusing system of courts, often with overlapping jurisdiction (figure 4.2). There is also a unitary federal court system, whose jurisdiction often overlaps with that of state courts (concurrent jurisdiction). Because issues of jurisdiction are sometimes blurred, a litigant may have a choice of bringing a case in one or more state courts or a federal court, and some crimes—for example, bank robbery and drug trafficking—violate both federal and state laws. In recent history, the jurisdiction of the federal courts has been expanded by statutory enactments of Congress in such matters as crime, commerce, civil rights, and taxation. Thus, a black litigant could opt to bring a civil rights action in federal court rather than in a state court in Dixie. The Racketeer Influenced and Corrupt Organizations (RICO) section of the Organized Crime Control Act of 1970 authorizes prosecution in federal court for the violation of certain state laws if the violations were committed in a certain pattern defined as racketeering (see Abadinsky 1985). Thus, in Cook County, Illinois, beginning in 1985, a number of state (circuit) court judges were prosecuted in federal court under RICO for accepting bribes.

State Courts

There are two basic types of courts: those that try cases (trial courts), and those that consider cases only on appeal (appellate courts) from a trial court or a lower appellate court. These courts are known by a confusing variety of names in different states, so we will use generic titles in this chapter (see figure 4.3):

1. Lower court = limited jurisdiction
2. Superior court = general jurisdiction
3. Intermediate court of appeals = appellate jurisdiction
4. Supreme court = appellate jurisdiction of last resort

Lower Court

There are criminal and civil parts of lower court. Soon after a person is arrested by the police, he or she is usually brought to the criminal part of *lower*

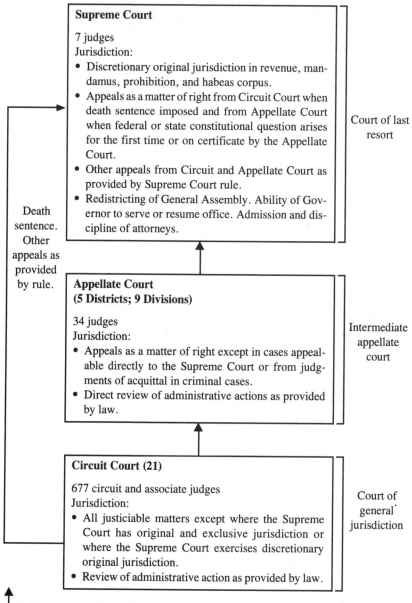

Figure 4.1. Organization of the Illinois courts.

Supreme Court

7 judges
Jurisdiction:
- Discretionary original jurisdiction in revenue, mandamus, prohibition, and habeas corpus.
- Appeals as a matter of right from Circuit Court when death sentence imposed and from Appellate Court when federal or state constitutional question arises for the first time or on certificate by the Appellate Court.
- Other appeals from Circuit and Appellate Court as provided by Supreme Court rule.
- Redistricting of General Assembly. Ability of Governor to serve or resume office. Admission and discipline of attorneys.

Court of last resort

Death sentence. Other appeals as provided by rule.

Appellate Court
(5 Districts; 9 Divisions)

34 judges
Jurisdiction:
- Appeals as a matter of right except in cases appealable directly to the Supreme Court or from judgments of acquittal in criminal cases.
- Direct review of administrative actions as provided by law.

Intermediate appellate court

Circuit Court (21)

677 circuit and associate judges
Jurisdiction:
- All justiciable matters except where the Supreme Court has original and exclusive jurisdiction or where the Supreme Court exercises discretionary original jurisdiction.
- Review of administrative action as provided by law.

Court of general jurisdiction

↑ Indicates route of appeal.

Figure 4.2. Organization of the New York State courts—1985.

Court of Last Resort	Court of Appeals

Intermediate Court of Appeals	Supreme Court Appellate Divisions (4 Divisions)

Courts of General Jurisdiction

Supreme Courts

Court of Claims	Surrogate's Courts	Family Courts	County Courts (Outside New York City)

Courts of Limited Jurisdiction

Civil Court (New York City)	Criminal Court (New York City)	City Courts (outside New York City)	District Courts (outside New York City)	Town and Village Courts (outside New York City)

court where the charges against the subject are read, a determination is made about the appointment of an attorney (if he or she cannot afford to hire one), and, if the case is a felony, bail will be set. If the charge is a misdemeanor or less (an offense or violation), it can be dealt with immediately or at a later date (in which case bail will be set). Some jurisdictions may use a justice of the peace or, as in Connecticut, part-time magistrates for processing minor cases without a jury. After initial processing in lower court, felony cases must be transferred to a superior court. Search warrants are also the responsibility of the lower court.

Depending on the state, the lower courts can include juvenile or family court, probate or surrogate court, county or municipal court, traffic court, justice of the peace or police court. In civil matters, if the money at issue is less than a specific amount, for example, $5,000, the case will be heard in the civil part of a lower court, and *small-claims* matters, for example, less than $500, will typically be heard in a court that bears that title or is sometimes known as *pro se* court. *Pro se,* or "for oneself," refers to matters in which litigants rep-

Figure 4.3. Structure of a State Court System.

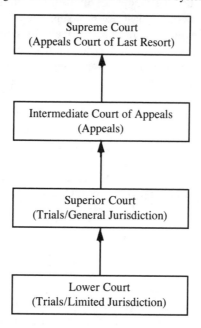

resent themselves rather than use lawyers. (Small-claims court will be discussed in Chapter 7.) Matters involving disputes above a certain dollar amount will be heard in a superior court.

Superior Court

There are criminal and civil parts of *superior court*. While this court is authorized to try any type of case, the criminal part typically deals only with felony cases. In some instances it may hear cases appealed from lower court. The civil part of the superior court can hear cases involving any type of non-criminal dispute, but it typically limits the cases it will consider to those involving a minimum dollar amount or issues of equity. Depending on the state, these courts are called superior court, circuit court, district court, supreme court, court of common pleas.

Intermediate Court of Appeals

The decision of a superior court in criminal and civil cases can be appealed (by the defendant in criminal cases; either litigant in civil cases) to the appellate court, and about half the states divide this court into an *intermediate court of appeals* and a court of last resort or supreme court. Appellate courts do not try cases, and evidence is limited to that already considered at trial by a superior court. The court bases its decision on the superior-court transcript and written briefs and oral arguments presented by the attorneys on behalf of and opposed to the appeal. The intermediate court of appeals was designed to reduce the workload of the court of last resort, although in many instances the result appears otherwise; that is, it appears to encourage more appeals. In some states the intermediate court of appeals is divided into districts; Illinois, for example, has five appellate districts, and a decision made by one district appellate court is not binding on any other district. Intermediate courts of appeal are usually called the court of appeals, although in some states they are called the superior court or appellate court. Cases are typically heard by panels of three judges.

Supreme Court

In states without an intermediate court of appeals, the *supreme court* must consider all appeals. Although the rules vary from state to state, in most the supreme court has some discretion over the cases it will consider: ''Almost everywhere the highest state court is not required to hear every appeal brought to it. The bigger the state and the higher the volume of litigation, the lower the likelihood that the state's highest court will decide any particular lawsuit'' (Neely 1985: 34). Criminal cases involving the death sentence are automatically appealed to the supreme court. The supreme court sits in the capital and hears cases *en banc* (that is, all of the justices sit in judgment). The decision of a supreme court is binding throughout the state, and the line of appeal from a state supreme court is directly to the United States Supreme Court—*the* court of last resort. The decisions of appellate courts, particularly those of a supreme court, are often elaborate legal treatises that provide the material for the case method and the rule of precedent, or *stare decisis*.

While the court system of every state approximates the pattern of organization just outlined, in states without a unitary system there is often a confusing maze of overlapping courts and jurisdictions, a situation that potential litigants may find quite dismaying but that knowledgeable lawyers may use to their advantage. Henry Glick (1983: 41) notes that court organization has ''demonstrated little logic or planning, because *adding certain new courts serves various political goals.*'' (Efforts to simplify the structure of state court systems will be discussed later in this chapter.)

Appellate Courts

A Rational Appellate Court

In his classic, *The Common Law Tradition,* Karl Llewellyn (1960) provides fourteen points against which to measure an appellate court:

1. *Law-conditioned officials.* The personnel must be trained and experienced lawyers who come to the appellate bench with years of active legal work.

2. *Legal doctrine.* There must be an accepted body of legal doctrines that are to be used in deciding specific cases. These doctrines serve to restrain appellate decisions.

3. *Known doctrinal techniques.* The legal doctrines must be used in a standard and generally accepted fashion.

4. *Responsibility for justice.* The justices must have an ingrained sense of duty to bring about a just result.

5. *One single right answer.* While there can often be in fact several answers, justices must act with an urge to find one answer alone that is the *right* one.

6. *An opinion of the court.* The decision must be made with a published opinion that "reaches far beyond the case in hand; the opinion has as one if not its major office, to show how like cases are properly to be decided in the future" (1960: 26).

7. *A frozen record from below.* The facts that the appellate court must consider should be largely the immutable record of the trial court.

8. *Issues limited, sharpened, and phrased in advance.* Lawyers must submit briefs that provide the justices with a basis for a decision.

9. *Adversary argument by counsel.* An appellate decision must be rendered only after written and oral arguments are presented by trained counsel. This assists in the predictability of outcome.

10. *Group decision.* "A group all of whom take full part is likely to produce a net view with wider perspective and fewer extremes than an individual . . . and continuity is likely to be greater with a group" (1960: 31).

11. *Judicial security and honesty.* The justices must be immune from personal or political retribution for their decisions.

12. *A known bench.* The appellate court establishes a way of looking at things that can be known to those who follow the court's decisions. This forms a tradition into which new justices are socialized.

13. *The general period-style and its promise.* A way of thought and writing must be closely associated with the court during particular periods. This enhances predictability—an inarticulate court produces excessive appeals by a confused or speculative bar.

14. *Professional judicial office.* The justices are full-time office holders who must not allow personal predilections to keep them from their responsibilities to the court.

The Appellate Decision

According to Judge Edward Re (1975b: 11–13), an appellate decision should contain:

1. an introductory statement or paragraph setting forth the nature of the case and the appeal;

2. the question presented in the appeal—What is the court being asked to decide?

3. the essential or salient facts;

4. the judicial discussion of the pertinent authority (precedent) that resolves or decides the question or issues presented (*ratio decedendi*); and

5. the precise disposition of the appeal.

Appellate-court (as well as all federal and many state trial) judges are assisted by law clerks and sometimes by staff attorneys. The clerks are usually recent law school graduates who perform research and draft initial, if not final, opinions. They typically serve for two years, and cynics sometimes remark that the literary style of some judges appears to change with the same frequency as their law clerks.

Federal Courts

The federal courts have jurisdiction over five types of cases:

1. those in which the United States is a party;

2. those involving foreign officials;

3. those involving parties from different states if more than $10,000 is involved[3];

4. those involving the U.S. Constitution and federal laws; and

5. those concerning specialty matters such as patent, copyright, customs, and bankruptcy.

The state courts share jurisdiction with federal courts in categories 3 and 4; the federal courts exercise exclusive jurisdiction in all other cases. "Only those state court decisions involving the federal Constitution and laws may be appealed to the federal courts" (Wheeler and Levin 1979:12).

In the unitary federal system, there are five categories of courts—as well as a number of very specialized courts and quasi-judicial agencies, for example, Court of Claims, Tax Court, Court of Military Appeals, Court of International Trade; and specialized courts of appeal such as the Court of Customs and Patent Appeals. The categories of courts are the following (see figure 4.4):

1. Magistrates = limited jurisdiction
2. District Court = general jurisdiction
3. Special District Court = specialized jurisdiction

Figure 4.4. Structure of the Federal Court System.[a]

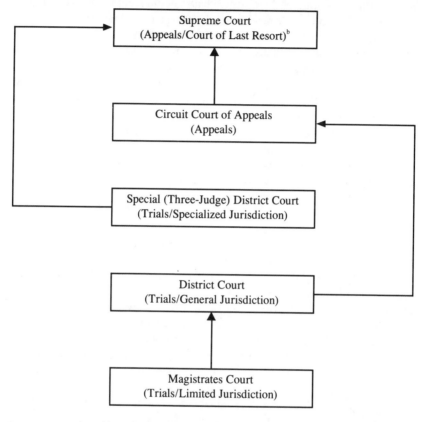

[a]Excludes specialized courts such as Court of Claims, Tax Court, Court of Military Appeals.
[b]Has original jurisdiction in a few very special cases.

4. Court of Appeals = intermediate appellate jurisdiction
5. Supreme Court = appellate jurisdiction of last resort

Magistrates

After an arrest is made, the subject may be brought before a judge in district court or, more frequently, before a U.S. magistrate. The magistrate is an attorney appointed by the judges of a district either for a term of eight years, or in the case of those who serve only part-time, for four years.

By statute, judges may assign a wide variety of pretrial work to magistrates. However, the Federal Judicial Center (1985: xi) notes, ''what is actually assigned to a magistrate depends upon a district's procedures for handling pretrial matters.'' Typically, in criminal cases, these judicial officers conduct pretrial hearings—reading of the charges, bail, appointment of counsel—and, if both sides agree, try misdemeanors. If the charge is a felony, the case will be sent to a judge of the district court. Magistrates are authorized to consider civil matters when the amount in dispute is less than $10,000, or when both parties agree to have the magistrate decide the case with or without a jury.

In many districts, magistrates preside over pretrial case conferences and pretrial motions, although the final decision may be reserved for a district court judge based on a report and recommendation from the magistrate. Magistrates may deal with Social Security cases and habeas corpus petitions from prisoners, although this may only involve submitting a report and recommendation to district court judges. Depending on local rules, the decisions of a magistrate can be appealed to the district court or directly to the court of appeals.

District Court

There are ninety-four federal district courts with about six hundred judges (in 1986 there were 576 judges and a number of retired—or senior—judges who assisted as trial judges). Each state, the Commonwealth of Puerto Rico, the District of Columbia, the Virgin Islands, Guam, and the Northern Mariana Islands have at least one district, while three states—New York, California, and Texas—have four. No district cuts across a state line (except the District of Wyoming, which includes Idaho and Montana portions of Yellowstone National Park). There are between one and twenty-seven judges assigned to each district, the largest being the Southern District of New York which is headquartered in Foley Square in the Borough of Manhattan. The district court usually tries civil (above $10,000) and criminal cases (misdemeanor trials and felonies), and deals with issues involving certain federal agencies. In the three territorial districts, the court also exercises local jurisdiction.

Federal district courts were established by Congress with a great deal of ambivalence. While such courts were favored by those who supported a strong national government, there was the question of states' rights. The Supremacy Clause (Article VI) of the Constitution stipulates that ''the authority of the United States, shall be the supreme law of the land; and the judges in every state shall be bound thereby, any thing in the constitution or laws of any state to the contrary notwithstanding.'' Thus, it was argued, state judges are required to enforce the Constitution, so federal courts would be redundant. It was not until the Judiciary Act of 1875 that district courts were empowered to hear civil suits involving at least $500 (if the dispute arose ''under the Constitution, laws, or treaties of the United States''). The jurisdiction of federal district courts has increased dramatically in recent times. As Stephen Wasby (1984: 33–34) points out, new statutes ''have led to increases in district court cases on such subjects as environmental protection, job discrimination, and education of the handicapped.'' About three-quarters of the civil cases, however, involve disputes between private individuals and businesses, and the United States is a party in the other 25 percent.

Appeals from a ruling by a district court go to the court of appeals, although in certain exceptional cases they may be appealed directly to the Supreme Court (for example, injunctions against state laws).

Special District Court

Under certain circumstances a special three-judge district court may be convened. Such panels include two district court judges and one judge of the circuit court. They were first established in 1903 to consider requests for injunctions (equity) against orders of the Interstate Commerce Commission (a federal regulatory agency). In 1910 the authority of these special courts was expanded to include cases in which the validity of a state law was being challenged; "it was felt that allowing single district judges to invalidate state laws gave them too much power, particularly over state economic regulation," notes Stephen Wasby (1984: 35). Their authority was again increased in 1913—requests for injunctions against state administrative actions—and in 1937—requests for injunctions against federal statutes. In 1976 Congress voted to limit the use of the special three-judge tribunal to congressional and legislative apportionment cases and to issues involving the Voting Rights Act of 1965 and the Civil Rights Act of 1964. Appeals from the decision of a special district court ruling go directly to the Supreme Court.

Court of Appeals

Until 1891, each Supreme Court justice would literally ride one of the federal circuits during recess and sit as a circuit court judge to hear appeals. To assist the justices, a circuit judge was appointed in each federal circuit. This, however, was insufficient. After the Civil War the phenomenal growth of the American economy led to an increase in government regulatory activity and, coupled with judicial activism on behalf of business and industry, produced a virtual breakdown in federal appeals by the 1880s (Howard 1981). In 1891 Congress created the court of appeals, although the position of circuit judge lingered until 1911; those who sit on the court of appeals are still referred to as circuit judges (Posner 1985). The courts of appeals were designed "to help the Supreme Court enforce the supremacy and uniformity of federal law" (Howard 1981: 3). In a number of respects this purpose has not been accomplished.

Although in theory the federal judiciary is organized into a typical pyramidal structure, in practice federal judicial power is widely diffused among judges who, writes J. Woodford Howard, Jr. (1981: 3), "are insulated by deep traditions of independence, not only from the other branches of government but also from each other." Local rules and custom distinguish one court of appeals from another. Some rely on oral argument in every case, while others allow it in only a small portion of the cases they consider; some provide long opinions with their decisions, while others, due to caseload pressures, frequently utilize summary dispositions—decisions without opinions, or very brief orders. Stephen Wasby (1984: 43) notes that in only two circuits (District of Columbia and the Seventh-Illinois) do judges of the court of appeals even work in the same courthouse. Geographic dispersion, he states, "coupled with rotation of panel membership, large caseloads, and ideological differences, can contribute to inconsistency within a court of appeals, limiting the courts' ability to produce uniformity in national law" and increasing the burden on the Supreme Court. Regionalism remains a source of disparity and conflict among the circuits, which can only be resolved by the Supreme Court (Howard 1981).

The defendant in a criminal case and the losing side in a civil case can appeal to the court of appeals in whose circuit the district court lies. There are twelve courts of appeals in eleven numbered circuits and the District of Columbia, with between six and twenty-eight judges; each circuit, except the District of Columbia, encompasses at least three states. (See Figure 4.5) A court of appeals sits in panels of three judges, although in exceptional cases the court may sit *en banc*—most or all of the judges in the circuit hearing the case. There are more than two hundred appellate judges and retired (senior) judges assisting them on circuit panels.

The jurisdiction of a court of appeals includes all of the cases decided by federal courts in its circuit and those of a number of federal administrative and regulatory agencies, such as the Federal Communications Commission and the Environmental Protection Agency. An appeal from the decision of a court of appeals must be taken to the Supreme Court. Under certain conditions, a case can be appealed from district court directly to the Supreme Court. This will occur when, for example, the case has been decided by a three-judge district court, or when a federal statute has been declared unconstitutional and the government is appealing, or when the issue is one of substantial national importance, such as the matter of the Nixon tapes.

Each circuit has a Supreme Court justice, with the two most senior justices assigned to two circuits. This is a link to an earlier era before the appeals courts were established as separate intermediate-level courts (Goldman and Jahnige 1985). On occasion, Supreme Court justices are asked to act on emergency petitions from their circuits when the Supreme Court is not in session. These petitions often involve cases of capital punishment, and the justice can order a stay of execution until the Court convenes. The courts of appeals must consider all

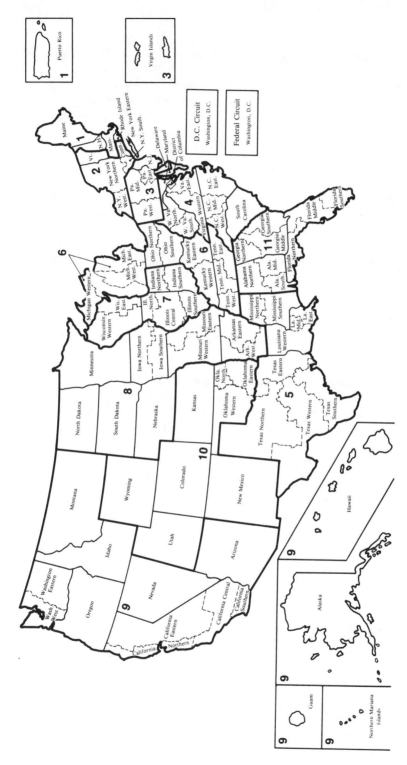

Figure 4.5. District and appeals court boundaries.

cases brought to them. Appeals from a decision of the circuit court go to the Supreme Court, which has discretion to choose the cases it hears.

Some circuit courts, by virtue of law or their geographic location, become magnets for certain types of cases. Certain appeals involving federal agencies must be brought in the District of Columbia, the site of the agency headquarters, while others have a choice; that is, the action may also be brought in the circuit court where the controversy developed. Because of its location in the financial capital of the United States, the Second Circuit (New York) is the site of a great deal of commercial litigation.

Appellate courts decide cases on the basis of written material—petition and case records—and sometimes after oral arguments from both sides. During oral arguments, the appellate court judges often assume an inquisitorial role with probing questions to the attorneys. The justices and their law clerks read the briefs submitted by each side and research previous decisions—precedent— that can have a bearing on the case at issue.

United States Supreme Court

Paul Freund (1961) states that the Supreme Court has three fundamental responsibilities:

1. *To resolve disputes between states.* These disputes often involve boundaries or the apportionment of interstate waters.

2. *To provide for the uniformity of federal law.* The Court has ultimate authority in the event of conflicting decisions by lower courts.

3. *To maintain the constitutional order.* The Court determines if executive or legislative actions conform to the Constitution.

Once an institution of little consequence and now an equal of the other branches of government, the Supreme Court makes decisions that affect the lives of every person in the United States (and sometimes persons beyond its borders). Since the historic precedent in an otherwise unimportant case, *Marbury v. Madison,* the Supreme Court has enjoyed the power to declare a statutory enactment void, unconstitutional. The Supreme Court became the interpreter of the law, not because the delegates at the Constitutional Convention declared it so, but because things worked out that way. In 1907, Justice Charles Evans Hughes stated it bluntly: ''We are under a Constitution, but the Constitution is what the judges say it is'' (in Harrell and Anderson 1982: 11).

The Constitution, which provides for a Supreme Court, does not state how many members it is to have; the first Court had six members, and the number, which is determined by Congress, fluctuated until well after the Civil War. The nine-member bench has become such a strong tradition, however, that in 1937 even an overwhelmingly Democratic Congress refused to increase its membership at the request of President Franklin Roosevelt (as was discussed in Chapter 2). According to the Constitution, the Court has original jurisdiction ''in all cases affecting ambassadors, other public ministers and consuls,'' and those in ''which the United States shall be a party'' (Article III, Section 2). In theory, the Court will also consider disputes between states, or between a state and the federal government, but it only rarely does so. Original jurisdiction is seldom exercised; by 1984 the Supreme Court had issued full opinions in only 164 such cases (Goldman and Jahnige 1985). In cases of original jurisdiction where the Court cannot reach a decision on the pleadings of the litigants, a senior district judge is usually appointed to hear testimony and make a finding and recommendation upon which the Court can act.

The Constitution is not explicit in stating the jurisdiction of the Supreme Court other than making it ''appellate.'' Therefore, its jurisdiction is subject to congressional modification. Originally, the Court was required to hear all cases that came before it on a *writ of error;* under common law, this was an order from an appellate court directing a trial court to send up its record of a case for review. In 1914, the Court was granted *certiorari jurisdiction,* according to which it could deny consideration to any petition that was not supported by four justices. This discretion was at first limited to certain state decisions— those favoring rights claimed under federal law—but in 1916 all cases involving alleged denials of federal rights were shifted to the Court's certiorari jurisdiction.

According to the Judiciary Act of 1925, some cases are technically outside the Court's certiorari jurisdiction. The ones, in theory, that it must consider are

1. cases from a state supreme court when either a federal law or treaty has been declared unconstitutional, or when a state law or provision of a state constitution has been upheld against a challenge that it is in conflict with a federal law, treaty, or the Constitution;

2. cases from a U.S. court of appeals when either a state law or provision of a state constitution has been ruled unconstitutional;

3. cases from any federal court when a federal law has been held unconstitutional and the United States—officers or agencies—is a party; and

4. cases required to be considered by a three-judge district court in which it has granted or denied an injunction.

In practice, however, the Court has considerable discretion over these ''mandated'' cases, which it frequently dismisses for ''lack of a substantial federal question'' or ''want of jurisdiction.'' Even when an appeal is accepted for review, the Court frequently disposes of it without any oral arguments by simply affirming the decision of the court below (Goldman and Jahnige 1985).

The Court is also empowered to receive cases for *certification*. In this case, a lower court—federal district court or court of appeals—requests (certifies) that the Court rule on a legal question in a pending case that it cannot resolve. If the Court accepts the certificate, the justices answer the question, which is then applied by the lower court in deciding the case. The procedure is rarely utilized. Even more rare is the use of Court authority to intervene into the activities of a trial court with an extraordinary writ ordering the judge to perform some act (*writ of mandamus*) or forbidding him or her from doing so (*writ of prohibition*).

The Court decides about three hundred cases a year (which is about 4 percent of all petitions presented to it), and less than half of these cases are granted a full hearing, that is, an oral argument by attorneys for both sides of the question. Of those receiving a full hearing, about 85 percent are subjected to a detailed opinion written by one of the judges voting in the majority (to which dissents are usually attached). The remaining cases and those for which no oral arguments were conducted are typically disposed of by a *per curiam* opinion in which the court states its opinion, but the author is not revealed, or by a brief memorandum order such as "dismissed," "vacated" (render void), or "reversed and remanded" (overturn the decision and send the case back to the court below for further consideration). The Court can also choose to affirm the judgment of the court below, although this type of decision does not serve as a precedent. Since the Court grants certiorari in less than 5 percent of the cases that are appealed, a lawyer who declares that he or she will take a case all the way to the Supreme Court is usually engaging in rhetorical excess. (However, most cases heard by the Court do result in reversals of the lower-court decision.) Many petitions come to the Court from prison inmates who do not have attorneys to see to it that legal papers are submitted in proper form. Often only a page or two, they rarely conform to any legal specifications and are placed in a special group (*in forma pauperis*— brought by paupers) and examined by the chief justice's law clerks. In other courts, these papers would typically be rejected for lack of proper form.

Each associate justice of the Court is entitled to employ up to four law clerks (the chief justice has more) who traditionally serve terms of one year. Recently, some justices have been keeping clerks on for a second year, and the Court has also hired some career law clerks to provide expertise and continuity. The selection of law clerks is up to each justice, and the position is quite prestigious; it usually goes to the top graduates of the elite law schools, based on recommendations from law professors or former clerks. The Court has declared itself immune from charges of employment discrimination, and its law clerks have been mostly white males. The law clerks examine and summarize petitions, review briefs, conduct research, and draft opinions. They often play a key role in selecting cases for certiorari consideration.

The Court has developed several rules governing its review of cases:

1. Cases must not be presented in a friendly, nonadversarial proceeding (to get an advisory opinion, for example); the dispute must be a real one.

2. The Court will not anticipate a question of constitutional law in advance of the necessity of deciding it.

3. The Court will not formulate a rule of constitutional law broader than is required by the precise facts to which it is to be applied.

4. If a case can be decided either on constitutional grounds or on the grounds of statutory construction or general law, the Court will rule only on the latter.

5. The Court will not decide the validity of a statute upon the complaint of a person who fails to show that he or she is injured by its operation (has "standing").

6. The Court will not pass upon the constitutionality of a statute at the request of a person who has benefited from it.

7. Whenever possible, the Court will avoid making a determination of the validity of an act of Congress.

The annual term of the Supreme Court begins on the first Monday in October and is known by the year in which it starts; the term ends toward the end of June. More than four thousand cases are received each year, ten- or twenty-page petitions replete with the records of previous court hearings. They are reviewed by the chief justice and his law clerks, who draw up a list of cases that the chief justice believes should be discussed by the full Court. The associate justices have summaries of the petitions and may add cases to the chief justice's list.

Henry Glick (1983) refers to "cues" that make a case stand out, thereby improving its chances for review; the reputation of the lower appellate judges; written dissents in the lower courts indicating controversy; the U.S. government being a party to the case and seeking review; the presence of race relations, civil liberties, or a variety of economic issues. The more cues, the greater the likelihood of review. When a case is rejected for review, the decision of the lower court stands.

Based on the "rule of four," or certiorari, the cases that the Court agrees to consider involve substantial federal questions and are usually decided on the basis of the written record and briefs submitted by the attorneys. In some cases, usually those involving important public issues, oral arguments will be scheduled and opposing attorneys will be given an opportunity to appear before the Court, which meets *en banc*. Justice William J. Brennan, Jr. states that he prepared for oral arguments by using his law clerks to help pick "to pieces every single case, the record, and briefs" (in Taylor 1986c: 10).

At the oral sessions each attorney is usually permitted half an hour to present his or her case and must be prepared to answer the often probing questions of the justices, some of whom may pepper the attorney with queries. The justices do not wait until the attorney is finished but often interrupt with questions. Written presentations are discouraged, although a lawyer may use notes. Stephen Wasby notes (1984: 175) that not only do the justices ask questions, but they also "make statements and suggest positions not raised by the lawyers." The purpose of a justice's questions and statements is often to influence his or her colleagues. Stuart Taylor, Jr. (1986a: 12) notes that there is some doubt as to the effect of oral arguments: "The arguments come after the opposing sides have filed long written briefs that state their cases in far more detail than can be done in 30 minutes of oral advocacy amid frequent interruptions from the bench." However, he states that in close cases where one or more justices may not have made a definite decision, "an especially good oral argument or an especially bad one may make a difference. A justice who is on the fence may be swayed." In some cases someone who is not a party to the case—interest groups or the U.S. government represented by the solicitor general—may, with the permission of the Court or the litigants, file an *amicus curiae* (friend of the court) brief advocating a particular outcome.

In order to appear before the Court, attorneys must be members of the bar of the Supreme Court, although temporary admission (*pro hac vice*) is usually granted if requested by another lawyer or agency employing the attorney. Membership requires the lawyer to have been a member of the bar in his or her home state for at least three years and to pay a small fee. Few applications are rejected, and the rejections are usually based on disciplinary violations back home. Many, if not most, lawyers request admission for status reasons and have no intention of practicing before the Supreme Court. Every attorney who appears before the Court receives a souvenir—two quills.

Solicitor General

As an employee of the Department of Justice, the solicitor general represents the United States in all cases before the Supreme Court. The office of solicitor general reviews every case in which the government was a losing litigant and determines whether or not to appeal the case. Stuart Taylor, Jr. (1986b: 8) notes that when the solicitor general appears before the Supreme Court, he has a distinct advantage over other attorneys: "Partly because his client is the Government, partly because his office has a reputation for professional excellence and a measure of independence, his arguments have usually carried special weight with the Court." He notes that while the Court hears about 4 percent of all petitions, more than 70 percent of those filed by the solicitor general receive hearings, and of those, the office has won a comfortable majority in every term since 1935–1936. While most lawyers appear in business suits, tradition requires the solicitor general to be attired in a morning coat and striped pants.

After the *en banc* session, the justices go over the cases with their law clerks and tentatively decide which way to vote. They then meet in conference to discuss the cases under consideration. The chief justice speaks first, and the discussion continues according to seniority. Prior to any final vote, justices may also distribute memos indicating their thinking and trying to influence their colleagues. Justices usually do not participate (*recuse*) in a case when they know the parties, in cases in which they were involved prior to their appointment to the Court, or when they have even a small, indirect financial interest, usually stock ownership. When a consensus develops, a vote is taken in reverse order of seniority (to prevent the more senior justices from exerting too much influence). The chief justice, if part of the majority, chooses an associate justice from the majority side to write the opinion of the Court; otherwise the opinion is written by the senior justice in the majority. The opinion is circulated to the other justices so they can offer changes, which, if accepted, means a redraft and re-circulation. Members may add their dissenting opinions to the final opinion, and sometimes a member of the majority will also provide a separate but concurring opinion in the case. Quite often the written opinion is as important as the actual vote since it provides the material for case law. The opinion of the Court is a closely guarded secret until it is announced and copies of the judgment sent to the lawyers and for publication—leaks are quite rare. The Court has the final word if it affirms the decision of the lower court; otherwise, the case may be sent back for further judicial action, often a retrial.

Judicial Administration and Reform

While operational agencies in the executive branch of government are organized bureaucratically, with day-to-day operations managed by a chain of command and carried out on the basis of a highly specialized division of labor, the judicial branch has typically resisted bureaucratization. What would be routine for an executive branch agency is often slow and inefficient in the judicial branch. While executive-branch operations are under the control of administrators who are, more or less, trained and experienced in management, the judicial branch is under the control of judges who may have little or no experience, and even less interest, in such mundane matters as providing adequate lighting, heating and cooling, clean washrooms, and bulletin boards for posting the daily court calendars. There is also the pressing problem of case management, promulgating the calendars, assigning judges, and maintaining and safeguarding case files. Legal education provides no exposure to court administration.

In the United States the judicial branch is also characterized by a lack of specialization. Judges are often confronted by cases with issues about which they have little knowledge or experience. A judge whose legal practice involved civil cases is found in criminal court, a criminal lawyer is found on the bench of juvenile court, and both may have to preside at a divorce hearing or antitrust case.

Mark Cannon notes that

> until recently judges typically proceeded without the advice of professional managers or the benefit of modern techniques of careful research, planning, evaluation and training. Even today, with court administrators having served for over ten years in many courts, judges are often slow to heed their advice and continue to rely on intuitions and predilections born of legal training and disposition to follow precedents. (1982: 36)

He points out that judges prize independence and that traditions of civility and camaraderie associated with the legal profession mitigate against a chain of command and formal rules of interaction among judges.

Administration

As we noted at the beginning of this chapter, no two state court systems are exactly alike, and the administration of each varies accordingly. While the federal system has some administrative responsibilities vested in the Supreme Court, there is no ministry of justice, the centralized system that exists in other democratic countries. In 1938, Congress transferred the management of the federal judiciary from the Department of Justice to the federal judges themselves. Because of opposition from Chief Justice Charles Hughes (1910–16, 1930–41), managerial control was not lodged in the Supreme Court. Instead, it is distributed throughout the federal judiciary (Howard 1981).

The Supreme Court promulgates rules for the lower courts but its control over budgetary matters and policy-making is minimal. The chief justice appoints the administrator for the Administrative Office of the United States Courts, but his or her responsibilities are limited to collecting statistics and other data in order to assist the work of the judicial branch.

Each federal circuit has a circuit judicial council, and in each of the federal districts there is a chief judge who has administrative responsibilities, but his or her ability to carry out policies is based more on the level of cooperation in a district than on any real powers that he or she can exercise—each judge is independent and appointed for life. In his study, Steven Flanders (1977: 8) found that in each district there were "great differences in the scope of court-wide policy on administrative matters and case management, and in the extent to which court-wide policy was enforced." In 1971 Congress passed the Circuit Executive Act, which provided for the appointment of a circuit executive in each federal circuit to provide managerial expertise in budgeting, information systems, personnel and training, facilities, furnishings, and supplies, research, and public relations. (For an evaluation of this position, see Macy 1985.)

While court administration can affect the level of justice dispensed in a system, judicial management has typically been the most primitive of all governmental services. The judicial branch was the last to take advantage of the revolution in information management that resulted from the use of computers. David Saari (1985: 32–33) points out that the courthouse has a natural aversion to change; the lawyers who dominate its operations

> are not interested in working in a typical executive type of bureaucratically dominated, centralized atmosphere, which they will resist by keeping courts locally controlled to suit their own professional interest. Thus the politically favorable, localized power and the professionalism trends [of the legal profession] join together to preserve that historical design concept of the judiciary from excessive bureaucratization that has overrun other institutions of society, especially executive-branch organizations and large businesses. This antibureaucratic strain of courts seems to explain many local examples and variations where the public and courts have rejected reform aimed toward centralized control.

Daniel McGillis and Lake Wise (1976: 14), in a monograph on efforts to provide a joint research and planning effort for local courts, note the extreme nature of localization in California:

> . . . 24 otherwise independent Municipal Courts [are] located in discrete judicial districts within Los Angeles County. Municipal Courts are trial courts, created by the California State Constitution and granted jurisdiction in cases involving misdemeanors, traffic violations, and small claims, as well as other civil matters where the amount in controversy is less than $5,000. Preliminary hearings in felony proceedings are also conducted in the Municipal Courts. . . . Each Municipal Court is an autonomous unit for the purposes of administration. Neither the formal authority at the state level nor the informal structure within the county can bind the 24 judicial districts of Los Angeles County into a coordinated whole.

Formal authority for the administration of all courts in California is vested in a state-level Judicial Council and its staff agency, the Administrative Office of the Courts, which promulgates rules that are binding upon all courts. However, note McGillis and Wise (1976: 14), "its work leaves untouched a myriad of court problems that affect the Municipal Court on a day-to-day basis. In no realistic sense does the Judicial Council or the Administrative Office of the Courts administer the trial courts, nor does it really 'oversee' their administration."

At the top of a state court system is the chief judge of the court of last resort, who usually has certain statewide administrative responsibilities. There may also be a judicial conference or similar entity that promulgates rules for the entire state judiciary and helps to resolve disputes, and the supreme court or the conference will have authority to remove judges for judicial misconduct. The day-to-day operations of a judicial district are the responsibility of the chief or presiding judge who may gain the position by election—the judges in the district make the choice from among their colleagues—or by tradition—for example, the judge with the most seniority who is not yet sixty-five. Paul Wice describes the duties of the presiding judge:

> His or her primary responsibilities are to keep the cases flowing in as efficient a manner as the administration of individual justice permits. [He or she will pressure judges to "move cases" whenever a backlog develops.] The other functions of this chief judicial officer vary depending upon local tradition and preferences but most perform the following tasks: (1) assign judges to various courts, (2) initiate disciplinary action against members of the bench, (3) act as spokespersons for bench to bar and general public, (4) preside over functions involving the bench, (5) serve as ex officio members of various committees within the court system, (6) decide administrative matters such as vacations and retirements of court members, and (7) plan and execute continuing education projects. (1985: 52–53)

Important managerial aspects of any court system are the responsibility of the clerk of the court, and in some systems the chief judge is assisted by a court manager, a professional who is responsible for many of the nonlegal aspects of the court system.

Clerk of the court. The duties and the title of the "clerk of the court" vary from state to state. In about one-third of the states there is a distinct elected office called county clerk. In other states, substantially similar functions of this official are performed by officers entitled clerk, circuit clerk, recorder of deeds, registrar of deeds, or even auditor. The clerk of the court may be elected or appointed and is responsible for maintaining the written records of the court and for supervising the work of the assistant clerks who attend all court sessions. According to the *Dictionary of Criminal Justice Data Terminology* (1981: 56), "The typical duties of the court clerk are receiving documents to be filed in the court record, assigning case numbers, scheduling cases on the court calendar, entering judgments and orders in the court record, preparing writs and warrants [for the judge's signature], and keeping the court records and seal," which must be affixed to all court documents if they are to be official. In some jurisdictions the clerk of the court prepares the court budget (Stout 1986).

Court manager. Court management is a relatively new profession, dating only to the 1960s; its practitioners oversee the administrative functions of the court under the general direction of the chief judge. In practice, the judges of the court play the role of a board of directors with the chief judge serving as chairman of the board; the court manager is the administrator or executive officer. Under this system, the judges determine policy that is implemented by the court manager. Many of the functions performed by a court manager were traditionally the duties of the chief judge. While the duties of court managers vary with the location and size of the court that employs them, their basic functions, according to the National Association for Court Management (Williamsburg, VA 23187-8798) include the following:

Personnel management. Administration of wage and salary systems; recruiting, selecting, training, developing, evaluating, counseling, and disciplining nonjudicial administrative staff; and facilitating personnel matters for judicial staff.

Fiscal management. Preparation of court budgets; administering accounting, purchasing, payroll, and financial control functions; and guiding the budget through state and local government review processes.

Caseflow management. Analysis and evaluation of pending caseloads, and preparing and implementing recommendations for effective calendar management.

Automated office management. Analysis, evaluation, implementation of management information systems to assist the court: word processors, telecommunications equipment, microfilm and microfiche devices and techniques.

Jury management. Management of the jury system in the most efficient and cost-effective manner.

Space and equipment management. Planning for physical space needs; purchasing and managing equipment and supplies.

Records management. Creating and managing uniform recordkeeping systems.

Information management. Collecting and providing management information to all departments and branches of government; publishing data on pending and completed judicial business and internal functions of the court system.

Court liaison. Acting as a liaison to other courts, public and private agencies, governments, and attorneys to promote the work of the court.

Public relations. Acting as a clearinghouse for the release of information to the media and the public, and educating the public about the work of the court.

Research and advisory services. Identifying problems and recommending procedural and administrative changes to the court.

Reform

Suggestions for reform at the federal level include adding additional judges to handle the increasing federal calendars, geographic realignment to better effect a balancing of court caseloads, delegating court management to professional managers, diverting certain cases for arbitration, and transferring mandatory jurisdiction over certain cases, for example, diversity of citizenship,[4] to the state courts. There have also been proposals for the establishment of additional specialized federal courts (similar to the U.S. Court of Tax Appeals) and pressure for the creation of another level of appeals courts in the federal system. But, in the assessment of J. Woodford Howard, Jr. (1981), none of these proposals can respond to the problems created by the decentralized nature of the federal judiciary.

The three related major administrative reforms for state court systems advocated by such groups as the American Bar Association and the American Judicature Society are court unification, court centralization, and unified budgeting.

Court unification. This is a consolidation and simplification of existing trial courts into a single superior court on a countywide basis; lower courts cease to exist. While the consolidated superior court has specialized divisions, such as juvenile court, civil court, small-claims court, misdemeanor court, felony court, all judges are equal and selected in the same manner—appointment, election, or merit (discussed in Chapter 5). The salary and authority of each trial judge is the same and, accordingly, judges can be allocated to whatever courts are in need during any particular period of time. With court unification, the neglect of the lower courts caused by judges aspiring to a superior-court bench would no longer be relevant.

Court centralization. This means placing statewide authority for court administration into a single office, that of the chief justice of the highest court or establishing the position of chief administrative judge. Says Ronald Stout (1986: 206), "Centralized management provides the state's highest court with the power to make rules, appoint managerial personnel, assign judges and nonjudicial staff, and prepare and execute a centralized, state-financed yearly budget." Under this system, there is a degree of uniformity rarely reached in more decentralized systems, and judges can be moved across counties on temporary assignments to reduce case backlogs. For example, in Illinois, which has unification and centralization, judges from downstate counties, where during the summer months there is a reduction in court calendars, are transferred to Cook County (Chicago) to help reduce calendar backlog there.

In New York, the court system is centralized under the state's chief judge, who appoints a chief administrator for the courts. The administrator operates under policy and standards approved by the court of appeals. The chief administrator is responsible for the day-to-day operations of the state's more than thirty-five hundred judges and nine thousand support personnel. He or she estimates the financial needs of the courts, designates administrative judges for the trial courts, transfers judges to balance work loads, hires nonjudicial personnel, prepares reports of the activities of the courts, and makes recommendations for legislation affecting the courts. Thomas Henderson and his colleagues (1984: 5) summarize the arguments for and against court unification and centralization:

> A simplified court structure and strong central direction . . . will increase uniformity of justice and enhance the managerial capability of the courts. Opponents of unification have countered that such changes will lead to a large central bureaucracy which will be insensitive to local concerns. In their view, rigidity will be substituted for individualized justice.

Unified budgeting. According to Ronald Stout (1986: 206), this "means that the budget for the court system is prepared at the state level, regardless of the source of funds, and that the executive branch does not have the authority to modify the budget request," since this would encroach upon the separation of powers. He notes that there are twenty-seven states in which the primary responsibility for funding the trial courts is unified. Since the ability to prepare and implement the budget is a prime feature of the exercise of power, unified budgeting and court centralization are closely related, if not necessarily intertwined.

Obstacles to reform. The options for restructuring a court system are limited by the constitutional requirements of separation of powers and the judicial norms of the adversary system; simplification and centralization that are available to other organizations may be inappropriate for the courts. Furthermore, many court-related functions have been relegated by law to other organizations such as the prosecutor, public defender, sheriff, corrections department, county commission, and clerks (Henderson, et al. 1984). Lawyers and court personnel ranging from bailiffs to judges are socialized into a particular system, and the familiar is often the most comfortable setting in which to spend one's working days. Private attorneys who have learned to negotiate the system enjoy certain advantages, and they are loath to give them up in the name of reform or efficiency—"If it ain't broken, why fix it?" As we will see in subsequent chapters, those who have the most to gain from greater efficiency, the public, are rarely exposed to the judicial system on any regular basis. Litigants and defendants are only peripheral players, whose time-limited participation in the judicial system has little or no impact. The very inefficiency of the system is often also a basis for additional personnel needs that provide patronage for the politicized judiciary.

Henry Glick notes that court reform is usually opposed by Stratum III attorneys:

> Lawyers who deal almost daily with local courts become accustomed to and dependent on existing court organization, procedures, and personnel. Their intimate knowledge of how local courts operate is an important key to their legal success. Changes in court structure disrupt their routine and create new uncertainties about how courts will behave. Justice delayed is not necessarily justice denied since delay may be part of a legal strategy to reach a negotiated settlement, to prepare a case more carefully, or to permit a lawyer to take on a larger volume of business than he or she can handle at one time. (1982: 23)

Trial lawyers frequently form associations to protect their legislative interests. Glick (1982) notes that rural and small-town lawyers also oppose court reform, particularly the streamlining of state courts if it means that the local judges will be transferred to a larger city.

As we might expect, the lawyers who are usually found in the forefront of efforts at court reform are from Stratum I; those attorneys are seldom found in court, particularly the state courts. In general, like the clients they represent, Stratum I attorneys are Republicans working in urban areas dominated by Democrats, and the clash over court reform often becomes embroiled in highly partisan politics.

The most significant impetus for a major reform, improving case management in criminal court, has been the Fifth Amendment's guarantee of a speedy trial and legislation based on court interpretations of the same. Burton Kreindel et al. note:

> In jurisdictions which had a strict speedy trial rule (i.e., the required dismissal of the charges against any defendant whose trial and dispositions had been unreasonably delayed beyond a fixed time period, such as 90, 120, or 270 days) and where there was public pressure on the judiciary to avoid any such dismissals, the various court organizations worked together to expedite the flow of cases. *The incentive in such courts apparently was not the goal of general improvement in the administration of justice, but the avoidance of the very visible public outcry seen in jurisdictions where a defendant is released and his case dismissed, not because he was found not guilty, but because of delays in the processing of his case through the court.* This incentive is particularly effective in those jurisdictions where the judiciary faces periodic elections. (1977: 35; emphasis added)

After this overview of the various levels of the judiciary, in the next chapter we will examine the key actors on the judicial stage—the judges, prosecutors, and defense attorneys.

Notes

1. Venue in criminal cases is relatively simple: it is where the crime is alleged to have taken place. In civil cases, however, it can be based on a number of factors; for example, where the cause of the action arose, or where the defendant resides or conducts his/her business, or where the plaintiff resides. For a full discussion of the issue of jurisdiction and venue, see Friedenthal, Kane, and Miller 1985: chapters 2 and 3.

2. The issue of state court jurisdiction over out-of-state defendants is filled with controversy, particularly when it involves the liability of foreign corporations whose products are sold in a particular state as part of the "stream of commerce."

3. This is referred to as *diversity jurisdiction*. Based on Article III Section 2 of the Constitution and the Judiciary Act of 1789, a litigant has the option of bringing an action in either state or federal court. The federal court, however, will apply the appropriate *state* law. The $10,000 figure was set by Congress in 1958. (Federal courts will not consider domestic relations or probate cases even if there is diversity.) There is some controversy over the motives behind diversity jurisdiction. Some scholars claim that its purpose is to protect commercial interests from hostile state legislatures that might pressure state courts. Others see diversity as a way of protecting out-of-state litigants against the prejudice of state courts (Friedenthal, Kane, and Miller 1985).

4. Federal courts have original jurisdiction over cases of at least $10,000 involving citizens of different states; this power originated out of a fear that state courts would be prejudiced in favor of their own citizens.

5

The Key Actors: Judges, Prosecutors, and Attorneys

At the center of the judicial system are the lawyers: judges, prosecutors, and attorneys who represent civil and criminal defendants and plaintiffs in civil cases. They share a common education—law school—and, given the nature of the practice of law in the United States, are interchangeable. That is, many judges were at one time prosecutors, and most were also defense attorneys. Private defense attorneys, particularly those in criminal practice, have often served as prosecutors. Lawyers who graduate from the elite law schools are seldom found among the ranks of these key actors, particularly those who practice in state courts. One reason is salaries, which are not competitive with those of a partner in a national law firm. Another is the need for political connections of a type typically shunned by those practicing in large law firms. Furthermore, lawyers working for the government, as judges or prosecutors, for example, are quite limited in the types of additional remunerative work they may perform, with teaching and lecturing usually posing the least possibility of a conflict of interest.

Judges

In chapter 4, we examined the role of the appellate judge, who determines issues of law on appeal. The trial judge, under our adversarial system of justice, is a referee responsible for enforcing the rules that govern criminal and civil cases. The trial judge has no interest in the outcome of a case before him or her, but must ensure that it has been accomplished fairly, according to codes of procedure, applicable statutes, common law, and case law. When a jury is used, the judge determines issues of law, and the jury determines issues of fact (the truthfulness and relevance of the evidence). When there is no jury, the judge determines issues both of law and of fact. Since judges commonly come to the bench after years of litigation practice, it is vital that they be able to quickly change hats—to make the transition from advocacy to neutrality. In contrast to judges in Continental Europe and Japan, judges in the United States receive no formal training before they assume their positions (although there is training available at state and national institutes); their training is primarily on the job. A judge's behavior on the bench is subject to few controls, the most important being the possibility of a reversal by an appellate court, which is always a blow to the professional standing of any trial judge. In states using some form of election, the judge can also suffer at the hands of the electorate.

Trial judges actually preside over few trials—most criminal and civil cases are settled without a trial. The role of the judge in bringing about these settlements varies from jurisdiction to jurisdiction (to be discussed in greater detail in Chapter 8), but mediation and conciliation skills are often as important, if not more so, than trial skills for the average judge. What a judge does in his or her chambers with parties to an action may be more important than what he or she does in the courtroom. In addition, a trial judge has courtroom administrative responsibilities, imposes sentences on criminal defendants, and conducts probation revocation hearings. How are persons with all the talents required of a judge selected for their positions?

Selecting Judges

The judicial system provides a rich source of political patronage and, accordingly, there are important political implications in any method used to select judges. Three basic methods are used along with a number of variations of each: (1) appointment by a chief executive, (2) election, and (3) merit system (and, although not discussed here, in two states the legislature chooses judges). Many states use a mixed system, with different judges selected through different systems. In New York, for example, all judges are elected except those serving on the court of appeals (court of last resort)—who are appointed by the governor—and some serving in courts of limited jurisdiction, such as the New York City Criminal Courts, whose judges are appointed by the mayor. In Illinois, all judges are elected, but the judges of the circuit court (general jurisdiction) appoint associate judges, who enjoy the same salary and authority as their elected colleagues (although they serve for only four years, instead of six). The Constitution does not provide a method for selecting federal judges.

Appointment

Appointment by a chief executive—a mayor, a governor, or the president—is used in some states and is the method by which all federal judges are selected. In the federal system (where all judges serve life terms), whenever there is a vacancy on a district court bench, the president (actually officials in the Department of Justice) will consult with the senior U.S. senator from that state if he or she is a member of the president's party. Otherwise, there will be consultation with the junior senator. If neither senator is of the same party as the president, consultation will involve the senior member of the House of Representatives from that state who is a member of the president's party. In any event, the member of Congress will be asked to submit a list of candidates to the Department of Justice. Each candidate is asked to fill out an extensive questionnaire that is used as the basis of an investigation conducted by the Federal Bureau of Investigation.

At some point the final list of prospective candidates is reviewed by the Standing Committee on the Federal Judiciary of the American Bar Association, which rates each candidate (a) exceptionally well-qualified, (b) well-qualified, (c) qualified, or (d) not qualified. A rating may also note that a majority of the committee found the candidate minimally qualified, while a minority found him or her unqualified; this rating is "qualified/unqualified." The ABA committee considers how long the candidate has been a member of the bar—not less than fifteen years—and the amount of trial experience (particularly for a district court appointment), reputation among the bar, scholarship (particularly for a Court of Appeals position, for example, publication of law journal articles and quality of any appellate decisions drafted by the candidate), and a rather vague quality known as "judicial temperament."

The president is under no compulsion to accept an ABA rating, but it can carry a lot of weight with the news media and with U.S. senators who must act upon any judicial nomination. Few candidates are publicly declared "unqualified" by the ABA, but such a rating can often stop an appointment. Richard Nixon, until the last days of his presidency, would not nominate any person rated "not qualified" by the ABA committee. However, in his last full day in office, Nixon nominated Thomas Meskil, the governor of Connecticut, to the Court of Appeals, despite an ABA rating of "not qualified," and he was confirmed by the Senate.

According to the unofficial, yet binding, rules of the U.S. Senate, which in many ways is a "gentlemen's club," a senator from the president's party in the state where a district court vacancy exists may veto any appointment by raising an objection in the form of *senatorial courtesy,* stating that the particular nomination is "personally obnoxious." Thus, in practice, while the president legally makes the nomination, the appointment process is not dominated by the president.

Although each federal appellate court circuit (except the District of Columbia and territorial circuits) includes several states, the selection process is similar. Court-of-appeals judgeships are informally allocated among the states of the particular circuit in rough proportion to the number of court-of-appeals cases that arise in each state. In this case, power over the appointment process is reserved for officials in the state to which the judgeship in question has been allocated (Posner 1985).[1]

The presidential nomination is referred to the Judiciary Committee, which conducts its own investigation and holds public hearings on all nominees. The committee will then vote on whether to send the nomination to the full Senate for confirmation. In most instances, judges are routinely approved by both the Judiciary Committee and the Senate. For appointments to the Supreme Court, the process is the same but no senator enjoys senatorial courtesy. For appointments to a state bench, it is the governor who makes the nomination, and senatorial courtesy is not customary.

Because the only formal qualification for federal judicial positions is that a district court appointee must live in the state where the vacancy exists (Supreme Court justices need not even be lawyers), presidential nominees have only infrequently been voted down by the Senate. In 1986, the Republican-controlled Judiciary Committee refused to vote out the nomination of a candidate for a district court judgeship in Alabama—the second judicial nominee in forty-nine years to suffer such a fate. The first candidate in forty-three years, nominated by President Jimmy Carter for a North Carolina district court, was rejected in 1980 (when the Judiciary Committee went against the wishes of the Democratic senator from North Carolina, whose candidate had been found ''qualified'' by the ABA).

Because of the importance of the Supreme Court, nominees are subjected to greater scrutiny, but there have been infrequent vetoes by the Senate—two when Richard Nixon was president. In the 1970 vote on G. Harrold Carswell, the Senate floor manager for his nomination, Roman Hruska (R-Neb.), responded to critics who accused Carswell of having mediocre legal qualifications: ''Even if he is mediocre, there are a lot of mediocre judges and people and lawyers. They are entitled to a little representation, aren't they, and a little chance? We can't have all Brandeises, Cardozos, and Frankfurters, and stuff like that there.'' His argument was apparently not persuasive and the nomination was defeated 51–45 (Lewis and Peoples 1978).

In addition to being able to pass an investigative screening and secure an ABA rating of at least ''qualified,'' becoming a candidate requires substantial political connections and quite often ideological compatibility with the appointing authority. While somewhat less important on a state level, it can be crucial in the case of federal judgeships. Democratic presidents tend to nominate liberals and Republicans, conservatives. Presidents Nixon and Reagan ran on pledges to appoint only conservatives—traditionalists—to the federal courts. However, in one instance the press reported that President Reagan was going to nominate a Republican woman lawyer who had been rated ''well-qualified'' by the ABA, but he subsequently backed down after conservatives criticized her support of "feminist" causes. Appointments to the Supreme Court also tend to involve geographic considerations, with presidents attempting to have all regions of the country represented on the Court. Religious, and more recently racial, gender, and ethnic considerations, have also all played a role in Supreme Court appointments.

Election

   Prior to the Jacksonian era, most judges were appointed by the governor or the state legislature; Jacksonian democracy led to the popular election of judges. State judges may be elected in a partisan election—one in which there is a party primary, and the candidates are listed as Democrats or Republicans (or with some other local party affiliation) in the general election—or in a nonpartisan election—candidates are not listed by any political affiliation. The nonpartisan election was a largely unsuccessful effort to remove judicial selection from the control of corrupt political organizations. In theory, the electoral system for selecting judges is clearly the most democratic, and it is the way we select the most important public officials in the other branches of government. But the nature of judicial office makes the electoral process controversial.

   The attorney-as-advocate must leave that role behind when becoming a judge. As a candidate for judicial office, an attorney is, accordingly, restrained by a canon of ethics from taking positions on partisan issues. While a candidate for legislative office is free to state a position on a host of controversial issues ranging from tax increases to prayer in public school, a candidate for judicial office is constrained from taking positions on such issues. A violation of the code of professional conduct (promulgated by the state supreme court) with respect to elections can lead to the loss of office (by a successful candidate) and even to disbarment. Thus, while campaigns for legislative and executive positions can be quite exciting, judicial elections are characteristically dull. The electorate is typically faced with a list of judicial candidates (in the 1986 primary in Cook County, Illinois, there were seventy-seven candidates for sixteen judicial positions) about whom little is known, and what is known usually has no bearing on the candidates' qualifications for judicial office—for example, ethnic background, race, religion, and, in partisan elections, party affiliation.

   In practice, three often overlapping variables control an election for judicial office: (1) political party support, (2) ethnicity or religion, and (3) position on the ballot. Let us look at these in reverse order of importance.

Position on the ballot. The position of a candidate on the election ballot (or voting machine) is governed by the election law and can be determined in several ways. In some states the position of all candidates is determined by a lottery drawing, at least in the party primary. In the general election, it may depend on the number of votes for governor cast at the last general election; the party receiving the highest number of votes gets the first position on the ballot. This is the preferred position because in jurisdictions that have a very long ballot—dozens of usually unknown candidates running for a wide array of offices—some voters have a tendency to vote only for the first few candidates. Judges are sometimes elected as a result of this totally inane process. In some states the names of candidates are randomly rotated from election district to election district—obviously the fairest method.

Ethnicity or religion. In judicial elections, voters are usually faced with a list of names of persons about whom they know little or nothing. Under such circumstances (as every politician recognizes), the voter is likely not to cast a vote for the particular office, or to vote for names with which the voter identifies on the basis of ethnicity or religion. Thus, Irish voters may vote for Irish-sounding names, and the same would hold for Italian, Jewish, German, Bohemian, Protestant and other voters. Judges have frequently been elected on the strength of their ethnic surnames.

Political party support. A circuit court (state court of general jurisdiction) judge in Chicago, "who had spent more time with a bottle of blended whiskey than with a volume of revised statutes," says David Axelrod (1983: 4, Sec. 4), "offered a surprisingly candid self-analysis: 'You know, I may not be much of a judge, but I'm one hell of a precinct captain.' " In order for an aspiring candidate for judicial office to appear on the election ballot, he or she needs to secure the signature of hundreds, sometimes thousands of voters on nominating petitions. The circulating of petitions is usually accomplished by the precinct captains of a political party. These persons also have the responsibility of getting out the vote. Better-organized political organizations, those with active precinct captains, usually dominate judicial elections.

In a partisan system, a primary election is required to determine who will have the right to appear on the ballot in the general election with a particular party affiliation. In most areas the primary election is controlled by a particular dominant political organization, Republican or Democrat. The leaders ("bosses") of such organizations select the party candidates, who, particularly for judicial office, are usually successful in the primary election. Since only a minority of eligible voters usually vote in any primary, and still fewer actually cast votes for judicial offices, the party stalwarts are able to dominate the election of judges by the discipline they can exert on party loyalists. In practice, it is the party leadership who typically determines who is elected to judicial office.

In some areas the election of judges does not provide the electorate with any choice, because the elections are uncontested. In general elections it is not unusual for candidates, judicial and otherwise, to be unopposed in districts where there is an absence of a viable two-party system. Thus, for example, judicial candidates in Chicago on the Democratic ticket usually run unopposed in the general election, while the same is true of Republican candidates in suburban and rural downstate areas.[2] In New York City, Democratic candidates for judicial office frequently run unopposed, while in some suburban and upstate areas, the same is true of Republican candidates. A 1984 study by the Fund for Modern Courts found that in the New York elections for supreme court (superior court) judges in the last six years, 87 percent were either uncontested or noncompetitive. In other words, either an opposition candidate did not appear on the ballot or the leaders of the Democratic and Republican parties made a deal to cross-endorse the same candidates (a frequent occurrence in New York) rather than leave it up to the electorate. Another study found the identical situation with respect to the election of civil court (lower court) judges in New York City (Fund for Modern Courts 1986). An editorial in the *New York Times* (Oct. 25, 1986: 14) referred to this system as a "form of election fraud," which "is perpetuated every time New Yorkers cast votes for judges."

In most states, no matter how the judge is initially selected, he or she must submit either to reelection, a nonpartisan retention or confirmation ballot, after a certain amount of time on the bench. In Illinois, for example, after a circuit court judge (general jurisdiction) serves for six years, and a supreme court judge has served ten years, his or her name will appear on the ballot of a general election, providing voters with an opportunity to vote for or against retention. In 1986, for example, the retention ballot in Cook County, Illinois, consisted of the names of thirty-nine judges. Judges who fail to receive a positive vote of at least 60 percent of those casting votes are removed from office. In 1986, one judge, who was strongly opposed by the police union, failed to win retention. In California, the seven justices of the supreme court are appointed by the governor for terms of twelve years (or less if they were appointed to fill unexpired terms). At the end of the term, a judge is subjected to a statewide retention ballot. In 1986, a successful campaign effort was launched by two political consulting firms against the retention of Rose Bird, chief justice of the California Supreme Court, and two associate justices, based on claims that they had refused to uphold the death sentence against scores of convicted murderers. Karl Llewellyn (1960) has taken issue with the retention vote, arguing that appellate court justices must be immune from personal or political retribution for their decisions.

Merit system. Efforts to reform the way judges are chosen have taken a number of forms, the most notable being that adopted in Missouri in 1940, known as the *Missouri Plan*. Twelve states that utilize merit systems copy, in whole or in part, the Missouri Plan.

The politics of Missouri were influenced for many years by the often corrupt politics associated with the Pendergast machine of Kansas City (see Dorsett 1968). The selection of judges by popular election suffered accordingly, and the leadership of the Missouri bar, with the support of the press, was successful in instituting a unique way of selecting some judges. Richard Watson and Rondal Downing (1969) describe the system's three basic features:

1. *Nominating commission.* There is a nominating commission for each level of courts to which the plan applies (some local courts continue to use popular election). The appellate commission, for example, is made up of seven members: three lawyers elected by the attorneys residing in each of the three courts-of-appeals jurisdictions into which the state is divided, three persons whose only legal qualification is residency in the same three jurisdictions and who are appointed by the governor, and the chief justice of the supreme court, who is the *ex officio* chairman.

2. *Governor's selection.* When there is a judicial vacancy in any applicable court, the nominating commission sends a list of three candidates to the governor, who is required to pick one of the three.

3. *Retention ballot.* After one year of service, each judge appointed under the system appears on a retention ballot: "Shall Judge _____ be retained in office?" If a majority of those casting votes on the question say yes, the judge remains in office for the full term (either six or twelve years, depending on the court). If the judge does not receive a majority of yes votes, the office is declared vacant and the nominating commission drafts a new list for the governor.

Most states utilize a modified form of the merit system, the salient feature being a nominating commission of lawyers and laypeople. In a survey to which forty-one states, the District of Columbia, Puerto Rico, and the Virgin Islands responded, Florence Rubin (1985) found that twenty-six states, the District of Columbia, and Puerto Rico have established judicial nominating commissions: twelve states, the District of Columbia, and Puerto Rico have judicial nominating committees that review candidates for all of the courts; nine states utilize different nominating commissions for each court level; and in the remaining five states, a commission reviews candidates only for certain courts—for example, the court of last resort in New York, the intermediate appellate court in Tennessee, and the general and limited jurisdiction courts in North Carolina. Only Puerto Rico excludes laypeople from serving on these commissions.

Pros and Cons of the Methods for Choosing Judges

The appointment of judges by a chief executive places the decision in the hands of a highly visible public official; it is the system that provides for the greatest level of accountability. A president or governor will be praised or criticized for his or her judicial appointments, a factor that encourages the appointment of qualified candidates. On the other hand, governors and presidents have, at times, shown a willingness to appoint persons of questionable ability or background. The appointment process removes the public from any direct participation in the judicial selection process.

The electoral method receives support from political party leaders in whom the power of judicial selection is largely vested. They argue that it is "democratic," that all other important public officials are elected by the people. The best defense of this position has been put forward by Edward Costikyan (1966), a reform leader of the Democratic Party of Manhattan ("Tammany Hall"). He asserts that the collective decision-making of district or ward leaders is superior to appointment by one person, a chief executive. He notes that judicial candidates selected by party leaders because of their political activity have had experience with the human problems that make up a large part of the court caseload, particularly in the lower courts. However, the electoral method of selecting judges receives little support from political scientists, bar associations, and newspaper editorials, because it places too much power in the hands of party officials. Furthermore, these party officials, who in reality select the candidates, are able to avoid accountability because the candidates are officially put into office by the electorate.

Judicial candidates in contested elections (or those facing retention elections) must raise funds for their campaigns and attempt to win over blocks of voters; either can compromise judicial neutrality. In fact, many of those who contribute to judicial campaigns are attorneys whose practice will bring them into the very courts whose judges they helped to elect. Samuel Rosenman states:

> I learned first hand what it means for a judicial candidate to have to seek votes in political club houses, to ask for the support of political district leaders, to receive financial contributions for his campaign from lawyers and others, to make nonpolitical speeches about his own qualifications to audiences who could not care less—audiences who had little interest in any of the judicial candidates, of whom they had never heard, and whom they would never remember. (Task Force on Administration of Justice 1967:66–67)

In an "Editorial" (1964:124–25) the *Journal of the American Judicature Society* referred to the nonpartisan election of judges as the worst of all the traditional methods. Under this system "having the same name as a well-known public figure, a large campaign fund, a pleasing TV image, or the proper place on the ballot are far more influential in selecting judges than character, legal ability, judicial temperament or distinguished experience on the bench."

In the 1973 election for chief justice of the New York Court of Appeals, the successful candidate spent more than $1.2 million and defeated a highly respected appellate judge. As a result, the legislature passed a merit system law for the state's highest court; now, a commission of lawyers and laypeople draws up a list of candidates, and the governor makes the final selection.

The merit or Missouri system has many supporters among editorial writers, the American Bar Association, and the American Judicature Society, who favor taking the courts out of politics. "At the very least," states U.S. district court judge Marvin Aspen (1987: 17), "merit selection will broaden the pool of potential judicial applicants to include many fine lawyers who have little hope of serving on the bench under present election procedures." However, under this system, accountability is almost completely absent, the selection process being diffused among a commission, the governor, and, finally, the electorate—and there is a great deal of voter disinterest in retention elections. Henry Glick (1983) notes that the laypeople appointed to commissions are usually closely aligned with the governor and support the governor's preferences. Furthermore, while in the appointed and electoral systems, political leaders are concerned with fulfilling political commitments—patronage—in the lawyer-dominated merit system, the focus is on the expected judicial attitudes and policies of potential candidates, a more personal concern. Glick (1983: 89) notes that all the research on the selection of state judges reveals that "while there are some differences among state judges, differences do not result from the particular selection system used and the Missouri plan does not produce judges with superior formal credentials for office."

Removing Judges

Russell Wheeler and A. Leo Levin point out the issues and delicate balance involved in dealing with judicial discipline. There is

> the need to preserve judicial independence and need to deal with the judge who cannot or will not properly discharge the functions of office. Moreover, the problems of defining unfitness are subtle and complicated: what some may perceive as judicial incompetence—characterizing, for example, comments to witnesses and attorneys as rude or insensitive—others may perceive as conduct well within the bounds of discretion that judges must have for the effective movement of cases. (1979: 3)

There are four basic methods for judicial discipline and removal, the first being the only one used in the federal system.

1. *Impeachment and Conviction.* Removing a federal judge involves the cumbersome and infrequently invoked impeachment process. Impeachment refers to the bringing of charges—analogous to an indictment in the criminal process—and as of 1986 only ten judges have ever been impeached, and of these only four were removed (two more resigned). Even federal judges who are convicted of crimes can only be removed from office by impeachment. The process begins in the House of Representatives, whose members vote on articles of impeachment. The articles are prosecuted in the Senate by members of

the Lower House chosen by their peers; they act as prosecutors before the Senate, which serves as judge and jury. According to the Constitution (Article I), "The Senate shall have the sole Power to try all Impeachments." This is usually handled by a panel chosen by the Senate leadership. The panel hears the evidence and makes a recommendation to the full body. The Constitution (Article I) provides that "no person shall be convicted without Concurrence of two-thirds of the Members present." All states have provisions for the impeachment of public officials, and the procedures generally follow the federal model.

In 1980 Congress enacted the Judicial Conduct and Disability Act, which provides for the judicial council in each of the twelve (appellate) circuits to consider allegations about the personal conduct and mental and physical condition of federal district court judges. If the council finds that a judge has engaged in conduct that is grounds for impeachment, it can request that the Judicial Conference[3] refer the matter to the House of Representatives for impeachment proceedings.

2. *Legislative Resolution.* More than half the states permit the removal of a state judge by a concurrent two-thirds vote of both houses, or by the governor with the concurrence of a majority vote of both houses.

3. *Recall.* Seven states, mostly in the West, have constitutional provisions for the recall of elected officials, including state judges. Recall requires circulating a petition, and if enough valid signatures are secured, the name of the official appears on the ballot at the next general election; the electorate votes yea or nay with respect to continuing the official in office.

4. *Commission System.* All states have commissions on judicial conduct that are usually responsible for investigating allegations against state judges and recommending censure or removal, the final decision usually being left to the state supreme court or other judicial panel.

Removing Judges in Illinois

The two-tiered discipline process provided for by the Illinois Constitution began in 1971 and is typical of many states.

The Judicial Inquiry Board has nine members: two are circuit (superior) court judges selected by the supreme court, and seven are appointed by the governor—three lawyers and four nonlawyers. The board has authority to receive or initiate complaints concerning judges and file them with the Court Commission. "The Board shall not file a complaint unless five members believe that a reasonable basis exists (1) to charge the Judge or Associate Judge with willful misconduct in office, persistent failure to perform his duties, or other conduct that is prejudicial to the administration of justice or that brings the judicial office into disrepute, or (2) to charge that the Judge or Associate Judge is physically or mentally unable to perform his duties."

The Judicial Inquiry Board prosecutes the complaint before the Court Commission: one supreme court judge, two appellate court judges, and two superior court judges. With the concurrence of three members, the Commission has the final authority to (1) remove the judge from office, (2) suspend without pay, or (3) censure.

In its first thirteen years, the board brought complaints against thirty-seven judges: eleven were dismissed by the Court Commission, ten resulted in suspensions ranging from one month to one year, eight resulted in reprimands and three in censure, three judges resigned before the hearing, and three judges were removed from the bench.

Source: Illinois Judicial Inquiry Board.

Removing Judges in New York

The New York State Commission on Judicial Conduct is comprised of eleven members, four appointed by the governor, three by the chief judge of the court of appeals, and one each by the speaker of the assembly, the majority leader of the senate, and the two legislative minority leaders. At least two of its members must be nonlawyers and four must be judges. Members serve staggered four-year terms, and they appoint an administrator who is charged with the day-to-day operations of the commission.

The commission receives or initiates complaints about the conduct, qualifications, fitness to perform, or performance of official duties of any judge in the state and conducts an investigation and a hearing, both of which are confidential until complete. If the commission finds cause for disciplinary action against a judge, its findings are made available to the public through the clerk of the court of appeals; the commission publishes an annual report of its activities. The commission has the power to admonish, censure, remove, or retire a judge based on its findings.

Source: Fund for Modern Courts.

Prosecutors

In common law, a crime was viewed not as an act against the state, but rather as a wrong inflicted upon the victim who was responsible for the arrest and prosecution of the offender. The common law courts would adjudicate the matter "much as they would a contract dispute or a tortious injury" (Kress 1976: 100). Jack Kress (1976) notes that the origins of the public prosecutor in the United States are in doubt: some trace it to the Dutch experience in New York where the sheriff acted as a prosecutor; some see its roots in the French *procureur* who operated under an inquisitorial system; others see its origins in the English experience with the king's attorney. In colonial America the prosecution of cases was the responsibility of a district attorney (the title varied), usually appointed by the governor and assigned to a particular county or region. "In this respect," says Samuel Walker (1980: 22), "colonial practice diverged from the custom in England, where private prosecutors handled all but the most important cases." By the end of the American Revolution, all states had enacted legislation establishing the office of public prosecutor, who was usually an elected county official. In the federal system, the Judiciary Act of 1789 provided for a United States attorney to be appointed by the president in each court district. Since then, the prosecutor has become the most powerful figure in the criminal justice system.

Federal Prosecutors

Since they need to be confirmed by the Senate, a senator's influence over the appointment of a U.S. attorney (USA) is similar to that over a district court judge. In 1870 Congress created the Department of Justice (DOJ) with the attorney general as its head. The attorney general supervises USAs and their assistants, organized-crime task-force attorneys, as well as investigative agencies such as the FBI and Drug Enforcement Administration. There is also a solicitor general in the DOJ who handles cases to be taken before the Supreme Court (see Chapter 4).

The position of U.S. attorney is one with a great deal of prestige and public visibility; the name of a USA is frequently mentioned in the local news media. Service as a USA can lead to higher office—a federal judgeship for example— or can be a springboard for elected office. Although he or she is part of the DOJ, a USA enjoys considerable autonomy and a great deal of discretionary authority. Subject only to being overruled by the attorney general (an infrequent occurrence), the USA decides which cases will be investigated and prosecuted.[4] Observers have noted that a U.S. attorney's relationship with the judges of his or her district is actually more important than the USA's relationship with the DOJ (Wasby 1984; Goldman and Jahnige 1985). The ability of the attorney general to hire and fire a USA depends on his or her influence with the president—the president appoints and only the president can fire a USA (Eisenstein 1978). When a new president takes office, incumbent USAs usually submit their resignation, even if their appointment has not expired.

State Prosecutors

Like his federal counterpart, the prosecutor in a state system receives a great deal of media attention, and in most states he or she enjoys complete autonomy; in all but a few states, the prosecutor is an elected county official answerable only to the electorate. In Alaska, district attorneys are appointed by the attorney general, who is a gubernatorial appointee; in Connecticut, the state's attorneys are appointed by the judges of the Superior Court for terms of four years; in Delaware and Rhode Island, the attorney general, a state elected official, is responsible for prosecuting all felony cases; in New Jersey, county prosecutors are appointed by the governor for terms of five years. In those states that elect prosecutors, the aspiring candidate, if he or she is to be successful, obviously needs the support of a political organization and campaign contributors. The office of prosecutor has served as an important source of political patronage, and it can investigate political enemies while protecting political friends. Being a prosecutor has often been seen as a stepping stone to higher public office. Most prosecutors aspire to higher office, and many important public officials were at one time prosecutors.

The prosecutor's office decides which cases are to be prosecuted, and for what criminal charges. While prosecutors (sometimes called the state's attorneys or district attorneys) cannot control intake—they are dependent on the police to bring cases—they can decide not to prosecute and, legally, need not provide any reason—although politically it might be a necessity in highly publicized cases. The prosecutor's office can decline to prosecute a case, dismiss it, accept a plea of guilty to a reduced charge, or prosecute it to the fullest extent allowable by law. The enormous discretion enjoyed by the prosecutor is the basis for much of the plea bargaining in criminal courts (which will be discussed in chapter 8).

Like a U.S. attorney, a county prosecutor employs assistants who do most (and in large counties all) of the actual trial work. In practice, as we shall see in later chapters, there are very few trials in either the criminal or civil courts. Most assistant prosecutors are recent graduates from law school who are using the prosecutor's office as an opportunity to gain trial experience. A typical assistant prosecutor works for about three or four years and then enters private practice, often to do criminal defense work. The prosecutor's office, then, is characterized by a great deal of turnover, sometimes due to electoral politics, but more often as a result of assistants leaving for more lucrative opportunities in private legal practice. James Fishman states:

> The legal profession is highly stratified with limited mobility. One's final position in the status hierarchy of the profession is heavily determined by the status position of one's first job as a lawyer. That, in turn, in influenced by the prestige of one's law school which, in turn, is influenced by the prestige of one's college which, in turn, is influenced by one's family socioeconomic background. Being an assistant prosecutor as the first job in one's legal career does little to enhance one's occupational mobility. (1979: 252)

Most assistants are not graduates of prestigious law schools, although there are some exceptions. The New York (Manhattan) County District Attorney has had an outstanding reputation ever since Thomas E. Dewey was elected to the position in 1937. Dewey, a Republican, became governor and was succeeded by his first assistant, Frank S. Hogan, a Democrat who remained district attorney until he retired thirty-four years later. The nonpolitical nature of the office and its reputation for excellence attracts many law school students who might otherwise enter corporate practice upon graduation. The office receives more than fifteen hundred applications for the approximately fifty annual vacancies (Barzilay 1983).

In some jurisdictions the decision to charge a suspect is left to the police (usually detectives), and the prosecutor's office receives the case only after charges against the subject have already been filed. In other jurisdictions the charging decision is controlled by the prosecutor from the beginning; an assistant prosecutor decides what, if any, charges should be filed. In still other jurisdictions, if a felony is to be charged by the police, the prosecutor must first give permission; the police can usually charge misdemeanors without any consultation.[5]

Early screening keeps weak and petty cases from overburdening the system; however, it can also result in faulty decisions since there may not be a great deal of information available about the case and/or the suspect so early in the process. Pamela Utz (1979: 110) states that in Alameda County, California, ''A case-weighting system was developed to force early evaluation of the seriousness of cases.'' The decision to charge a felony, she notes, ''would be based on a careful evaluation of whether a case truly warranted prison, and on the practical likelihood of later sustaining the charge.''

The prosecutor's office may be organized to handle cases horizontally, vertically, or in a mixture of the two methods.

1. *Horizontal prosecution.* This is the predominant mode of handling cases in more populous counties. Each assistant prosecutor is assigned to handle a different step in the judicial process. (See Chapter 6 for these steps.) Some are assigned to receive and screen cases as they enter the system. Some will be assigned to the lower courts to deal with bond hearings, probable-cause hearings and misdemeanor cases. If a felony case is sent to the grand jury or superior court, it will be managed by assistants assigned to those bodies. If a case is appealed, it will be handled by assistants who specialize in appeals. (Those who are familiar with basketball will recognize this method as the *zone defense.*) Horizontal prosecution in felony cases means that a victim or complainant will have to deal with a different assistant prosecutor at each stage of the judicial process. The victim may feel tossed about, receiving little personal attention, and this can be costly in terms of cooperation.

2. *Vertical prosecution.* This system is used in smaller jurisdictions where the prosecutor's office is not overburdened by the mass of cases that characterize most metropolitan areas. Each assistant prosecutor is assigned a caseload—

Figure 5.1. Differences in how prosecutors handle felony cases. Outcome of felony cases presented to prosecutor.

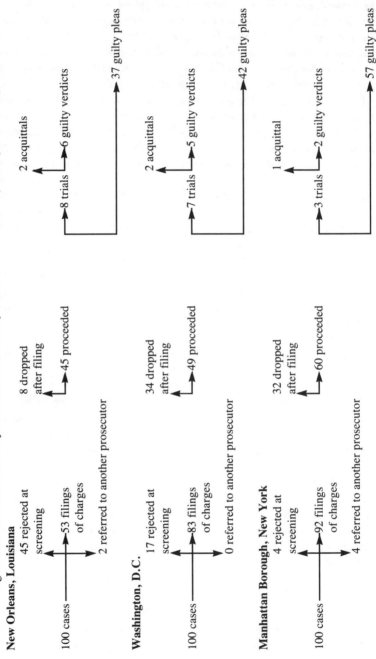

Source: Zawitz 1983:55.

a number of specific cases—for which he or she has total responsibility. The assistant picks up the case after the decision to charge has been made and stays with it until the final disposition. (Those familiar with basketball will recognize this method as the *man-to-man defense.*) The victim or complainant has the comfort of one assistant throughout the entire judicial process; he or she does not have to discuss the case anew with each new assistant. Unfortunately, this method can be quite costly in terms of personnel. As we will discuss later, it is often difficult to gather all of the primary and secondary actors in court at the same time, with the necessary files and exhibits needed for the case to move forward. Quite often an assistant prosecutor will find that he or she is prepared for trial but other actors or records are either missing or not prepared, and the case will be rescheduled for another date. With horizontal prosecution, the clerk will call the next case and the prosecutor will deal with that one; with vertical prosecution the entire day may be wasted.

3. *Mixed prosecution.* This system takes advantage of the strengths inherent in horizontal and vertical prosecution. Most routine cases will be handled in a horizontal (cost-effective manner), while certain targeted cases, those involving organized crime or serious repeat offenders, for example, will be subject to vertical prosecution. In using this mixed method, the prosecutor may set up special bureaus—such as a homicide bureau, a rackets bureau, or a serious-offender bureau—with assistants and investigators who have special training or experience in dealing with these types of cases.

Like the police, a prosecutor is responsible for enforcing the law, and in so doing acts in the name of "the people," (actually in the name of the United States of America or the State of _____). Unlike the police, however, a prosecutor has an additional responsibility: *justice.* A police officer having the minimum level of evidence necessary to effect a lawful arrest—*probable cause*—must, in the case of a felony, arrest the suspect. The prosecutor, however, requires a much higher level of evidence—*beyond a reasonable doubt.* As an officer of the court, the prosecutor must be concerned with the possibility of prosecuting a person who is innocent or, at least, one against whom the evidence is not sufficient to justify a verdict of guilty. To prosecute would be unjust. This explains why prosecutors will often dismiss cases, or declare *nolle prosequi* (or simply "nol pros"; this is a formal entry on the record by the prosecutor that he or she will not prosecute the case any further; a similar entry may be made by the plaintiff in a civil case). Differing levels of proof play an important role in plea bargaining (which will be discussed in chapter 8).

Defense Attorneys

In civil matters, neither the plaintiff nor the defendant is constitutionally entitled to an attorney. However, in criminal cases the complainant is represented by a government attorney—the prosecutor—and the defendant has a constitutional right to be represented by "competent" counsel. Criminal justice in the United States is based on an adversarial model, and the defense counsel is one of its cornerstones. Within this adversarial system of justice, the attorney for the accused has a singular purpose: as an advocate, he or she must use every lawful means to exonerate or, failing that, to mitigate punishment. Questions of justice, of guilt or innocence, which should concern the prosecutor, are not the responsibility of defense counsel—at least not in the United States. Monroe Freedman (1975) notes that in totalitarian countries such as Cuba, it is the responsibility of the lawyer not to argue that his or her client is innocent but rather to determine if the client is guilty, and, if so, to seek the sanction necessary to best provide rehabilitation—even if that means execution. Lon Fuller (1961: 34) argues that under our adversarial system, an attorney who refuses to defend a client because he thinks he is guilty "is wrongfully usurping the office of judge and jury."

In the United States, only agents of government must be dedicated to truth-finding. Defense counsel is under no comparable obligation; his or her role is to defend the client whether innocent or guilty. In fact, defense counsel is required to throw up roadblocks in the face of the truth to prevent the admission of evidence that may be wholly reliable, such as a murder weapon seized in violation of the Fourth Amendment or a truthful but involuntary confession. Freedman argues that

> in the adversary system, it is not the role or function of the advocate to act upon conclusions of ultimate facts such as guilt or innocence. That function is assigned to the judge or jury, which bases its decision on the adversaries' presentation of their clients' cases. Thus, the fact of guilt or innocence is irrelevant to the role that has been assigned to the advocate. (1975: 57)

A public defender (Bellows 1983: 8) writes:

> It is an axiom of criminal defense practice that you represent your guilty clients as zealously as you do your innocent ones (not that you can always tell the difference). [A] client who you *really* believe is innocent . . . does not happen very often. In fact, it happens rarely enough to be considered remarkable. One of the awkward truths about being a public defender is that you are in the practice of representing people who are, indeed, guilty as charged.

The right to counsel existed in colonial America, although often in practice rather than in law. In Connecticut since 1750 it had been the custom to appoint counsel for defendants who requested attorneys, although there was not a statutory provision until 1818. Pennsylvania and Delaware in 1701 provided all criminal defendants with the same privilege of counsel as their prosecutors, and South Carolina did the same in 1731. Most states made the same provision regarding the right to counsel in their post-revolutionary constitutions (Mc-

Donald 1983). The Sixth Amendment provides that "the accused shall enjoy the right . . . to have the assistance of counsel for his defense." In 1928 the Supreme Court (*Johnson v. Zerbst*) ruled that an indigent defendant is entitled to counsel in a federal criminal prosecution. In 1932 the Court ruled (*Powell v. Alabama*) that an indigent defendant accused of a capital offense in a state court is also entitled to counsel at public expense. In 1963 the Court ruled (*Gideon v. Wainwright*) that all indigent defendants accused of felonies are entitled to counsel at state expense; and in 1972 the Court (*Argersinger v. Hamlin*) extended the right to counsel for indigent defendants accused of misdemeanors for which the penalty includes possible imprisonment. William McDonald (1983) states that these decisions established the importance of lawyers in criminal cases as basic for justice. They asserted the value of the legal profession for ensuring equality in the midst of gross inequalities.

In the United States today, there are three ways to accomplish the right to counsel: (1) engaging a private attorney, (2) public defender systems, and (3) assigned counsel.

Private Defense Counsel

Relatively few lawyers in private practice handle criminal cases on a regular basis, and most of them are solo practitioners or work within law firms of less than four partners or associates (Wice 1978). The professional and private life-style of the criminal attorney usually falls far short of the glamorous portrayals in books and movies and on television. Paul Wice (1978) presents a portrait of the private criminal attorney that is instead rather depressing. He (private criminal attorneys are almost invariably male) must be concerned about continually securing clients, and in some jurisdictions this requires unlawful kickbacks to other attorneys or persons working in criminal justice (e.g., clerks, police officers, bailiffs) for referrals. He must worry about being paid because his clients are usually poor and, since they are not drawn from the ranks of boy scouts, may refuse to pay when a case is over; the hours are long and a great deal of time is spent simply waiting in, or traveling to, courthouses:

> The private criminal lawyer is usually at his office for an hour or two prior to his morning court appearance and will return home there in the late afternoon for a few additional hours. He may also be found in his office on weekends and on those rare days when no court appearances are required. For the bulk of the day, however, the criminal lawyer will be in the courthouse. His time will be spent roaming hallways, waiting for appointments, chatting with his fellow practitioners over rancid coffee, and occasionally carrying out professional responsibilities before a judge. (1978: 129)

The private practice of criminal law is not only physically demanding but, Wice notes, it has significant social and psychological costs:

> The private criminal lawyer obviously suffers from guilt by association. The public reflexively links the client with his attorney and fails to appreciate the professional and constitutional responsibility which the latter must exercise. The public seems to reason that if a lawyer chooses to defend a guilty man, then the lawyer must himself also be tainted with some guilt. (1978: 91)

Because his clients are poor financial risks, the private criminal attorney usually requires at least part of his fee in advance—"upfront money." In many cases this is the only fee he will receive. Since the fee any single client can afford to pay is relatively low, the criminal attorney must substitute quantity for quality. That is, he must have numerous clients to maintain a profitable criminal practice, and he cannot spend too much time on any single case since the fee is rather inelastic and extra time will not necessarily result in additional payment.

It is not unusual for an attorney to find himself prepared for a hearing that fails to take place, because, for example, the defendant, complainant, or other principal fails to appear, or records have been misplaced. Because of the likelihood that any one case scheduled for a court hearing on a particular day will result in a continuance, private attorneys, like airlines, usually overbook. (Airlines may book more passengers for a flight than the plane has seats, under the assumption that everyone will not actually show up for the flight, and every empty seat represents lost income.) Case management becomes a preoccupation as the attorney rushes from courtroom to courtroom juggling his cases, frequently requesting continuances. In New York City, for example, Nancy Jacobs and Ellen Chayet (1986) found that 43 percent of the criminal cases were adjourned at least once due to defense-counsel trial-scheduling conflicts. Since the prosecutor can object to and a judge need not grant a continuance, the attorney needs to maintain good relations with the other key actors. This has implications for plea bargaining that will be discussed in chapter 8.

Public Defender

The public defender is a counterpart of the prosecutor; that is, he or she is a government official. Instead of representing "the people," however, the public defender represents the interests of indigent defendants. And unlike most prosecutors, the public defender is usually appointed, not elected. The reason for using an appointment system is quite simple: on what would an aspiring candidate for public defender base his or her campaign? "If I am elected, more defendants will go free, and others will serve less time in prison"? While a candidate for prosecutor can engage in a great deal of law-and-order rhetoric and promise to be tough on criminals, the aspiring public defender is quite limited in what he or she can do to attract votes.

There are statewide and local public defender systems. According to the government publication *Criminal Defense Systems*:

> Under statewide public defender systems, an individual is designated by statute as the State public defender and is charged with developing and maintaining a system of representation for each of the counties in the State. In such systems, there is usually a governing board that shares responsibility with the State public defender for the operation of the program. Most statewide systems are part of the executive branch, but others may operate as part of the judicial branch, as independent State agencies, or as independent nonprofit organizations. (1984: 3)

Local public defenders are usually part of county government, and they are often appointed by the county legislature on a recommendation from the judiciary. An independent nonprofit organization is used in New York City, however, where the Legal Aid Society represents all indigent criminal defendants except those accused of murder. The society is governed by a board of directors "that's a Who's Who of prominent lawyers, businessmen, and educators" (Pileggi 1982: 30). It was founded over one hundred years ago as *Der Deutsche Rechtsschutz,* an association to help German immigrants. This limitation and the German name were soon dropped in favor of helping the poor of all nationalities. As opposed to public defender offices, which handle only criminal matters, the Legal Aid Society has a civil division.

While public defenders are the primary providers of criminal defense services in only 34 percent of all counties in the United States, they serve 68 percent of the nation's population; 43 percent of the largest fifty counties in the nation are served predominantly by a public defender program (*Criminal Defense Systems* 1984). Like the prosecutor's office, a public defender's office may be organized horizontally ("zone defense"), vertically ("man-to-man defense"), or in a combination of the two. Like the prosecutor, the public defender employs assistant or deputy defenders, who may be full- or part-time, and investigative personnel. Like the prosecutor's office, that of the public defender suffers from a great deal of personnel turnover. The position of an assistant is attractive to lawyers who are interested in gaining a great deal of criminal trial experience in a relatively short period of time.

Like providers of other forms of welfare, the public defender may be resented by the recipients of his or her services. In addition to this attitude toward receiving a necessary beneficence, there is the common folk wisdom that "you only get what you pay for!" Jonathan Casper points out that

> what attracts defendants to private lawyers is, for a large number of them at least, the notion that, because of the financial exchange between lawyer and client, the lawyer will be more committed to the defendant's interests. It is money that provides a sense of control, the leverage to insure that lawyers will listen to their clients, take instructions from their clients, and generally exert themselves on their clients' behalf. Moreover, not only does the client fail to pay, and thus lack

this leverage over public defenders, but someone else does. And that someone else is "the state"—the very same institution that is proceeding against the defendant. Thus, the public defenders suffer not only from the fact that they are imposed upon defendants rather than being selected, and from the absence of financial exchange, but they are employed by the enemy. (1978: 4)

Paul Wice (1983: 41) contrasts the public defender with the private criminal attorney. He notes that, through the development of their reputation as a successful advocate, private criminal attorneys can improve their economic condition. "Public defenders," he writes, "will receive their salaries regardless of the outcome of the case, but private attorneys know that their economic worth is directly related to how well they satisfy their clients." Despite the bleak picture of the private practice of criminal law, Wice notes, "Private attorneys are motivated to offer several benefits usually unavailable at the public defender's office. Although these advantages may not be related to the ultimate disposition of the case, they nevertheless do heighten the prestige of private criminal lawyers in the eyes of their clientele." There are two major advantages of private lawyers:

1. They can provide personalized attention, sometimes referred to as "handholding." The large caseloads typical of a public defender's office results in cases being handled horizontally, with clients being represented by different attorneys at various stages of the judicial process. Clients do not have their own attorney and cannot drop in for a review of their case in a secluded office. In addition, among criminal clientele, there is prestige in having one's own attorney.

2. Private lawyers are more willing to take an aggressive stance toward both the judge and the prosecutor on behalf of the client. Private criminal attorneys have been found to be much more willing to risk contempt citations and other forms of judicial anger than public defenders, who are often assigned to a specific judge for a length of time; confrontations with the judge could make things quite difficult for the public defender. (Some observers, however, have found the opposite—that private attorneys are more willing to compromise, and public defenders more aggressive. This issue will be looked at again when plea bargaining is discussed in chapter 8.)

But public defenders have some advantages, too. As opposed to most attorneys in private practice who handle criminal cases, they have access to their own law libraries and at least limited use of investigators. "Additionally," says Wice (1985: 65), "the public defender is clearly a criminal specialist," and furthermore, "because of his continued involvement with the prosecutors and judiciary, the public defender can frequently develop a working relationship in which the exchange of favors, so necessary to greasing the squeaky wheel of justice, can directly benefit the indigent defendant."

Assigned Counsel

About 60 percent of the counties in the United States use court-appointed private attorneys as the primary method for providing legal representation for indigent criminal defendants. These are primarily rural counties with small populations whose limited number of cases do not justify a salaried public defender system. Even in counties that use a public defender system, many defendants are represented by private attorneys appointed by the trial judge. There are two reasons for this. First, when public defenders are unable to handle their caseloads adequately, especially during certain peak seasons, judges will supplement them by appointing private counsel. Second, the court will appoint attorneys when there is conflict of interest because one attorney or law firm (the public defender's office fits this definition) is representing a codefendant. There is always a potential conflict of interest because, for example, one defendant may agree to testify against another defendant in return for leniency.

Private attorneys in most jurisdictions are assigned by individual judges on an ad hoc case-by-case basis. In some jurisdictions, however, the assignment of private counsel is more systematic and involves an administrator who oversees the program and develops standards and guidelines. In a few jurisdictions, responsibility for appointment is given to the public defender or clerk of the court. In a small number of jurisdictions, a private attorney or law firm is under contract to provide legal services for indigent criminal defendants (*Criminal Defender Systems* 1984). In most jurisdictions, a list of attorneys who have requested to be considered for appointment provides the basis for assigning private counsel. Compensation for assigned counsel is usually based on a fee schedule for in-court and out-of-court hours spent on a case. The hourly fee varies with the jurisdiction, and, sometimes, with the complexity of the case. In any event, the hourly fees are typically less than what an attorney would normally expect for representing a private client—but payment is guaranteed.

Legal Aid

While a criminal defendant, in virtually all instances, is entitled to be represented by competent counsel, persons with civil grievances or defendants in a civil action have no such constitutional entitlement: justice has a price that poor Americans cannot afford to pay.

Jerold Auerbach (1976) notes that in the years just before and immediately after the First World War, there was fear of civil unrest that intensified with the Bolshevik Revolution in Russia. The foreigners who had fueled the industrial revolution were now seen as potential revolutionaries. Strikes and mass demonstrations for higher wages, better working conditions, and a forty-hour workweek were viewed as the forerunners of radical upheavals. The American Bar Association argued that it was the influx of foreigners who lacked an understanding of American values, and not class injustice, that was at the heart of the problem. It was important to educate the alien elements, to show them that they had a stake in the American system. Law and courts, not strikes and violence, are the American way, said the ABA. The bar had a responsibility, a noblesse oblige, to promote justice under law.

Legal Aid Societies

As noted above, the Legal Aid Society in New York was founded by German-Americans in 1876 to assist their compatriots who were being preyed upon by confidence men. The society subsequently expanded its services to the poor generally, and other cities followed the New York example. A society was formed in Chicago in 1886 to aid young women being lured into prostitution by offers of legitimate employment. By the turn of the century there were legal aid societies in six cities, and in 1909 the first bar-association-sponsored legal aid society was established. Most societies, however, were supported by private contributions, and the expansion of legal aid was primarily the result of the efforts of Arthur von Briesen, a Prussian immigrant who served the Union during the Civil War. He warned potential contributors that the alternative to legal aid was civil strife and political disorder—given the times, a realistic approach to raising money. As fear of social unrest increased, so did the expansion of legal aid societies. Although there were only fifteen by 1910, that number increased to forty-one in the next decade, and by 1923 there were sixty-one. In 1914, Reginald Haber Smith, a young Harvard Law School graduate, became the head of the newly formed Boston Legal Aid Society. He was appalled by the lack of legal services for the poor, and traveling on a Carnegie Foundation grant, toured the United States visiting legal aid societies and courts. The result was a book, *Justice and the Poor* (1919). As a result of his efforts, the National Organization of Legal Aid Organizations was formed, and the ABA established a standing committee on legal aid.

Legal aid societies limited their assistance to the "deserving poor," that is, those who were employed, and the cases accepted were those too petty for any private attorney—the societies wanted to avoid competing with the private bar. The continuing inability of legal aid to even begin to address the issue of equal justice under law led to the establishment of the Legal Services Corporation and public interest law firms.

Federal Legal Services

In 1965, as part of President Lyndon B. Johnson's War on Poverty, Congress authorized funding for legal aid for the poor in civil and criminal cases under the Office of Economic Opportunity (OEO). The program came in the wake of urban riots, much as the impetus for earlier legal aid was the unrest of the first two decades of the twentieth century. As opposed to the earlier effort, legal services had the support of the president of the ABA, Lewis F. Powell, Jr., who was later appointed to the Supreme Court by President Nixon. Bar groups, however, wanted assurance that the legal services attorneys would not compete with local private practitioners. Under OEO legislation, neighborhood law offices were opened by local groups with federal funding. However, soon after the first offices were opened, they were swamped by more needy clients than they could properly represent (Johnson 1974). A review of program goals led to the conclusion that the funding being provided by the federal government would never even begin to meet the needs of the poor. A new strategy developed. Instead of handling the problems of the poor simply on an individual basis, legal services attorneys would work for law reform that could affect large numbers of poor persons—the instrumental use of law.

This goal was advanced by the quality of attorneys attracted to the legal services program; law school graduates who would normally be destined for corporate practice were energized by the prospects of social action through law. During the entire history of the legal aid society, no staff attorney had ever taken a case to the Supreme Court, but between 1967 to 1972, legal services attorneys took 219, 136 of which were decided on their merits, and 73 of these were won (Johnson 1974).

By 1973 there were over nine hundred legal services offices around the country employing close to five thousand lawyers. They initiated class-action suits against powerful interests. They forced federal and local governmental agencies to pay benefits to poor persons as mandated by welfare legislation; they forced the public schools to admit children of illegal aliens; they forced public hospitals to provide free abortions to indigent women; and they initiated litigation to force officials to improve jail conditions. The legal services attorneys upset business and farming communities by litigating to enforce state and federal statutes with respect to wages and working conditions. In addition to its efforts on behalf of farm workers, California Rural Legal Assistance forced the state to increase Medicaid and other welfare payments. Then-Governor Ronald Reagan was unsuccessful in his efforts to cut off funding for the group.

In 1974 Congress created the Legal Service Corporation to insulate the activities of legal services lawyers from increasing political pressures. Soon after Ronald Reagan was elected president, however, he moved to abolish the program by asking Congress to cut out all appropriations. Congress refused, although funding was cut back by 25 percent and significant restrictions were placed on the types of cases legal services lawyers could handle. The 1974 legislation provided for a governing board of eleven members appointed by the president, and in his continuing efforts to destroy the program, President Reagan nominated opponents of legal services to the governing board. In the first three years of his presidency, he nominated twenty-six people for the board, all opponents of legal services, none of whom were confirmed by the Republican-controlled Senate. The battle over the role of government in providing legal assistance for the poor continues, with the ABA on the side of continued funding and many political conservatives in opposition.

Public Interest Law

According to the Council for Public Interest Law (CPIL) (1976: 3), "Public interest law is the name that has been given to efforts to provide legal representation to interests that historically have been unrepresented and underrepresented in the legal process." There are two types of public interest law programs:

1. Some programs "focus on policy-oriented cases, where a decision will affect large numbers of people or advance a major law reform objective." Cases are selected because they have the potential to extend beyond the particular litigants, for example, those involving the environment or civil rights (CPIL 1976: 7).
2. Other programs "are designed to provide legal services to underserved groups on matters of immediate concern only to the parties directly involved," such as those provided by legal aid societies, public defenders, and neighborhood legal services offices (CPIL 1976: 7).

The first type of public interest law is of rather recent vintage. Historically, the judicial branch often thwarted legislative efforts designed to improve the situation of disadvantaged portions of our population: blacks, workers, children, mentally ill, the poor. While those on the left of the political spectrum historically advocated legislative remedies, those on the right found comfort in the courts. Over the years, however, the legislative branch became increasingly tolerant of activities that often denied equal protection and due process. The activism of the Supreme Court headed by Earl Warren gave impetus to those seeking to use the judicial branch to advance liberal causes that had failed in the legislative branch. Policy-oriented public interest law emerged from this perspective.

The public interest law firm is generally an independent tax-exempt corporation operating under a board of trustees and funded chiefly by foundation grants and individual contributions. Typically, these firms combine traditional legal activities with research, publication, organizing, and public education. One of the best-known public interest firms is the Legal Defense Educational Fund of the National Association for the Advancement of Colored People (NAACP). The CPIL (1976:34) notes that "virtually all subsequent public interest legal endeavors have followed in some respects the early example of the

NAACP'' (see the box, ''National Association for the Advancement of Colored People'').

National Association for the Advancement of Colored People

Founded in 1909, the NAACP was originally a lobbying and educational group, but gradually increased its activities to include litigation through its Legal Defense Educational Fund (LDEF), which became independent in 1939. By 1921 the NAACP had won court cases on voting, housing, and grand juries, and it was the LDEF that litigated the issue of school segregation culminating in the decision of *Brown v. the Board of Education.* The strategy used by the NAACP to challenge segregation was based on two major points, which are described by Rosemary Salomone (1986: 41): ''First sue for equal schools [as per the *Plessy* decision] on the theory that the cost of maintaining a dual system would prove so prohibitive as to speed the abolition of a segregated system. Second, pursue desegregation on the university level where it was likely to meet the least resistance. Then proceed incrementally to the elementary and secondary level.''

The model developed by the LDEF (CPIL 1976):

—used fulltime, salaried staff attorneys;
—avoided routine service cases in favor of those that affected issues beyond the immediate concern of individual litigants;
—assumed a proactive posture, seeking out cases with issues that could bring about changes in the way in which political and social institutions dealt with blacks;
—raised funds from widespread membership efforts;
—rejected the accumulation of big cases in favor of cases that promised incremental victories that built a favorable legal climate and fostered a positive public and legislative climate that could be converted into changed behavior patterns; and
—created a network of private attorneys to follow up on court victories and convert the rights won in court into practical substantive benefits.

Public interest law firms usually specialize in a particular area of advocacy and litigation. The Trial Lawyers for Public Justice (TLPJ) is a Washington-based public interest law firm that seeks damages on behalf of victims of government and corporate misconduct. Cases accepted by the firm must have a far-reaching effect on public interest litigation and set precedents for similar actions. Such cases generally have the potential for large monetary damage awards to alleviate the suffering of the victim and punish the wrongdoer. The case must involve unique legal issues that demonstrate a creative use of law for the public good. The firm has brought suit against a number of companies on behalf of persons harmed from exposure to toxic chemicals and against government officials for failing to protect persons from contaminated water. TLPJ has utilized the federal Clean Water Act, which allows citizens to file suit against companies to force compliance with federal law in order to improve water quality by halting pollution through punishing offending companies with steep fines. The firm's activities are supported by private contributions, settlement fees, and *pro bono* work by numerous attorneys. TLPJ attorneys have been fighting against legislative efforts to limit the size of awards in personal injury cases.

The Washington-based Center for Law and Social Policy was established in 1969 by four attorneys in the District of Columbia in order to work on behalf of the poor and the physically and mentally disabled. In addition to its advocacy efforts, the center sponsors a law school clinic for which approximately twenty law school students a year receive academic credit. Equal Rights Advocates of San Francisco specializes in cases involving employment and employment-related discrimination against women. The firm chooses cases that will have an impact—either because of the number of people who will be affected by the results or because of the legal principle that will be established—with respect to pay equity, sexual harassment, access to nontraditional jobs, or pregnancy-based discrimination. The Center for Public Representation (CPR) is headquartered in Madison, Wisconsin, where it operates a clinical program with the University of Wisconsin Law School. CPR specializes in issues relating to health-care cost containment, particularly for senior citizens.

A more recent development in the field of public interest law has been the establishment of firms with expressly conservative or pro-business agendas. The Washington Legal Foundation (WLF) was established in 1976 to promote "free enterprise and economic growth." WLF actively opposes the efforts of "so-called public legal advocates" who have "sought more judicial intrusion into our lives and marketplace, and more protection for dangerous criminals at our expense." (WLF Annual Report 1984: 3). "WLF successfully counters the activities of well-financed, anti-business, pro-criminal activists like the ACLU [American Civil Liberties Union], Ralph Nader and the Environmental Defense Fund who seek to implement a political agenda which they could not possibly achieve at the ballot box" (WLF Annual Report 1985: 1). The National Chamber Litigation Center (NCLC) was founded in 1977 as a public policy law firm for the U.S. Chamber of Commerce. The NCLC represents the business community in issues of national concern before the courts and regulatory agencies.

Now that we have set out the various roles for judges, prosecutors, and attorneys, in the next chapter we will examine the "scripts" used by these key actors on the stage that is the criminal court.

Notes

1. Thus, the appointment of federal district court judge J. Skelly Wright of New Orleans to the Fifth Circuit Court of Appeals was vetoed by Louisiana's senators using senatorial courtesy. Judge Wright's firm stand in desegregation cases had made him quite unpopular; he was eventually appointed to the Court of Appeals for the District of Columbia, a circuit outside the power of southern senators.

2. From 1974 to 1984, 71 percent of Circuit Court judgeships in Chicago were filled by candidates who ran unopposed in both the primary and general elections (Aspen 1987).

3. The Judicial Conference, which was established in 1922 as the Conference of Senior Circuit Judges, strives to provide uniformity of policy throughout the federal judiciary. Among the matters with which it has dealt are ethical standards for judges and other court personnel and qualifications for nonjudicial court personnel. Through its committee structure and director of the administrative office, the conference presents legislative proposals to Congress and prepares the budget for the federal judiciary (Wasby 1984).

4. About 40 percent of the work of the U.S. attorney's office involves civil matters, often as defense counsel for the government in tort actions (Eisenstein 1978).

5. In many states, city ordinances duplicate state misdemeanor provisions, and minor offenses therefore may be prosecuted under state law or under the local ordinances (Kamisar, LaFave, and Israel 1986: 26). Local ordinances are typically prosecuted by the city attorney, who often has the title of corporation counsel.

6

The Criminal Court Process

In the last chapter we examined the key actors in the legal system, all of whom are attorneys, and in previous chapters we looked at the role of attorneys in the appellate process. In this and the following chapter, we will look at a public stage on which attorneys are the stars; the scenario: criminal, civil, and juvenile trials. The trial brings together two opposing attorneys whose combat in an adversarial system is refereed by a judge. In some cases the judge also acts as a finder of fact; in other cases this responsibility is left to a jury. In this chapter we will be concerned with the criminal jury trial.[1]

Corpus Delecti

Literally meaning "the body of the crime," *corpus delecti* refers to the substance (or the body) of the alleged violation of the criminal law. It includes two elements which must be proved in order to sustain a criminal charge: *actus reus* and *mens rea*.

Actus reus refers to the need to prove that a violation of the criminal law actually occurred. It is a description of the criminal behavior; for example, according to the criminal law of Illinois (chapter 38: 19–3A), "A person commits residential burglary who knowingly and without authority enters the dwelling place of another with intent to commit therein a felony." Thus, it must be proved that the defendant entered the dwelling place of another without permission of the legal occupant for the purpose of taking property or harming the occupant. The defendant's fingerprints found inside a dwelling to which he had never been given legal access, and possession of household items belonging to the occupant which the defendant had not been given permission to possess, would constitute evidence of *actus reus*.

Mens rea literally means a "guilty mind" and refers to the question of intent. In order to prove the *corpus delecti* the prosecutor must be able to show that the defendant had a wrongful purpose—wilfulness—in carrying out the *actus reus*. Thus, a person lawfully employed by a moving company who mistakenly entered the wrong apartment and mistakenly removed household items was devoid of *mens rea*. *Mens rea* may also be absent as a result of infancy or mental incapacity. However, a person who injures or kills another by accident has *mens rea* if he or she was acting in a reckless manner, for example, driving under the influence of alcohol or drugs. Behavior that is a gross deviation from the standard of care expected of a reasonable person may constitute *mens rea* if it involves a conscious and unjustifiable risk of harm to others. A defendant can also raise an *affirmative defense:* he may claim self-defense or entrapment, for example, that government trickery induced him to commit a crime that he was otherwise not predisposed to commit.

Due Process

In a criminal action the state is arrayed against an individual defendant, and this inherent inequality requires that certain specific procedures be followed, or the defendant cannot be found guilty and punished according to law. Thus, there is an inherent tension between society's desire for the control of crime and the value we place on liberty—Herbert Packer (1968) refers to this as a conflict between two models of criminal justice—crime control and due process.

1. The *Crime Control Model* "is based on the proposition that the repression of criminal conduct is by far the most important function to be performed by the criminal justice process" (1968: 158). Effective crime control requires a high level of efficiency: the system must be able to apprehend, prosecute, and convict a large proportion of criminal offenders. The system, however, must respond to a great many cases with only limited resources. Consequently, efficiency demands that cases be handled speedily, with a minimum of formality and without time-consuming challenges. This efficiency can be accomplished only by a presumption of guilt (1968: 160): "The supposition is that the screening processes operated by the police and prosecutors are reliable indicators of probable guilt." To maximize crime control, after this screening the system must move expeditiously to conviction and sentencing. The crime control model is characterized by a high level of confidence in the ability of police and prosecutors to separate the guilty from the innocent. It is a model that tends toward inquisitorial system of justice, and conflicts with the due process model.

2. The *Due Process Model* is based on the assumption that the criminal justice system is deficient and stresses the possibility of error:

Figure 6.1. The criminal justice process.

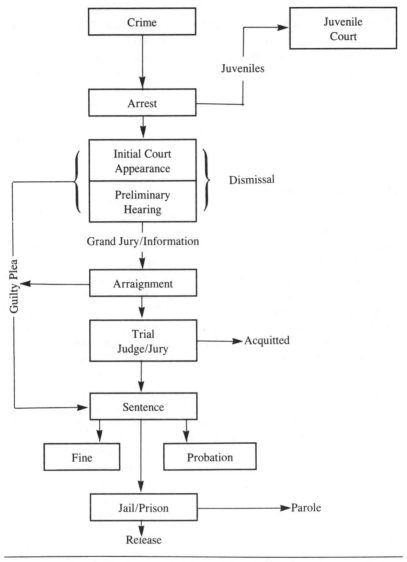

People are notoriously poor observers of disturbing events—the more emotion-arousing the context, the greater the possibility that recollection will be incorrect; confessions and admissions by persons in police custody may be induced by physical or psychological coercion so that the police end up hearing what the suspect thinks they want to hear rather than the truth; witnesses may be animated by a bias or interest that no one would trouble to discover except one specially charged with protecting the interests of the accused (as the police are not). (1968: 163)

Due process confronts crime control and its need for efficiency and speed with an obstacle course of formalities, technicalities, and civil rights (1968: 166): "Power is always subject to abuse—sometimes subtle, other times, as in the criminal justice process, open and ugly. Precisely because of its potency in subjecting the individual to the coercive power of the state, the criminal justice process must . . . be subjected to controls that prevent it from operating with maximal efficiency." The due process model requires the system to slow down until it "resembles a factory that has to devote a substantial part of its input to quality control" (1968: 165)—due process guarantees.

Due Process Guarantees

A finding of guilty must be beyond a reasonable doubt. While this legal concept cannot be quantified, it would certainly be far in excess of 50 percent. In other words, if a juror cannot, based only on the evidence presented and admitted at the trial, conclude, beyond any reasonable doubt, that the defendant committed the crime alleged, the juror must vote for a verdict of "not guilty."

Second are a series of guarantees that are part of the Constitution or Supreme Court rulings based on the Constitution. It should be noted that while the Court determines the minimum levels of due process to which a defendant is entitled, states have the sovereign power to provide rights beyond those embodied in the Constitution, and some states provide additional rights.

Right to Remain Silent

According to the Fifth Amendment, a person cannot "be compelled in any criminal case to be a witness against himself." Thus, the government must prove the allegation beyond a reasonable doubt, and the defendant is protected from having to assist in this endeavor. The basis for providing this protection is the long history of coerced confessions. Furthermore, the Supreme Court ruled in 1966 (*Miranda v. Arizona*) that before a suspect can be questioned by the police, he or she must be informed of the right to remain silent, as well as the right to counsel. In 1984, the Supreme Court, in a 5–4 decision (*New York v. Quarles*) ruled that "overriding considerations of public safety" may justify questioning a suspect in custody without providing the warnings contained in *Miranda*. The *public safety exception* was the result of a woman's complaint to two New York City police officers that she had been raped and that the suspects had entered a nearby supermarket. The officers entered the store and apprehended one of the suspects, who was found to be wearing a shoulder holster. One of the officers asked whether he had a gun. The suspect nodded toward a pile of boxes and said, "The gun is over there." The Court ruled that the unattended firearm represented an immediate danger to public safety, and the gun and the statement were admitted into evidence.

In 1985 the Court handed down a decision in the case of *Oregon v. Elstad* that affected the Miranda decision. Pursuant to an arrest warrant, the police went to the home of an eighteen-year-old suspect and explained to him that they thought he was involved in a burglary. He responded, "Yes, I was there." An hour later at the police station, the officers informed the suspect of his *Miranda* rights. He indicated that he understood and gave a full confession. On appeal the Court ruled that the statement "I was there" was inadmissible; however, the Court ruled that the second confession was valid despite arguments that it was an extension of the original inadmissible confession and was thereby tainted.

In a 1986 decision (*Moran v. Burbine*), the Court ruled that a suspect's *Miranda* rights were not violated when the police misled his attorney. Brian Burbine had been arrested for the brutal murder of a woman. An assistant public defender telephoned the police station where Burbine was being held and was told that there would be no questioning until the next day. The suspect was not informed of the call. About an hour later, Burbine was advised of his rights and confessed to the murder. The Court ruled that "events occurring outside of the presence of the suspect and entirely unknown to him, surely can have no bearing on the capacity to comprehend and knowingly relinquish a constitutional right." In that same year, the Court ruled (*Colorado v. Connelly*) that confessions of mentally ill defendants are admissible: A criminal suspect's "perception of coercion flowing from the 'voice of God,' however important or significant such perception may be in other disciplines, is a matter to which the United States Constitution does not speak."

Right to Counsel

The Sixth Amendment guarantees the accused "the assistance of Counsel for his defence." In 1963 the Court ruled that states must provide counsel for all indigent defendants in felony cases (*Gideon v. Wainwright*), and this was subsequently extended to misdemeanor cases where imprisonment might result (*Argersinger v. Hamlin*). Moreover, the right to appointed counsel is not limited to court, but extends to any time the police wish to ask a suspect questions (*Miranda*).

Right to Bail

The Constitution is rather vague with respect to bail. While the Eighth Amendment prohibits "excessive bail," no definition of "excessive" is provided. Persons accused of capital offenses are usually held without bail, and in 1987, the Supreme Court ruled (*United States v. Salerno*) that defendants who are found to constitute a danger to public safety may be held without the setting of bail. Furthermore, for a person without any means, a bail of even $25 can be excessive, while some drug dealers find no difficulty raising a million dollars for bail. In some states, bail bondsmen, who are privately licensed entrepreneurs, will provide a defendant's bail for a fee, generally 10 percent of the bond. If the defendant fails to return to court as required in the bail agreement, the bond is forfeited. Bail bondsmen employ skiptracers to apprehend bail jumpers and, in any event, jumping bail is an additional criminal offense for which a judge issues a warrant.

Many defendants are released without the need for a cash bond or its equivalent (such as title to a car or house); this is known as *released on recognizance* (ROR) and is a pledge to return to court on the appointed date to stand trial. In some jurisdictions there are programs designed to maximize the number of persons who can qualify for ROR. The best known of these programs, the Manhattan Bail Project, was developed by the Vera Foundation in New York City and copied by a number of jurisdictions. Defendants are interviewed by pretrial investigators (who are sometimes law students) and the results are entered on a point-scale form (see figure 6.2). Michael Kirby describes the use of the point scale:

> A number of items dealing with the defendant's ties in the community (e.g., employment, residence, and family ties) and relevant criminal justice factors (such as prior record, current charge or prior bail violations) are included in the scale. Normally a defendant is given plus or minus points for each item. The information obtained in the interview is then verified by referring to records, employers and family members. If the defendant has attained a certain number of points, a recommendation is made to the court for release. (1977: 1)

Persons who are unable to effect a release on bail are held in custody in a jail, usually a county facility, which in most jurisdictions is operated by the sheriff. This subjects legally innocent persons to punishment, separates them from family, friends, and employment, limits them in assisting their attorneys in the defense process, and adds to the overcrowding that is characteristic of most county jails. While incarceration is most always an unpleasant experience, in a county jail it is even more so. Most detention facilities provide few opportunities for recreation, and they are usually understaffed and overcrowded, subjecting the inmates to the real possibility of physical and/or sexual assault by other prisoners.

The basic purpose of bail is to guarantee a defendant's return to court, but it is often used as a form of preventive detention. When there is strong belief that the defendant will return to crime, a judge, often on the recommendation of the prosecution, will set bail at a level that is impossible for the defendant to

Figure 6.2. Original Vera Point Scale—Manhattan Bail Project.

To be recommended, defendant needs:
1. A New York area address where he can be reached, and
2. A total of five points from the following categories:

Interview	Verified	
		Prior Record
1	1	No convictions.
0	0	One misdemeanor conviction.
−1	−1	Two misdemeanor or one felony convictions.
−2	−2	Three or more misdemeanor or two or more felony convictions.
		Family Ties (In New York area)
3	3	Lives in established family home and visits other family members (immediate family only).
2	2	Lives in established family home (immediate family).
		Employment or School
3	3	Present job 1 year or more, steadily.
2	2	Present job 4 months or present and prior 6 months.
1	1	Has present job which is still available. OR Unemployed 3 months or less and 9 months or more steady prior job. OR Unemployment Compensation. OR Welfare.
3	3	Presently in school, attending regularly.
2	2	Out of school less than 6 months but employed, or in training.
1	1	Out of school 3 months or less, unemployed and not in training.
		Residence (In New York area steadily)
3	3	1 year at present residence.
2	2	1 year at present or last prior residence or 6 months at present residence.
1	1	6 months at present and last prior residence or in New York City 5 years or more.
		Discretion
+1	+1	Positive, over 65, attending hospital, appeared on some previous case.
−1	0	Negative—intoxicated—intention to leave jurisdiction.

Total Interview Points

Interview Verified

Recommended   Not Recommended

Source: Kirby, 1977.

make. The use of bail in this manner, while not illegal, is quite controversial. It involves predictions of future behavior, always a questionable undertaking with important moral and legal aspects. The judge's bail decision is influenced by the defendant's previous criminal record, his or her previous behavior while out on bail, roots in the community, the attitude of the prosecutor, and publicity that the case may have generated.

Right to a Speedy and Public Jury Trial

The Sixth Amendment guarantees that "in all criminal prosecutions, the accused shall enjoy the right to a speedy and public trial, by an impartial jury."

While the term "speedy trial" is not defined in the Constitution, most states and the federal government have statutes specifying the amount of time allowed from arrest to trial. According to the federal Speedy Trial Act, a defendant must be brought to trial within one hundred days of his or her arrest. In Illinois, statutes require that the defendant be brought to trial within 120 days if incarcerated, or 160 days if free on bail; otherwise, the case must be dismissed. In 1972 the Court (*Barker v. Wingo*) ruled that determination of whether a particular defendant has been denied a speedy trial is to be made on a case-by-case basis, and the Court established several tests by which to judge the delay: (a) length of the delay, (b) reasons for the delay, (c) timely assertion of the right to a speedy trial, and (d) prejudice to the defendant as a result of the delay. The Court indicated an interest in preventing oppressive pretrial incarceration, minimizing the anxiety and hardship of the defendant, and avoiding hampering the defense—delay that hampers the defense can result in the denial of a fair trial, which violates the Fifth and Fourteenth Amendments.

While the Sixth Amendment protects criminal defendants from being tried in secret, can a defendant waive this right or demand a closed trial?[2] In 1986 the Court ruled that the First Amendment's freedom of the press cannot be overcome by a defendant's assertion that a public trial will be prejudicial. In 1986 (*Press-Enterprise Company v. Superior Court of California*), the Court ruled that judges may bar the press and the public from pretrial hearings in criminal cases only as a last resort to assure a fair trial, and only after stating why it is necessary to conduct the hearings in secret. Chief Justice Warren E. Burger, writing for the majority, pointed out that "one of the important means of assuring a fair trial is that the process be open to neutral observers."

In addition to the trial itself, in 1984 the Court ruled unanimously that trial judges must also ordinarily permit the public and news media to attend the jury selection proceedings (*Press-Enterprise v. Superior Court*).

Right to Confront Witnesses

The Sixth Amendment requires that the defendant "be informed of the nature and cause of the accusations; to be confronted with the witnesses against him; to have compulsory process for obtaining witnesses in his favor." Thus, the defendant can subpoena a witness to testify in his or her defense and has the unlimited right to cross-examine adverse witnesses (discussed later in this chapter).

Exclusionary Rule

This legal principle (sometimes referred to as the "poisoned fruit doctrine"), which is based on the Fourth and Fourteenth Amendments, prohibits evidence obtained in violation of the Constitution from being used in a trial.

Thus, even evidence that proves a defendant's guilt beyond a reasonable doubt, cannot be entered into evidence at trial if it was secured in an unconstitutional manner (*Weeks v. United States*, 1914; *Mapp v. Ohio*, 1961). This rule is the Court's way of controlling the behavior of law enforcement agents, by rendering certain improper activities not worth the effort (since their fruits will be inadmissible).

In 1984 (*United States v. Leon*), the Court ruled that when the police act on a defective warrant, the exclusionary rule need not apply, since its purpose is to control the behavior of the police, not of judges (who issue warrants). That same year, the Court established the doctrine of *inevitable discovery* as an exception to the exclusionary rule in *Nix v. Williams* (which was a continuation of a famous 1977 case, *Brewer v. Williams*). Robert Williams was suspected of killing a ten-year-old girl, and two hundred volunteers were combing the Des Moines, Iowa, area searching for her body. Although the police had promised the suspect's attorney that they would not question him, as they were driving Williams across the state, they asked him to think about the fact that "the parents of this little girl should be entitled to a Christian burial" for their daughter. His response was to lead the police to the victim's body.

In the 1977 case decision, the Court ruled that the "Christian burial" speech had violated the suspect's constitutional rights by inducing him to incriminate himself outside his lawyer's presence. Williams was tried again, and the prosecutors did not offer into evidence any incriminating statements of the defendant, nor did the state attempt to show that Williams had directed police to the body. The trial judge admitted the prosecution's evidence as to the condition of the body and related physical evidence on the grounds that the prosecution had shown that even if Williams had not been improperly interrogated, the victim's body would nevertheless have been found by the search party. In its decision, the Court gave recognition to the principle of inevitable discovery.

In *Colorado v. Bertine* (1987) the Court created an "inventory exception" to the exclusionary rule when it stated that police need not secure a search warrant to look into closed containers found in a confiscated vehicle. Police found illegal drugs in a closed back pack after a drunk-driving arrest. The Court ruled that police were following standardized procedures by opening closed containers and listing their contents during a vehicle inventory. The Court noted that knowledge of the precise nature of property found in vehicles for which the police have a responsibility, helps to guard against claims of theft, vandalism, or negligence. In *Maryland v. Garrison* (1987) the Court established a "reasonable mistake" exception to the exclusionary rule. Police officers in Baltimore, acting on a valid search warrant, entered the wrong apartment in a multiunit dwelling where they found illegal drugs. The Court ruled that under the circumstances—two apartments on a floor that the police reasonably believed contained only one apartment—the Constitution had not been violated. Later in

1987, the Court appeared to move in a different direction. In *Arizona v. Hicks* (1987) the Court ruled that police officers acting on a warrant to search for illegal weapons could not even slightly move stereo equipment suspected of being stolen to check the serial numbers.

Double Jeopardy Prohibited

The Fifth Amendment forbids double jeopardy by stating that no persons shall "be subject for the same offence to be twice put in jeopardy of life or limb." Once a defendant has been acquitted, that is, found not guilty, he or she can never be tried again for the same crime. Jeopardy becomes applicable in a jury trial when the jury is empaneled and sworn, and in a bench trial when the judge begins to hear evidence. The Court has permitted separate trials in federal and state courts based on the same act (for example, murder in a state court, and civil rights violations based on the murder in federal court), and in more than one state. The Court ruled (*Heath v. Alabama*, 1985) that two states may prosecute a defendant for the same criminal act without violating the Fifth Amendment. Larry Heath was sentenced in Alabama and Georgia for hiring two men to kidnap and kill his pregnant wife. She was kidnapped from their home in Alabama and shot to death in Georgia. In order to avoid a possible death sentence, Heath pled guilty in Georgia to a noncapital offense. He was subsequently tried and convicted of the same charges in Alabama and sentenced to death. The Court ruled that because each state is sovereign, the defendant had committed separate offenses against the law of each and, therefore, the convictions were an exception to the double jeopardy clause.

Joinder of offenses. An issue related to double jeopardy occurs when a defendant is alleged to have violated several statutes based on the same act or several acts that are somehow connected: "Most often, local law grants the prosecutor the option to bring either separate prosecutions or a single prosecution when the several charges arose from the same criminal episode" (Israel and LaFave 1980: 31). However, a prosecutor who opts for separate prosecutions runs the risk of crossing the somewhat nebulous line that constitutes double jeopardy and, in any event, state law and court decisions will typically bar cumulative sentences: "the maximum sentence will be limited to that available for the highest offense on which a conviction is obtained" (1980: 34). At times the court will order two or more indictments or information to be tried together (joined) if they could have initially been the subject of a single indictment/information.

Crime control versus due process. The conflict between the crime control and due process models of criminal justice can be conceived of as a zero-sum continuum: court decisions or legislation that moves criminal justice toward one model does so at the expense of the other. Exceptions to the exclusionary rule, for example, while they may increase police efficiency in certain instances, lessen the ability of the courts to control police misconduct.

Crime Control	Due Process
efficiency	liberty

Pretrial Procedures

Before we begin looking at the steps of the process used in the adjudication of criminal defendants, we need to note that its details vary from state to state and even between jurisdictions in the same state. Therefore, this chapter will present a generalized version of the criminal trial process that may not exactly match that of every jurisdiction. (For an overview, see figure 6.3, The Flow of Felony Cases.)

Criminal cases usually begin with a summary arrest (that is, an arrest without a warrant) by a police officer acting on his or her own—having seen a crime committed—or on behalf of a civilian complainant, usually the victim of a crime. In either event, the evidence needed to effect a lawful arrest is known as *probable cause*:

> that set of facts or circumstances based on reliable information or personal knowledge or observation by an officer which reasonably show and would warrant an ordinary prudent man in believing that a particular person has been guilty of, is threatening, or is about to commit some offense against the law. (Texas Criminal Justice Council 1974: 161)

Except for some minor offenses (usually involving a motor vehicle), the perpetrator will be transported to a police facility, fingerprinted, photographed, and given the opportunity to make one or more telephone calls. (At this point the procedures vary, and the following are those most frequently encountered.) If the charge is a misdemeanor, a lesser crime for which most jurisdictions provide a penalty of no more than one year of imprisonment, the suspect may be allowed to post bond and appear in court on a subsequent date. If the subject is unable to post bail, or if the charge is a felony, that is, a crime punishable by more than one year of imprisonment, he or she will be transported to a lower court for an initial hearing or, in misdemeanor cases, arraignment within twenty-four hours after the arrest. The charges will be read, the need for assigned counsel considered, (in misdemeanor cases a plea will be entered), and bail will be set. In misdemeanor cases, the charge(s) may be disposed of at this stage in a process often referred to as *rough justice*.

Figure 6.3. The flow of felony cases.

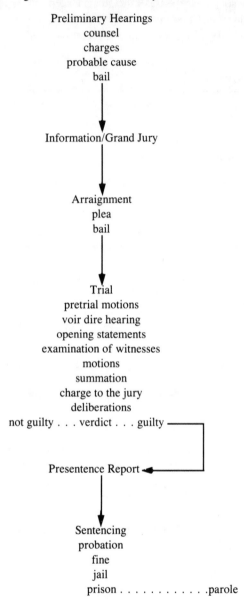

Preliminary Hearings
counsel
charges
probable cause
bail

Information/Grand Jury

Arraignment
plea
bail

Trial
pretrial motions
voir dire hearing
opening statements
examination of witnesses
motions
summation
charge to the jury
deliberations
not guilty . . . verdict . . . guilty

Presentence Report

Sentencing
probation
fine
jail
prison . . . . .parole

Rough Justice in the Lower Courts

Most criminal cases begin and end in the lower courts. Because of the large volume of cases entering this part of the criminal justice system, efficient case processing is the primary focus. Efficiency requires speed, but the various due-process guarantees to which every criminal defendant is entitled slow down the process considerably. In an effort to avoid delay, judges in the lower courts typically disregard the niceties of due process, and they are assisted in this process by both the prosecutor and the defense counsel. Defendants may be processed collectively, or at such a high rate of speed that individualization is virtually impossible. Dismissals and pleas of guilty predominate, and to the casual or uninformed observer the scene is confusing and not at all like popular portrayals of justice. It is rough justice. A study by the chief administrative judge in New York revealed that on average lower-court judges in that city spend a mere 3.4 minutes on each case ("No Trial—and No Punishment Either" 1986). An editorial in the *New York Times* (August 18, 1986: 22) referred to the lower courts in New York as dispensing "cattle-car" justice. In Chicago, where this writer has worked for a number of years, processing occurs so swiftly that defendants are often unaware of the fact that their cases have been dismissed—the inconvenience of several hours in a dank and often foul-smelling police lockup being viewed as sufficient punishment—for innocent and guilty alike.

In order to avoid legal complications that cause delay, the key actors must gain the cooperation of the defendant. This is accomplished by treating him or her in a lenient manner. Thus, defendants who waive their rights, who do not object to the speedy processing, receive an outcome considerably more lenient than that to which they might otherwise be entitled. Defendants who insist on the full array of due-process rights will get them—but there is often a price. Such defendants may be viewed as disruptive, as lacking in any show of contrition and, therefore, deserving of more severe treatment. If convicted, they will receive sentences in excess of the norm, and in the meantime they may be subjected to relatively high bail and a stay in the county jail while awaiting trial. It is no small irony that offenders who raise no objections and quickly plead guilty are often able to avoid incarceration, while those who insist on their innocence may be imprisoned, even if for only a short period of time.

Felony Cases

In felony cases, the prosecutor may send a case to the grand jury or present evidence at a preliminary (probable-cause) hearing and file an information setting forth details of the alleged offense, such as date, time, and place.

Grand Jury

In the federal system a grand jury is a body of twenty-three citizens empowered to operate with a quorum of sixteen, and requiring twelve votes for an indictment. In the fifty states, however, while the minimum varies considerably, nowhere does the maximum of grand jurors exceed twenty-three. While some states adhere to the federal rule of twelve for an indictment, in others the range is anywhere from four to nine (Frankel and Naftalis 1977). Like those serving on a petit, or trial jury, grand jurors are selected from the voting rolls. They meet in secret to consider evidence presented by the prosecutor. The use of a grand jury dates back to twelfth-century England, and it remained an arm of the king, part of his law enforcement and prosecutorial responsibilities. In the American colonies, grand juries routinely defied governmental authority, and as revolution approached, grand juries were generally sympathetic to those resisting British rule, refusing, for example, to indict opponents of the Stamp Act. It was during this period that the grand jury gained a reputation as a protector of the individual against unwarranted prosecution and, as a result, was incorporated into the Fifth Amendment: "No person shall be held to answer for a capital, or otherwise infamous crime, unless on presentment or indictment of a grand jury." England, which originated the grand jury, abolished it in 1933, and the Supreme Court has never applied this Fifth Amendment requirement to the states (Emerson 1983). Thus, while the federal government operates under the grand jury requirement, states differ in their use of this body.

In some states (see figure 6.4), the grand jury is required for all crimes; in other states, it is required in cases of felonies or capital crimes, while in a number of mostly midwestern and western states, the use of the grand jury is optional for the prosecutor. Even where the use of a grand jury for bringing charges is optional, Deborah Emerson notes that

> under certain circumstances prosecutors may prefer to use the grand jury or be forced to do so by events outside their control. For example, a grand jury indictment may be used to file charges when the defendant cannot be located and the time limits allowed for prosecution under the statute of limitations are about to be exceeded. Similarly, the secrecy of the grand jury may allow defendants to be charged and taken into custody before they can pose potential danger to a witness's safety or flee from the jurisdiction. In addition, the need to protect the identity of undercover agents, the ability to test a witness before a jury, or the opportunity to involve the community in case screening may be contributing factors. (1983: 13)

In Arizona, however, Emerson (1984: 142) found that prosecutors favored the probable cause hearing when the witness was considered to be in danger. In Pima (Tucson) and Maricopa (Phoenix) counties, prosecutors used the probable-cause hearing since the testimony can be preserved for use at trial, which removes one of the primary motivations for witness tampering. The hearing also provides some backup for the state should a witness not be available to testify at trial.

Since the members of a grand jury are not agents of the government—they act as representatives of the citizenry—the extensive due-process rights typically enjoyed by a criminal defendant are not relevant to grand jury proceedings. The activities and hearings of the grand jury are secret; sixteen states permit the subject of a grand jury inquiry to have an attorney present at the hearing, but counsel is permitted only to give advice, and in the other states and the federal system, an attorney is not even permitted to accompany his or her client at the hearing. There is no right to present evidence, or to cross-examine adverse witnesses. While the subject can refuse to answer any questions whose answers may be incriminating, he or she can be granted immunity and, under the threat of being jailed for contempt, be required to answer all questions.

There are two types of *immunity:*

1. *Transactional immunity* provides blanket protection against prosecution for crimes about which a person is compelled to testify.

2. *Use immunity* prohibits the information provided by a person from being used against him or her, but the person can still be prosecuted using evidence obtained independently of his or her testimony before the grand jury.

The grand jury can receive virtually any type of information, even that which would not be admissible at a trial, such as certain types of hearsay and evidence that was secured in violation of the Fourth Amendment—the exclusionary rule does not apply to the grand jury (*United States v. Calandra*, 1974). If a majority of grand jury members vote in support of an indictment, they return a *true bill*.

In every state and the federal system, the grand jury may also be used for investigation. This body has broad investigative authority, including the power to subpoena persons and documents. In those states where statutes permit and in the federal system, the grand jury is used to investigate the operations of law enforcement and other government agencies, particularly when corruption is suspected, and the activities of organized crime. In addition to handing down indictments, a federal grand jury (impaneled under the Organized Crime Control Act of 1970) and those of several states are permitted to issue reports. Federal organized-crime grand juries have the power to publish reports at the completion of their terms on certain types of noncriminal misconduct by public officials, although on the state level, Marvin Frankel and Gary Naftalis note, the practice is extremely varied:

> Many states prohibit grand jury reports, and those that permit them commonly circumscribe the grand jury's power. Grand juries are generally prohibited from commenting on purely private activity, and reports criticizing publicly

Figure 6.4. Requirements for grand jury indictment to initiate prosecutions.

Grand Jury Indictment Required[a]	Grand Jury Indictment Optional	Grand Jury Lacks Authority to Indict
All Crimes	Arizona	Pennsylvania[d]
New Jersey	Arkansas	
South Carolina	California	
Tennessee[b]	Colorado	
Virginia	Idaho	
All Felonies	Illinois	
Alabama	Indiana	
Alaska	Iowa	
Delaware	Kansas	
District of Columbia	Maryland	
Georgia	Michigan	
Hawaii	Missouri	
Kentucky	Montana	
Maine	Nebraska	
Mississippi	Nevada	
New Hampshire	New Mexico	
New York	North Dakota	
North Carolina	Oklahoma	
Ohio	Oregon	
Texas	South Dakota	
West Virginia	Utah	
Capital Crimes Only	Vermont	
Connecticut	Washington	
Florida	Wisconsin	
Louisiana	Wyoming	
Massachusetts[c]		
Minnesota		
Rhode Island		

[a] With the exception of capital cases a defendant can always waive his right to an indictment. Thus, the requirement for an indictment to initiate prosecution exists only in the absence of a waiver.

[b] The information on the laws of Tennessee derives exclusively from our statutory analysis. No survey instrument was returned from that state.

[c] In Massachusetts, felonies punishable by five years or less in state prison may be prosecuted on the basis of a complaint in the District Court. However, if this option is selected instead of prosecuting the case in Superior Court following an indictment, the defendant may not be sentenced to state prison but only to 2 1/2 years in the House of Correction. Capital offenses and felonies punishable by more than five years in prison must be prosecuted by indictment.

[d] The grand jury in Pennsylvania has investigative powers only and does not have the authority to issue indictments.

Source: Deborah Day Emerson, *The Role of the Grand Jury and the Preliminary Hearing in Pretrial Screening* (Washington, D.C.: U.S. Government Printing Office, 1984).

elected officials tend to be allowed only where statutory authority exists. Finally, as a rule, grand jury reports may be disclosed only with court approval. (1977: 32)

While grand jury reports cannot command any particular performance, the widespread publicity they receive usually encourages action by government officials.

The original purpose of the grand jury was to protect a person from being subjected to prosecution in the absence of sufficient evidence. Since the grand jury hears only one side of the case, however, it very seldom votes for *no true bill*, and there are many observers who feel that its original purpose has been distorted into being a tool of the prosecutor. (For a review of issues concerning reforming the grand jury, see Emerson 1983, 1984).

Preliminary Hearing

If the grand jury is not used, the lower-court judge will have witnesses sworn and hear testimony from both prosecution and defense counsel. This process is similar to, but more informal than, the trial process, since its only purpose is for a judge to determine whether there is enough evidence—probable cause—to justify continuing the case. In effect, this hearing reviews the sufficiency of evidence used by the police officer to justify an arrest. If no probable cause is found, an infrequent occurrence, the subject is released. If probable cause is found, the prosecutor will file an information and the defendant will be arraigned in superior court.

Arraignment

After a probable cause hearing and the filing of an information, or a grand jury indictment, an arrest warrant is issued and the subject is brought before a judge in superior court for arraignment.[3] He or she is informed of the charges and, if indigent, an attorney will be appointed; bail is set or (if previously set) reviewed; and the subject enters a plea: (a) not guilty, (b) not guilty by reason of insanity; (c) guilty; or (d) nolo contendere—no contest. The latter has the same effect as a plea of guilty, but it cannot be used as evidence of a criminal conviction at any subsequent civil trial related to the criminal act. Persons who refuse to enter a plea have a plea of not guilty automatically entered for them. In practice, most pleas at arraignment are ''guilty,'' since there has usually been an agreement to enter a plea of guilty in exchange for some form of leniency. (Plea bargaining will be discussed in Chapter 8.) Defendants who plead not guilty or not guilty by reason of insanity are ready to be tried. (Those who plead guilty or *nolo contendere* are ready for a sentencing hearing.)

The Jury

The use of trial juries goes back to colonial America and was made part of our Constitution by the Sixth Amendment. The Supreme Court has interpreted the Constitution to require jury trial only when the possible sentence is imprisonment for six months or more, although some states provide jury trials for all criminal defendants. While most states and the federal government use twelve-person juries, the Supreme Court has determined that juries with as few as six persons are constitutionally permissible except in cases involving a capital crime. In most states jury decisions—verdicts—are required to be unanimous, or else the result is a *hung jury* and a retrial or dismissal of the charges. The Court has ruled that jury verdicts of 10–2 (used in Oregon) and 9–3 (used in Louisiana) are constitutionally permitted. If six jurors are used, however, the decision must be unanimous.

The jury selection process involves seven steps (see figure 6.5):

1. *First master list.* This is usually the voting rolls, which by their very nature contain the names of citizens over the age of eighteen. In some jurisdictions the rolls of the motor vehicle bureau or the tax rolls are used because some persons choose not to register to vote in order to avoid jury duty.

2. *First juror list.* Names are selected at random from the master list.

3. *Questionnaires.* Persons on the first juror list are mailed questionnaires to determine if they are qualified. Most jurisdictions require that the jurors be citizens of at least eighteen years of age, who are able to read, write, and understand the English language, be residents of the court's jurisdiction for at least one year, and be free of any felony convictions and physical or mental handicaps that would make them unable to render jury service. Otherwise-qualified persons may be exempted for a variety of reasons, depending on the statutes and customs of the jurisdiction, for example, law enforcement officers, doctors, lawyers, and mothers of infants. Jurors may also be excused from service based on personal hardships, for example, the owners of small businesses. Persons may also receive a temporary postponement based on a hardship that is time-limited, for example, teachers during the school year or farmers during the harvest season. Evasion of jury service is a significant problem in some jurisdictions, and sometimes trial courts have to shut down because not enough of those summoned appear for service.

4. *Second master list.* Based on the questionnaires, a second master list is developed and jury service summonses are sent out. Those responding are screened as disqualified, exempt, excused, or qualified.

5. *Report for service.* Those who are qualified are directed to report to a central jury room where they constitute the jury pool.

6. *Impaneled.* The members of the jury pool are sworn in as jurors.

7. *Voir dire.* A panel of jurors is brought into a large courtroom in which the key actors are present in addition to the defendant. Each member of the panel is questioned by the judge, the prosecutor, and the defense counsel. (In some jurisdictions only the judge questions the jurors, although the attorneys may submit questions to the judge.) There are two purposes for the *voir dire* (meaning to speak the truth) hearing: first, to determine if any of the jurors is unfit to serve on this particular jury, for example, is familiar with the defendant or victim, is prejudiced, or has heard a great deal about the case as a result of pretrial publicity, and, second, to allow the attorneys for the prosecution and defense some discretion in determining who will serve on the jury. These goals are achieved by use of the *challenge for cause* and the *peremptory challenge*.

Either attorney can argue that a juror is not fit to serve based on certain information that was revealed as a result of the questions asked by the judge or the attorneys. A challenge for cause must be upheld by the judge, in which case the juror is excused. Peremptory challenges can be used by either attorney to excuse any juror without having to state a reason. Some jurisdictions do not permit peremptory challenges and, in any event, their number is limited from two to twenty-six, depending on the statutes and the seriousness of the charges. The voir dire hearing continues until a jury is chosen and *impaneled*, which means they are administered an oath by the court clerk "to well and truly try the case." In many jurisdictions one or two additional, or alternate, jurors are chosen in case a regular juror becomes ill or cannot serve for some other reason.

In 1986 the Supreme Court ruled that prosecutors may not use their peremptory challenges to exclude blacks from juries because they believe that such persons may favor a black defendant. In *Baston v. Kentucky* the Court overruled a 1965 decision on the same issue. The court determined that

> although a prosecutor ordinarily is entitled to exercise permitted peremptory challenges "for any reason at all, as long as that reason is related to his view concerning the outcome," the Equal Protection Clause forbids the prosecutor to challenge jurors solely on account of their race or on the assumption that black jurors as a group will be unable impartially to consider the state's case against a black defendant.

The decision also made it easier for a defendant to raise the issue. The Court's decision noted, "Once the defendant makes a prima facie showing [that black jurors were excluded], the burden shifts to the state to come forward with a neutral explanation for challenging black jurors." This decision may hasten the move to abolish the peremptory challenge, a position supported by Justice Thurgood Marshall in his concurring opinion.

In *Griffith v. Kentucky* and *Brown v. United States* (1987) the Court ruled that the decision in *Baston* would apply retroactively. (The ruling for retroac-

Figure 6.5. The jury selection process.

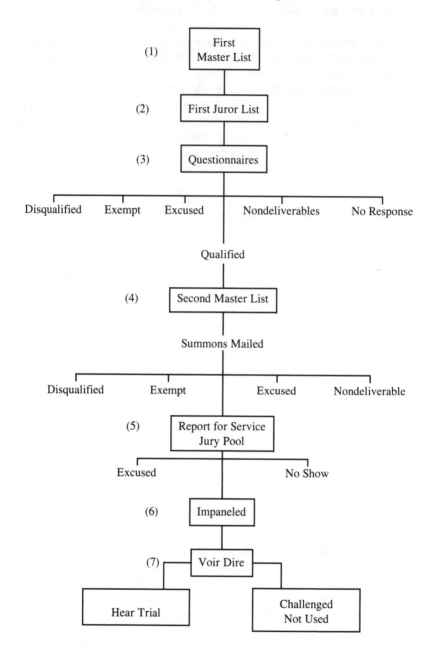

tivity represents a significant shift from the Court's previous approach to rulings on criminal procedure.)

That same year, the Court ruled that prospective jurors who state that they could not under any circumstances vote for the imposition of the death penalty could be excluded for cause. In *Lockhart v. McCree*, the Court ruled that the so-called *death-qualified* jury, "unlike the wholesale exclusion of blacks, women or Mexican-Americans from jury service, is carefully designed to serve the state's concededly legitimate interest in obtaining a single jury that can properly and impartially apply the law to the facts of the case at both guilt and sentencing phases of a capital crime." (In most states that authorize the death penalty, the jury first decides on guilt, and then, after a hearing, determines whether the death sentence should be imposed.)

Scientific jury selection. Scientific jury selection refers to the use of the tools of the social sciences to assist attorneys in the jury selection process. Morton Hunt (1982: 70) summarizes the approach:

> . . . a few dozen sociologists, psychologists, market researchers and others—use public opinion surveys, in-depth interviews, computer analyses correlating jurors' backgrounds and attitudes and laboratory simulations of impending trials to help lawyers select jurors likely to favor their side, exclude those likely to be hostile to it, and present their cases in ways psychologically designed to benefit from the unconscious needs and motives of the jurors.

The social scientists attempt to identify the type of person most likely to be favorable to their side, as well as those most likely to be hostile, for use at *voir dire* hearings. In some programs a simulated jury-selection process is conducted and the "jurors" selected are paid to participate in a mock trial that helps to prepare attorneys for the actual case being litigated. After the mock trial the "jurors" are interviewed to determine the best trial approach, the one most likely to convince a real jury: what questions should be asked, how to speak, what clothes to wear—all in an effort to enhance the attorney's influence on the prospective jury.

There are a number of firms that will provide this service (Hunt 1982; Andrews 1982), and it is expensive. For that reason, except in isolated cases, scientific jury selection usually occurs only in civil cases where the outcome can involve millions of dollars. The best known criminal case where this approach was used (by the defense—it would be too costly for the prosecution) involved a twenty-year-old black female inmate, Joann Little (sometimes spelled Joan or Joanne). In 1974, while being held in the rural Beaufort, North Carolina, jail on a burglary charge, Little stabbed a white, sixty-two-year-old night jailor to death with an icepick. Little claimed that the jailor had used the icepick to force her to commit an act of oral sodomy, and while there was conclusive evidence of a sex act, it could not be determined if the jailor had perpetrated a rape or had been lured to his death.

Because of the racial and gender implications, Joann Little received assistance which she otherwise would not have been able to afford. Social scientists conducted a public opinion poll among residents in the counties of the Beaufort area and the degree of prejudice uncovered caused the court to grant a change of venue to Raleigh (Wake County). Subsequent surveys of a sample of Wake County voters revealed a profile of friendly and unfriendly jurors that assisted lawyers at the *voir dire* hearing. The five-week trial ended with a jury deliberation that lasted only seventy-eight minutes—Joann Little was acquitted. The cost of the scientific jury services contributed to the Little defense was estimated at $300,000—the potential for exacerbating already existing inequities in our system of justice is obvious.

Instructions to the Jury

The members of a jury are given specific instructions by the judge with respect to their responsibilities as jurors. They are cautioned against discussing the case with anyone, including fellow jurors, and against reading or listening to anything pertaining to the case. They are directed to report any person who attempts to discuss the case with them, since this may constitute a crime—jury tampering. In particularly sensitive cases, or when there is a great deal of news coverage of a case, the jurors may be sequestered. This can happen after the trial is over and the jury is sent to deliberate, or from the time they are impaneled. In such cases, the jurors are held in a form of protective custody, in a hotel or motel guarded by bailiffs, deputy sheriffs, or marshals. What they read or view on television is monitored and subjected to censorship, and their telephone conversations with family or friends are restricted accordingly. Each court day they are transported by a special bus to and from the courthouse under guard. The sequestering continues until the jury reaches a verdict or until they are dismissed by the judge if they are a hung jury.

Evidence

It was noted above that evidence secured in an unconstitutional manner cannot be admitted at trial. Jurors must also be protected from evidence that may be misleading or prejudicial. This includes *hearsay*: an assertion made by a testifying witness about a statement made out of court by someone else. Hearsay is considered inherently prejudicial because opposing counsel does not have an opportunity to test the reliability of the evidence by cross-examining the person who originally made the statement at the time it was made. "The speaker may have been joking, or guessing, or even deliberately lying'' (Friedenthal, Kane, and Miller 1985: 464). There are, however, many exceptions to the general prohibition against hearsay evidence. The jury, after all, is made up of laypeople, and it is the responsibility of the judge—acting on motions or objections from counsel—to prevent improper testimony from being entered as evidence. There are two fundamental types of evidence, direct and indirect.

1. *Direct evidence*. Direct evidence proves a fact directly. It is testimony provided by an eyewitness (which in law also includes hearing and the senses of taste, smell, and touch). An example of eyewitness evidence would be a statement such as ''I observed the defendant exit the liquor store with a firearm in his right hand and a paper bag in his left hand.''

2. *Indirect evidence or circumstantial evidence*. This type of evidence does not prove a proposition directly. For example, a bullet recovered from the body of the victim matches that fired from a revolver owned by the defendant. Jon Waltz (1983: 14) states that circumstantial evidence, however, ''is frequently far more persuasive than direct evidence.'' Evidence such as fingerprints and hair samples is often more reliable than that provided by an eyewitness, particularly when the latter is based on the testimony of an untrained civilian, often the victim. Persons who are threatened or otherwise subject to the trauma of a crime are notoriously poor observers.

These two types of evidence come in three basic forms, which are described by Jon Waltz (1983: 14) as the following:

1. *Testimonial evidence* is that which is presented orally by a witness in court and under oath, although occasionally it takes the form of a sworn pretrial written deposition.

2. *Tangible evidence* is any physical exhibit, which can be
   (a) *real evidence*, such as the actual murder weapon, contract, drugs; or
   (b) *demonstrative evidence*, which is usually a visual aid such as a drawing of the crime scene or an anatomical model.

3. *Judicial notice* are those matters that are subject to common knowledge or certain verification through reference to such highly reliable sources as calendars or medical dictionaries. Such matters need not be proved, but the judge will ''instruct the jurors to take them as fully established without any necessity of formal proof through witnesses or exhibits.''

Court Personnel

Before proceeding to the trial, we should note the presence of persons other than the key actors. There will be one or more bailiffs (deputy sheriffs, court officers, marshals) responsible for maintaining order and security, and guarding prisoners. There will be a clerk who maintains the records and may call the cases. And there will be a court reporter who records all proceedings in the courtroom, especially the testimony of witnesses. The reporter uses a small typewriter-like stenographic device, which in the hands of a skilled operator permits simultaneous recording. The stenographic record is transcribed by typewriter and becomes the official record of the trial. In some jurisdictions, in addition to the court reporter, a tape recorder may be used.

The Trial

The centerpiece of the adversarial process is the trial, a battle between two attorneys that must be conducted in accordance with established procedures.

Pretrial Motions

Before the jury is brought into the courtroom to hear opening statements and the presentation of evidence, the defense attorney has an opportunity to make pretrial motions, which are oral and/or written pleadings. The five most common are the following:

1. *Motion to dismiss.* This motion is routinely made and routinely denied. Defense counsel claims that the information or indictment is insufficient to justify a trial.

2. *Motion for a change of venue.* The defense argues that a fair trial is not possible in the current jurisdiction because of the amount of pretrial publicity. If the judge agrees, the trial will be moved to another jurisdiction.

3. *Motion for a bill of particulars.* This motion is an attempt by the defense to obtain the details of the prosecution's charges, of the occurrences to be investigated at trial. This allows the attorney to place limits on the evidence offered by the prosecution; it must be *material*, that is, clearly related to the items in the bill of particulars, or it will be excluded as immaterial on an objection by defense counsel.

4. *Motion for discovery.* This permits the defense to have access to the evidence the prosecutor plans to use at the trial. This allows the attorney to prepare his or her defense. In many, if not most jurisdictions, discovery is informal, and opposing counsel is routinely allowed to review evidence.

5. *Motion to suppress.* This motion seeks to invoke the exclusionary rule. If successful, it often leaves the prosecution without important evidence and requires a nolle prosequi or dismissal of the charges.

Side-Bar

At times during a trial, the prosecutor or the defense will approach the bench and request a side-bar, or a private conference with the judge. This is usually done at the side of the bench away from the jury, and opposing counsel must be present because any ex parte discussion—having only one party present—with the judge is improper. This brief conference conducted out of hearing of the jurors usually involves the question of admissibility of certain evidence, or it may be used to inquire if certain questions can properly be asked of a witness. If the issue cannot be decided quickly, the judge will have the jury removed and hear arguments in open court on the matter.

Opening Statements

Before any evidence is presented, each side is allowed to address the jury in the form of a general outline of the case he or she intends to present. It has a parallel in the introduction of a term paper or scholarly article. The prosecutor states his or her intentions and the nature of the evidence to be relied upon: "Ladies and gentlemen of the jury, the state intends to prove that on. . . ." The defense may decline to present an opening statement; it is up to the prosecution to prove the defendant guilty beyond a reasonable doubt, and the defendant has no corresponding responsibility. An opening statement also provides advance notice to the opposition of the line of prosecution or defense. There is no time limit for an opening statement; it is at the discretion of the judge. The defense may object to any overstatements by the prosecution, or the prosecutor's opening statement may be used by defense counsel at summation to bring the prosecution's credibility into question for failing to prove what was set forth in the opening statement. At the conclusion of opening statements, it is time for the prosecutor's case-in-chief: the presentation of evidence.

Presentation of Evidence

Evidence must be presented by a witness who is called, sworn in by the court clerk, and directed to take the witness stand, which is a raised chair at the side of the judge's bench. A witness may testify on matters he or she saw, heard, or has knowledge of through one or more of the senses. Hearsay may not be presented as evidence; this is generally the repeating of a statement made by a third party (literally hear and say) or a belief not based on the witness's direct observation, material that cannot easily be subjected to the test of cross-examination. For example, a third party who testifies "I was told by the defendant's girlfriend that he robbed . . ." will not normally be permitted to continue. There are, however, many exceptions to the hearsay rule.[4] In general a witness cannot offer his or her opinion or conclusion unless it has been established that he or she is an "expert."

However, lay opinion with respect to matters such as duration of time, height, weight, or the speed of a vehicle is commonly allowed into evidence. Expert witnesses—scientists, medical doctors, handwriting analysts—can offer their professional opinions and conclusions, or they can be asked to respond to a hypothetical question that has a bearing on the case.

Witnesses, particularly police officers, are used to identify physical (or forensic) evidence such as documents, photos and diagrams of the crime scene, fingerprints, bloodstains, weapons. Without such identification, an item cannot be admitted into evidence as "Exhibit A" or "B" or "C."

This involves the *chain of custody*. The prosecutor must be able to prove that the piece of forensic evidence being presented to the jury is without any doubt the same item that was retrieved at the scene of the crime or during a subsequent investigation. This is not as easy as it may sound. The trial usually occurs months, if not years, after the crime. The evidence has passed through a number of hands, for example, those of the police officer who responded to the scene, the technician who analyzed it, and other police officers or clerks involved in transporting and filing and storage for use at the trial. Each person handling the evidence must record that fact by writing out his or her name, the date, time, and purpose. It must be shown that the evidence was properly secured, that only authorized persons had access to it, and that they properly recorded every time they had custody of the item.

Each person in the chain can be required to testify, and any broken link can render the evidence inadmissible. Poor police practices—for example, failing to properly secure the crime scene from the public and/or other police officers—can raise doubts about evidence. If many police officers were walking around the crime scene, each can be called to testify by the defense. This can be problematic for the prosecution because the jury can grow quite bored, and the more officers, the greater the chances of contradictory testimony.[5]

In the adversary system of justice (as opposed to an inquisitorial system) used in this country, the examination of a witness involves a series of questions. The questions and their responses must be narrow enough for opposing counsel to have the opportunity to object—to claim that the jury is about to hear testimony that is inadmissible. If such testimony does occur, and the attorney objects, the judge will order it stricken from the record and instruct the jury to disregard it—which may be easier said than done. Questions cannot be *leading*, that is, queries that suggest their own answer, such as "Isn't it true that the defendant owned a firearm?" as opposed to the more permissible question, "To your knowledge, did the defendant own a firearm?" The exceptions are preliminary questions to establish some basic facts; for example, "You reside at 1776 Northern Boulevard?" or "Is it correct that you are employed as a carpenter by the Winthrop Construction Company?" During a side-bar, counsel may request permission from the judge to ask a leading question, stating the reason for wanting to ask such a question—to help the witness remember an item, for example.

Opposition counsel can object to any question or answer on the grounds that the attorney is leading the witness, or for any other procedural defects, for example, that it is immaterial and irrelevant or that it requires an opinion or conclusion. The judge determines whether to uphold the objection or to overrule. If the objection is sustained, the opposing attorney may make an *offer to prove*, which is dictated to the court reporter out of hearing of the jury. If an objection is overruled, the attorney may *make an exception*, which has the effect of arguing the court made an error, thereby preparing the record for a possible appeal.

Cross-Examination

After the prosecutor has completed his or her direct examination of a witness whom he or she has called, the defense has an opportunity to cross-examine. Cross-examination has several purposes. It is used to challenge a witness's testimony, for example, by questioning his or her memory or vision. The attorney may attempt to impeach the credibility of the witness, for example, by asking questions about any criminal record, history of mental illness or alcoholism—any information that will tend to blemish the reputation of the witness in the eyes of the jury. The attorney may ask for the details of any previous relationship with the defendant. As with direct examination, the prosecutor can object to any questions.

Re-Direct and Re-Cross-Examination.

After the defense counsel has had an opportunity to cross-examine an adverse witness, the prosecution can ask additional questions of the witness with respect to any new matters that have been brought out during the cross-examination in an effort to re-establish the testimony or rehabilitate the witness. Questions that go beyond those new areas raised on cross-examination can be objected to by defense counsel. After the prosecution has completed the re-direct, defense counsel can re-cross-examine. This process can continue until both sides have no further questions or the judge intervenes.

After all prosecution witnesses have been subjected to direct and cross-examination, re-direct and re-cross-examination, the state rests; the prosecution's case-in-chief has been presented. At this point the defense may ask for a *directed verdict*; this means that the jury is removed from the courtroom and the judge is requested to render a verdict of not guilty based on insufficient evidence having been presented by the prosecution. It is extremely rare for a judge to agree to a directed verdict, and the motion is usually done to preserve some legal rights on appeal. At this point the judge may dismiss certain counts of a multicount indictment or information, based on insufficient evidence, but the trial will continue on the remaining counts.

In many jurisdictions, defense counsel may now present an opening statement summarizing the evidence that will be used to counter the prosecution's case. Then he or she has an opportunity to present witnesses, who may or may not include the defendant. According to the Fifth Amendment, a defendant cannot be forced to testify. Furthermore, if a defendant opts not to testify, this cannot be used against him or her when considering the question of guilt or innocence; this will be explained to the jury by the judge. If, however, the defendant decides to testify, the defendant-as-witness can be subjected to vigorous cross-examination by the prosecutor, who will attempt to impeach his or her credibility. As part of the impeachment process, questions about past criminal behavior, which would not ordinarily be permitted, are relevant and permissible. Furthermore, if the defendant decides to testify, a refusal to answer any questions can be used as evidence, an issue the prosecution will usually stress to the jury during closing arguments. Having a defendant with a serious criminal record testify is, obviously, a calculated risk for the defense.

Witnesses called by the defense are questioned by defense counsel—direct examination—and cross-examined by the prosecution. Re-direct and re-cross-examination continue as with the witnesses called by the prosecution. After the defense has rested, the prosecutor is permitted to call further witnesses for the purpose of *rebuttal*, which is testimony designed to refute the testimony of defense witnesses. If the prosecution has introduced new evidence or has delved into new matters, the defense is entitled to a *rejoinder*, which is testimony restricted to new defense evidence to refute the prosecutor's rebuttal. In practice, however, a judge seldom allows a rejoinder. On rare occasions when there is a surprise witness, it is during rebuttal or rejoinder that he or she is usually called to testify.

Final Motions

After both sides rest, without the jury present, the defense can renew the motion for a directed verdict of acquittal or a *demurrer*—a pleading that the prosecution has not provided sufficient evidence to allow the case to be decided by the jury. If the motion or demurrer is sustained, the trial is over and the defendant is acquitted. If denied by the judge, summations or closing arguments are in order.

Closing Arguments or Summations

The prosecutor is allowed to address the jury, presenting remarks that summarize the case he or she has presented, usually highlighting important testimony. Summations are not evidence, and the jury is informed of this by the judge. The defense is provided with the same opportunity, typically stressing the weakness of the state's case and the need to find a defendant guilty beyond a reasonable doubt. Attorneys for the state and for the defendant are both allowed considerable leeway during summations, and these can sometimes be quite dramatic. Improper remarks by the prosecutor, however—those that are inflammatory, for example—can provide a basis for appealing an adverse jury decision. After the defense closes, the prosecutor is permitted a rebuttal, but this is typically limited to those areas discussed by the defense in summation; new lines of argument are not permitted. In some states, if the defense has not called any witnesses, he or she is entitled to first and last closing arguments. There are no specific time limits for closing arguments, which may last only a few minutes or, in complex cases, run for a few days.

Charge to the Jury

The judge now charges the jury. He or she explains their responsibilities and the options they have as jurors, for example, in addition to a verdict of guilty or not guilty, in a multiple-count indictment or information, they can find the defendant guilty on some counts and not guilty on others. The judge will carefully cover the law applicable in the case, stating the issues and defining terms with which a layperson may not be familiar. In many states the attorneys are permitted to submit suggestions to be included in the instructions to the jury, and the judge will indicate those that are acceptable, and those that are not. Defense counsel may object to any ruling on suggestions, which is recorded by the court reporter providing the basis for an appeal in the event of an adverse verdict.

The judge instructs the jurors in two areas, which are described by Reid Hastie, Steven Penrod, and Nancy Pennington:

> First, the judge informs the jurors what their task consists of during deliberation and what procedures they should employ in reaching a verdict. The procedures defined by the judge generally include the instruction that the juror is to regard the defendant as innocent until proven otherwise; that the burden of proof is on the prosecution; that the juror's task is to determine the facts on the basis of credible evidence; that certain information may be regarded as evidence, such as direct testimony of witnesses, charts and exhibits, observations of the witnesses, and reasonable inferences drawn from the testimony; that other information may not be regarded as evidence, such as statements and questions posed by the attorneys, or race and background of defendant; how to assess the credibility of testimony, such as each witness's opportunity to observe, possible bias, character, and contradictions in testimony; what constitutes a reasonable inference as opposed to unwarranted speculation; and what is the meaning and application of the standard of proof, namely beyond a reasonable doubt, in assessing the truth of

allegations. The second portion of the judge's instructions defines for the jurors a complete set of possible verdicts, of which they must choose one. (1983: 17)

Jury Deliberations

The jury retires to the jury room and elects a foreman, unless they are in one of the states where the foreman is automatically the first juror who was chosen. The room is guarded by a bailiff and no one is permitted to enter without an explicit request from the foreman, via the bailiff, to the judge. At times, the jurors may request the court reporter to read some testimony or to review some forensic evidence. The manner in which the jury proceeds is not governed by law or custom; each jury is independent, not bound by precedent. Deliberations can take less than an hour, although this is rare, or a few days. As noted above, the jurors may be sequestered, or they may leave at the end of the court day, even when they have not reached a verdict.

If all the jurors agree to a verdict, it is signed by the foreman, and read aloud in court by the foreman, the bailiff, or the court clerk. The members of the jury may be polled, each juror being asked by the judge if this is his or her decision. After the verdict is read, the jury is dismissed by the judge "with thanks." Jurors are now free to discuss the case with anyone they choose—the press, the prosecutor or defense attorneys. In a Connecticut rape case in which the jury was deadlocked, the defense attorney hired a member of the jury to act as a consultant at the retrial. The attorney was interested in finding out what arguments had been most effective. Nevertheless, the defendant was convicted at the second trial (Johnson 1986).

If, despite repeated encouragement from the judge, the jury cannot reach a unanimous decision, it is a hung jury. The prosecutor must decide if he or she wishes to retry the case, and this often depends on the number of jurors who voted for a conviction. For example, an 11–1 vote for conviction would almost invariably result in a retrial.

Sentencing

If the defendant is found guilty, he or she enters the sentencing stage. Sentencing in the United States can be determinate or indeterminate. Indeterminate sentencing is based on a positive approach to crime and criminals; determinate sentencing is based on a classical approach.

Positive School

Positivism, as formulated by Auguste Comte (1798–1857), is a method for examining and understanding social behavior. Comte argued that the methods and logical forms of the natural sciences—the scientific method—are applicable to the study of humans as social beings. Social phenomena, Comte stated, must be studied and understood by observation, hypothesis, and experimentation in a new discipline he called sociology. The positive approach to the study of crime and criminals became known as criminology, whose early efforts are often identified with the Venetian physician Cesare Lombroso (1835-1909).

In his book, *L'uomo delinquente (The Criminal Man)*, Lombroso argued that the criminal is an evolutionary primitive, a throwback to earlier developmental stages through which noncriminal man had already passed (Lombroso 1968). Lombroso's stress on the physiological characteristics believed indicative of criminality have been abandoned (although there are contemporary theories of criminality centering on physiological causation). His lasting contribution, however, is the use of scientific methods to study crime and criminals, and there are serious legal implications in such an approach.

Positivism maintains that we can understand the cause of criminal behavior, and that crime is simply not "evil" persons acting in an "evil" manner, but rather, it is behavior caused by psychological or environmental variables. But if crime is caused by factors over which the offender has little or no control, how can he or she be held legally accountable for the criminal behavior? This is a problem with deterministic bases such as positivism for explaining crime. Positivism, however, provides a basis for rehabilitative efforts as a response to criminal behavior and it led to the establishment of the indeterminate sentence.

Indeterminate Sentence

While the indeterminate sentence can be traced back to the nineteenth century (see Abadinsky 1987), contemporary use dates back to the years following World War II. Toward the end of the war, Governor Earl Warren of California, responding to a prison scandal, instituted a new approach to penology: *corrections*. Instead of merely punishing criminals, the California system would attempt to rehabilitate offenders using the latest scientific approaches: prisons became correctional institutions, wardens became superintendents, and guards became correction officers. "Treaters"—psychiatrists, social workers, teachers—were sent into the correctional institutions. Since it is not possible to know in advance how much time will be needed to "correct" a specific offender, the indeterminate sentence was instituted and became the cornerstone of the corrections approach.

Under the indeterminate sentence, which continues to be used by most states, an offender is sentenced to a minimum number of years and a maximum number of years, for example, a sentence might be three years to nine years—written 3-0-0/9-0-0. It is the parole board, not the judge, who determines when the offender is to be released from prison (which, according to the corrections approach, is a correctional facility)—in 3-0-0, or 4-0-0, or 5-0-0, all the way up to 9-0-0. The members of the parole board review the inmate's record, efforts at rehabilitation, past criminal history, future plans, and make release decisions within the parameters set by the judge's sentence. Inmates not paroled become eligible for release prior to the expiration of their sentence through the mechanism of "time off for good behavior," usually one-third off the maximum. An inmate serving 3-0-0/9-0-0 could be paroled after serving three years, but, assuming good behavior, would more likely be released after 6-0-0. Persons paroled or released on good time come under the supervision of a parole officer for the remainder or a portion of the unserved sentence.

The California system of corrections spread to every state in the nation. It was, however, criticized by those on the right of the political spectrum for releasing criminals before the expiration of their sentence. Critics on the left argued that the indeterminate sentence actually kept persons in prison longer than they would have been made to stay if punishment had been the sole basis of incarceration. Under the indeterminate sentence, persons sent to prison for crimes of similar severity would not all serve the same amount of time—some would be paroled before others—which amounted to unequal justice. Furthermore, critics pointed out, parole boards often returned offenders to prison for violating the conditions of their release, that is, the rules of parole (see figure 6.6). By the mid-1970s, criticism increased as research into rehabilitative efforts failed to reveal any significant level of success in preventing recidivism, that is, a reversion to criminal behavior. By 1980, a number of states, including California, had switched back to a classical philosophy and determinate sentencing.

Classical School

Classicalism is an outgrowth of the eighteenth-century period known as the Enlightenment or the Age of Reason. Classical issues of crime and justice are associated with the works of Jean Jacques Rousseau (1712–78) and Cesare Bonesana, Marchese di Beccaria (1712–78), usually referred to as Cesare Beccaria. Rousseau (1945) set forth the notion of a *social contract*, a mythical state of affairs wherein each person agrees to a pact whose basic stipulation is that conditions of law are the same for all—that all men are created equal. In Rousseau's words (1945: 45), "The social contract establishes among the citizens an equality of such character that each binds himself on the same terms as all the others, and is *thus* entitled to enjoy the same rights as all the others."

Beccaria decried the unjust and disparate manner in which laws were enforced and punishment meted out in eighteenth-century Europe. Instead, he argued, all men are created equal, and punishment should be meted out with perfect uniformity. In his *Essay on Crime and Punishment*, published in 1764, Beccaria wrote that laws should be drawn precisely and matched to punishment intended to be applied equally to all classes of men. The law should stipulate a

Figure 6.6. An example of rules of probation and parole.

PHILADELPHIA COURT OF COMMON PLEAS
OFFICE OF COURT ADMINISTRATION
ADULT PROBATION DEPARTMENT

RULES OF PROBATION AND PAROLE

_____
NAME OF PROBATIONER/PAROLEE

_____
POLICE PHOTO NUMBER

_____
BILL AND TERM NUMBER

_____
SUPERVISING DISTRICT

The Honorable Judge _____ has placed you on probation and/or parole and expects you to comply with the following Rules of Probation/Parole:

1. Report to the Probation/Parole Officer as directed and permit the Officer to visit you at your home or place of employment when necessary.

2. Respond promptly to any summons to appear in court.

3. Report any change of address to your Probation/Parole Officer within 72 hours, and do not leave Philadelphia without permission from your Probation/Parole Officer.

4. Make every effort to seek and maintain employment, and promptly inform your Probation/Parole Officer of any change in your employment status.

5. Obey all federal, state, county criminal laws and city ordinances.

6. You may not unlawfully possess, use, sell or distribute controlled substances of any kind.

7. You may not possess firearms or any other deadly weapons.

8. Notify your Probation/Parole Officer within 72 hours of any new arrest.

You will also comply with the following special conditions of Probation/Parole:

_____
_____
_____

ACKNOWLEDGEMENT OF PROBATIONER/PAROLEE

I have read, or have had read to me, the foregoing rules and conditions of my Probation/Parole; I fully understand them and agree to follow them.

_____
WITNESS

_____
SIGNATURE OF PROBATIONER/PAROLEE
(NOTE: If signed by a mark, two witnesses must execute this instrument.)

_____
WITNESS
30-806

_____
DATE

PROBATIONER/PAROLEE

particular penalty for each specific crime, and judges should mete out identical sentences for each occurrence of the same offense (Beccaria 1963). The pictorial representation of the classical school appears on many courthouses and judicial documents in the form of Lady Justice carrying scales and wearing a blindfold.

The classical position, which is a cornerstone of our system of criminal justice, posits the concept of *free will*: that every adult is endowed with the ability to discern right from wrong and, furthermore, has a choice of being law-abiding or criminal. The commission of a crime is seen as a rational choice—in modern criminal law this is known as *mens rea*—and the actor is thus responsible for his or her behavior. Free will, of course, is an oversimplification, since one's position in society determines the degree of choice with respect to being law-abiding or criminal—we are not all created equal. In too many instances, society does not offer a viable alternative to crime for many of our poorer citizens, a situation reflected by the nature of our prison population for more than two hundred years. In any event, the classical school provides the philosophical basis for the determinate sentence.

Determinate Sentence

Used in about a dozen states, the determinate sentence requires a judge to impose a specific number of years for each particular crime, for example, nine years (9-0-0) for robbery. The offender is required to serve the entire sentence minus time off granted for good behavior in prison (usually a maximum of 50 percent off the sentence). In practice, determinate sentences can be classified according to the amount of discretion enjoyed by the judge. In California, for example, discretion is narrow. For each class of offense there is a *presumed sentence*, which the judge must impose. A slight increase, one or two years, is permitted on a sustained motion for *aggravation* on the part of the prosecutor, or a similar reduction in sentence on a sustained motion by the defense for *mitigation*. In Illinois, which switched from indeterminate sentencing in 1977 judges have enormous discretion—in contradiction to the principles of classicalism. Under certain circumstances, for example, a judge can set a determinate sentence for serious felonies anywhere from six to sixty years.

Determinate sentencing has been criticized for failing to deal adequately with the issue of disparity due to the influence of a prosecutor in determining the sentence via plea bargaining (discussed in chapter 8). It has also led to the demise of rehabilitative programming in many prisons.

Presentence Investigation Report

In some states the sentencing judge is required to order a presentence investigation (psi) report; in other jurisdictions it is discretionary. (The box

"Presentence Investigation" indicates the kinds of information found in a psi.) The presentence report has several purposes, the most important being to serve as a guide for the judge in the exercise of his or her sentencing discretion, especially when a sentence of probation instead of imprisonment is being considered. In most jurisdictions the report is given to the judge, prosecutor, and defense counsel and becomes a subject at the sentencing hearing. (The psi also assists correctional authorities to classify prisoners and probation and parole agencies to supervise offenders.)

In some jurisdictions, for example in Illinois, the Judge has very wide discretion, and therefore the presentence report may be quite important. In other states, such as California, the judge has limited discretion, which renders the presentence report relatively unimportant. It should be noted (and will be discussed further in Chapter 8) that most cases end not with a trial but with a negotiated plea of guilty. This makes the presentence report unnecessary, although in some jurisdictions a similar (pre-plea) report is submitted to provide a basis for plea bargaining.

Presentence Investigation

The presentence investigation (psi) by the probation department has as its primary purpose assisting the judge to render a sentencing decision based not only on the criminal record but also on the social and psychological background of the offender (see Abadinsky 1987). The psi report typically contains information on the following items:

Offense
  Official version
  Statement of police officer, complainants, victims
  Defendant's version of the offense
Prior Juvenile and Criminal Record
Family History
  Defendant
  Parents and siblings
  Spouse and children
Education
Health
  Physical
  Mental
Employment History
Military Record
Financial Condition
Evaluation and Summary
Recommendation

Sentencing Hearing

The Supreme Court has ruled that a defendant who has been convicted has a right to be represented at sentencing by an attorney. The attorney can muster facts and present them in a manner most likely to benefit the defendant in his or her attempt to win some form of leniency from the court. The prosecutor and the defense are permitted to address the court, each advocating an outcome in this final scene of the long adversarial process. The judge's degree of discretion varies depending on the statutes of the particular state. Generally, if the subject is eligible by law, the judge can sentence him or her to a term of probation, to the county or the local jail (for terms of one year or less), or to a state prison.

Appeals

The appeal of a verdict of guilty requires submitting a notice of appeal and elaborate documents, including a transcript of the trial. In 1963 (*Douglas v. California*), the Supreme Court ruled that an indigent defendant is entitled to state-appointed counsel on the first appeal following a felony conviction. The appellate court cannot act as a trial court, that is, receive new evidence concerning the facts already established at the original trial. It is limited to addressing new theories or legal arguments regarding the law applicable to these facts. In order to preserve the right to appeal, defense counsel is required to raise objections to errors committed at trial, objections that allow problems to be corrected immediately by the trial judge. These objections become part of the trial record upon which the appeal is based. While in general appeallate courts will review only those claims that were properly presented at trial, there are a number of exceptions designed to protect the defendant's rights (Israel and La-Fave 1980). The appellate court (as noted in Chapter 4) can uphold the verdict, overturn it, or order it reversed and remanded to the trial court for a new trial.

Probation and Parole Violation

Persons sentenced to probation and those released on parole or "good behavior" typically come under the supervision of a probation or parole officer. The former is usually part of the judicial branch; the latter is always part of the executive branch, although some states combine probation and parole (p/p) in the same agency under the executive branch. In any event, these officers have responsibility for enforcing the rules and regulations to which a probationer or parolee/conditional releasee is required to abide. If the p/p officer alleges that the rules have been violated, an administrative process will be implemented.

For probation violations, a preliminary hearing (as per *Gagnon v. Scarpelli*, 1973) will take place before a judge—if possible, the one who imposed the original sentence of probation. At the preliminary hearing, the judge will determine if there is sufficient evidence—probable cause—to indicate that the probationer violated one or more of the conditions of probation in an important respect. If so, he or she can be held in custody for sixty days pending a revocation hearing. At the preliminary and revocation hearings, the probationer will have an opportunity to confront and question adverse witnesses, be represented by counsel, and provide evidence on his or her own behalf. At the revocation hearing, the judge will consider the probationer's entire record while under supervision—for example, his or her employment record—in addition to the rule violations and make a decision whether to continue probation or sentence the offender to incarceration.

For parole violations, the process is similar, except that the hearing is not part of the judicial system but, rather, is held under the administrative authority of the parole board (as per *Morrissey v. Brewer*, 1972). The preliminary hearing is typically conducted by a hearing officer and the revocation hearing by members of the board of parole. At the revocation hearing, members of the parole board determine whether the violation is serious enough to warrant returning the parolee to prison.

Now that we have completed our examination of the criminal process, in the next chapter we will move to the civil side of the courthouse.

Notes

1. For a criminal attorney's intimate look at a jury in New Jersey considering a 1982 murder case, see Wishman 1986. For a detailed look at another murder trial see Heyman and Kenety 1986. Valerie Hans and Neil Vidmar (1986) have produced a most lively and informative look at the American jury system using as examples highly publicized cases such as those involving John DeLorean, Joann Little, Jean Harris, and John Hinckley.

2. This is an issue only for criminal trials because the public has no constitutional right to attend a civil trial.

3. In some jurisdictions, if the defendant has pleaded guilty to an information, thus bypassing the grand jury, the arraignment will occur at the preliminary hearing.

4. For example, in conspiracy cases, hearsay evidence is admissible for the purpose of tying together defendants who comprise the combination or confederation that is the basis for the criminal allegation.

5. For other serious problems with respect to the gathering of physical evidence at crime scenes by police departments, see Peterson 1974.

7

Civil and Juvenile Courts

In Chapter 6 we examined the process by which criminal matters are resolved in the United States. In this chapter we will look at the procedures used to resolve civil disputes and the unique operations of the juvenile court.

Civil Litigation and Adjudication

As noted in chapter 4, the courts are often called upon to decide broad issues of public policy such as school desegregation, legislative reapportionment, and antitrust actions, in addition to resolving more narrowly drawn conflicts. According to Jethro Lieberman (1981) civil litigation can accomplish three desirable goals:

1. provide for the compensation of those who have been injured,
2. serve to deter future harms or actions which are potentially harmful by the knowledge that some types of behavior can result in costly suits, and
3. cause the termination of ongoing harms or the reformation of institutional systems that perpetuate them.

The resolution of a dispute between private parties involves a lawsuit. Kenneth Holland lists its elements:

a. A lawsuit is a conflict about private rights between two individuals motivated by self-interest. A typical civil action involves a *tort:* a suit based on allegations of damages caused to the plaintiff by the defendant.

b. The dispute is about events that happened in the past—events that disturbed a preexisting social harmony.

c. A third party stands as a passive and impartial umpire who, after hearing arguments offered by each party in the presence of the other, resolves the dispute in accordance with preexisting legal rules.

(d) The court must hear the plaintiff's claim, and the parties initiate and control the definition of the issues, the development of facts, and the presentation of law. (1982: 17–18)

"To prevail in a lawsuit," notes Jethro Lieberman (1981: 18), "the plaintiff must prove both that the defendant committed an act that caused injury and that the act was a legal wrong." Moreover, continues Lieberman (1981: 19), modern litigation often involves the transformation of once lawful acts into legal wrongs. "Through a steady stream of legislative enactments and judicial pronouncements, the citizen's right to redress has grown apace," replacing, for example, "the doctrine of caveat emptor (let the buyer beware) and related rules, with stringent duties of care on those who act," such as manufacturers, hospitals, and units of government.

The expansion of the role of the judiciary has also led to an increase in lawsuits whose primary purpose appears to be the harassment of opponents. In an effort to thwart these "frivolous" lawsuits, the federal judiciary toughened Rule 11 of the Federal Rules of Civil Procedure to ensure that every legal filing is grounded in fact and not designed "for any improper purpose such as to harass or to cause unnecessary delay or needless increase in the cost of litigation." If a judge finds that a lawyer has violated Rule 11, he or she can be forced to pay the costs and legal fees expended by their opponents in defending against the improper action. The amended Rule 11 requires attorneys to inquire into the merits of their cases before proceeding, invalidating a "pure heart, empty head" defense.

Critics argue that the new rule has created just another means of harassing opponents through the use of civil litigation, and has increased the amount of time required for litigation—the opposite of what was intended. There is also fear that the possibility of sanctions for bringing a legal action may serve to keep attorneys from filing innovative cases with legal theories that require the passage of time before being accepted (Lewin 1986). For example, in 1986 new legal theories that could significantly expand liability for negligence were developing throughout the countries that share the English legal heritage— Canada, Australia, and the United States (see Kristof 1986b).

The Civil Trial Process

For the most part, the adversarial process used in criminal trials is also used in civil trials, with some important differences. First, a litigant must have *standing*—that is, he or she must have a personal stake in the outcome of the controversy so that the adversarial model will be fully operative. Thus, for example, in order to challenge the constitutionality of a particular statute or executive action, a litigant must be prepared to show that he or she has been or will be harmed—an *injury in fact*—unless the court provides a remedy. Ideological opposition or a general grievance, for example, against a particular policy of government is not sufficient to provide standing. Thus, a taxpayer who wants a court to halt covert military aid to contras fighting in Nicaragua, on the theory that it is an unauthorized expenditure of taxpayer's money, "may be told that since the injuries he alleges are not personal to him his suit will be dismissed for lack of standing," note Richard Lempert and Joseph Sanders (1986: 23–24). "The Court will not even examine the accusation that tax money is being illegally spent, although this may well be the case."

The second difference is that a finding for the plaintiff—the party bringing the action—is based on a *preponderance of the evidence,* an amount just over fifty percent, not the more stringent beyond-a-reasonable-doubt standard. Third, many of the extensive due-process guarantees that accrue to a defendant in a criminal case are not applicable in a civil proceeding. The Seventh Amendment guarantees the right to a jury trial in lawsuits "where the value in controversy shall exceed twenty dollars." While the Seventh Amendment has not been made applicable to the states, almost all states have similar constitutional guarantees (Friedenthal, Kane, and Miller 1985). Fourth, neither plaintiff nor defendant is constitutionally entitled to counsel; in other words, government has no legal obligation to provide an attorney to an indigent party involved in a civil action. A fifth difference is that civil juries often have less than twelve members, and they are not sequestered, and in civil actions involving issues of equity (nonmonetary matters requesting specific performance—discussed in Chapter 1), there is not a constitutional right to a jury trial.[1] Finally, and most important, while a criminal action can only be brought by the government—by a state or federal prosecutor—most civil actions are brought by private parties, although the government is sometimes a plaintiff or a defendant.

Filing a Civil Complaint

A civil action is known by the name of the plaintiff and the name of the defendant—*Smith v. Jones*—and the plaintiff's name appears first. Typically, the plaintiff's attorney pays a fee and files a *complaint* or *petition* with the clerk of the proper court, setting out the facts on which the action is based, the damages alleged, and the judgment or relief being sought. The clerk issues a summons, which is attached to a copy of the complaint, and both are served on the defendant by personnel from the sheriff's office, a U.S. marshal, or a private process-service agency.

The summons directs the defendant to file a response—a pleading—within a certain amount of time, usually thirty days, or suffer a judgment of *default*. A default judgment requires that the defendant be served personally—not by proxie—although there are some alternative methods, for example, registered mail accompanied by an announcement in the legal section of a newspaper or a copy affixed to the defendant's residence or business (a form of service known as "nail and mail"). The defendant's attorney can now respond to the allegations, sometimes alleging wrongdoing on the part of the plaintiff.

Jurisdiction

As noted in chapter 1, there is a code of civil procedure that governs such matters, and the first issue that must be determined is *jurisdiction,* which can at times become quite complex. For example, what if the plaintiff and defendant live in different counties, different states, or even different countries? What if the damages occurred in a third county or state? Some actions are local, for example, mortgage foreclosures, and can be brought only in the county where the property is located. Other actions can be transitory; that is, they may be brought wherever the defendant is found and served with the summons, such as a tort action for personal injuries. The plaintiff is required to establish that the court has jurisdiction to rule on the issue being presented.

Pretrial Activities

The activities prior to a civil trial are quite extensive and, in practice, usually lead to an out-of-court settlement. The delay after filing and preliminary motions may last several months, and roughly 75 percent of the cases are resolved during that time without a trial. There are often pretrial conferences with the judge, whose purpose is to facilitate a settlement.

Motions

There are a number of motions that can be made by defense counsel:

—a *motion to quash* asks the court to void the summons as not having been properly served;

—a *motion to strike* asks the court to excise parts of the petition as irrelevant, improper, or prejudicial;

—a *motion to make more definite* asks the court to require the plaintiff to be more specific about the complaints that are alleged, for example, to describe the injuries in greater detail so the defense will be better able to respond;

—a *motion to dismiss* argues that the court lacks jurisdiction, or that the plaintiff has not presented a legally sound basis for a cause of action against the defendant even if, in fact, the allegations are true.

—a *motion for summary judgment* is based on a claim that there is no genuine issue of material fact and, therefore, the undisputed portion of the case should be eliminated from trial; if the undisputed issues are crucial, the entire case may be determined without a trial.

The defendant's response can deny the allegations, admit some and deny others, or admit them all and plead extenuating circumstances—an excuse. The defendant may also file a *cross-complaint,* which may be part of the response or filed separately. It asks for relief or damages from the plaintiff and sometimes from others. The plaintiff may then file any of the above motions against the cross-complaint, except the motion to quash. Either party can now file a reply in answer to any new allegations raised by the other party.

Discovery

"The term 'discovery' encompasses the methods by which a party or potential party to a lawsuit obtains and preserves information regarding the action" (Friedenthal, Kane, and Miller 1985:380). As part of the discovery stage, the civil process utilizes a legal device, the deposition, that is absent from criminal cases. The *deposition* is an out-of-court procedure whereby plaintiff and defendant and any witnesses are placed under oath and asked questions by opposing counsel on matters not otherwise privileged and that relate to the pending case. The questions and their answers are recorded by a private court reporter engaged for this purpose. If relevant answers are not forthcoming, either side can submit written questions—known as *interrogatories*—for the other side to answer under oath. While a respondant need not answer a question deemed improper, the interrogating party can seek a court order to compel an answer. Discovery may also involve the production of documents such as a contract or lease and may require the plaintiff to undergo an examination by a medical doctor chosen by the defendant or the court in order to substantiate claims of injury.

Depositions are particularly useful for narrowing down the issues involved, and they provide each side with an opportunity to evaluate the case and to better prepare for trial. The deposition can also be used in court as a basis for impeaching subsequent testimony that is in conflict with the sworn out-of-court record. A deposition is not a matter of public record and, thus, the press has no right to access until it is released by virtue of a court order.

Conferences

After depositions and discovery, but before trial, the attorneys appear before the judge, usually without their clients, in order to come to an agreement on certain uncontested factual issues—*stipulations*—such as the date and time of the incident, photos, sketches, and other routine evidence. The purpose of stipulations is to make the trial process more efficient and cut down on the time necessary for completion. Often this part of the process can result in a settlement without the need for a trial. Like criminal cases, most civil cases are settled without resort to trial.

Trial

The civil and the criminal trial are conducted in the same manner, with opening statements, witnesses called by the plaintiff and then the defense, direct examination, cross-examination, re-direct, re-cross-examination, closing arguments, charge to the jury, deliberations, and the verdict. A judge may preclude the case being sent to the jury by ruling in favor of a motion for a directed verdict. At the close of the presentation of the opponent's evidence, either defense or plaintiff can argue that the evidence is either so compelling or so weak that only one outcome would be proper.

The plaintiff typically makes the first opening statement and the final closing argument (paralleling the role of the prosecutor in criminal trials). Usually the plaintiff is a witness, and the defendant may also opt to testify. In closing arguments, the plaintiff's attorney summarizes the case in a manner that points to the defendant's liability and stresses the losses that the plaintiff has suffered. Defense counsel claims that the defendant is not responsible for the injury or loss, or that the compensation claimed is too high. Civil trials may involve complex legal and scientific (for example, medical or engineering) matters that need to be simplified in order to be understood by the jury. Under such circumstances, the judge may utilize a legal device known as the *special verdict*. Instead of a verdict for or against the defendant, the jury responds to a series of written questions of fact posed by the judge. Based on the jury's answers, the judge determines the outcome of the case. A verdict in favor of the defendant by judge or jury ends the trial; a finding for the plaintiff requires a judgment. A trial judge may reduce a jury award that is excessive, or order a new trial when the verdict goes against the clear weight of the evidence, or reverse a verdict that is unreasonable given the facts presented at trial and the legal standard to be applied (Lempert and Sanders 1986). (This is known as a *judgment notwithstanding the verdict*.)

Jack Friedenthal, Mary Kane, and Arthur Miller raise an important question with respect to the civil jury verdict: Must all of the jurors agree on each of the issues?

> Consider, for example, a personal injury action in which plaintiff alleges three separate factual bases for finding that defendant was negligent. Suppose that the jurors split eight to four against a finding of negligence on each of these bases, but as to every determination, a different four jurors thought that negligence had been established. Thus, despite their disagreements on the specific factual issues, all twelve jurors find defendant at fault and return a verdict for plaintiff. (1985: 461)

The court may become aware of this situation as the result of a post-verdict poll of the jury and, the authors note, courts have split on the matter of letting the verdict stand: the trend seems to be in favor of upholding the verdict. "The result turns on whether the particular jurisdiction views the proper role of the jury merely to decide specific factual issues or to determine the overall outcome of the case'' (1985: 461–62).

Judgment

There is no sentence in a civil case; the next step is a determination by the judge or jury of the remedy or damages to be assessed. Once the judge enters a judgment against the defendant, if appropriate, the plaintiff can ask to have the court clerk issue an order to execute the judgment, which is delivered to the sheriff. This document commands the sheriff to take possession of the defendant's property and sell it at auction to satisfy the judgment, or a lien can be placed against the defendant's salary—garnishment—and a certain amount of money must be taken out each payday by the employer for the plaintiff. If the defendant fails to carry out the provisions of the judgment, the plaintiff can ask for a contempt order that can result in arrest and imprisonment.[2]

The civil courts are handicapped by an oppressive caseload, and it is not unusual for a tort action to take as long as five years before reaching the trial stage. When plaintiffs have a choice of courts, they usually choose the one with the least amount of delay, although travel considerations also have to be taken into account. The court of choice may be located some distance from the plaintiff and his or her attorney. Efforts to deal with the problem of delay have included the establishment of specialized courts and administrative bodies.

Specialized Courts and Administrative Bodies

The civil division of a state court system frequently has specialized courts for such matters as divorce (a family or domestic relations court), settlement of estates (probate court), cases of juveniles (to be discussed shortly), and small-claims cases.

Small-Claims Court. Small-claims courts have jurisdiction to settle cases when the money being contested is not above a certain amount, usually $500 or $1,000, depending on the statutes of the jurisdiction. The first small-claims court was established in 1913 by the Cleveland Municipal Court. The simplified process required no pleadings and only a very nominal filing fee; the participation of lawyers was discouraged. By 1920 other cities—Chicago, Minneapolis, New York, Philadelphia—had established small-claims courts based on the Cleveland model. In that year, Massachusetts adopted a statewide small-claims court; every lower court judge was required to establish special sessions for hearing all claims under $35 (Harrington 1985). Contemporary small-claims courts siphon off less complex cases for handling in a less formal manner than is typical in most other trial courts. Filing fees are low, and a summons can often be served by certified mail or by the sheriff for a small fee. The plaintiff need not engage an attorney, and defendants are rarely represented by counsel.

Although these courts were supposedly designed for the "little man," the citizen whose case does not involve enough money to interest a lawyer on a contingency basis, it has frequently been used by collection agencies, utility companies, and retailers as a relatively cheap and efficient way to move against persons allegedly owing small amounts of money. Steven Weller and John Ruhnka (1978: 3) note that "no issue with respect to small claims court has evoked more controversy than the question of whether collection agencies should be permitted to use these courts." Some states, such as New York, have enacted legislation prohibiting this use of small-claims courts. In their research, Weller and Ruhnka found a number of problems with the small-claims court:

> The defendant was largely ignored by most of the courts that we studied, and defendants without attorneys appeared to be significantly disadvantaged in many cases. Small claims litigation was not inexpensive for litigants who lost wages or who hired an attorney. A substantial number of individual litigants reported difficulties in learning their legal rights and in learning how to prepare for trial. Finally, we found that small claims courts are presently not being used by large numbers of consumer plaintiffs. (1978: 10)

Administrative bodies. In addition to specialized courts, governmental agencies have established administrative bodies (a number of which were mentioned in chapter 1) that have quasi-judicial authority to adjudicate certain types of cases. For example, a worker's compensation board determines whether an employee's injury was job-related, thus qualifying for worker's compensation. Motor vehicle departments may have hearing boards that make determinations about revoking driving licenses, and many states have boards that rule on matters involving civil rights and cases of alleged discrimination. There are also a number of programs for dealing with issues that would otherwise become part of the caseload of the civil courts (alternative dispute resolution will be examined in chapter 8).

Appeals

A losing litigant can appeal an adverse decision. However, under our adversarial system it is the obligation of the appellant's lawyer to draw to the court's attention, in his or her brief, relevant portions of the trial record for review. "The [appellate] court does not independently search the record for errors below, but leaves the decision of what needs review to the litigants" (Friendenthal, Kane, and Miller 1985: 601). In general, appellate review is limited to errors that were objected to by the aggrieved party's attorney at trial and thus appear in the trial record; attorneys cannot offer new evidence. "Errors that are not objected to below or arguments that are not raised at trial generally cannot be raised for the first time on appeal" (Friedenthal, Kane, and Miller 1985: 598).

Juvenile Justice

Because the goals of juvenile justice and the procedures of juvenile court are so different from both the criminal and civil processes, we will examine them separately. We will briefly review the historical development and legal foundations of the juvenile justice system, as well as the procedures of the juvenile court.

Societal attitudes toward children have varied throughout the ages, from early Christian beliefs which stressed their innocence and frailty to the eighteenth-century view of children as potential "little devils" in need of close supervision and strict discipline. In America, children became creatures to exploit. Child labor was an important part of economic life, and the children of the poor labored in mines (where their size was an advantage), mills, and factories under unsanitary and unsafe conditions.

The Supreme Court reflected the prevailing belief in laissez faire capitalism and would not intervene—statutes prohibiting children under twelve from employment and limiting the workday of youngsters over twelve to ten hours were ruled unconstitutional or routinely disobeyed. Increased immigration, industrialization, and urbanization drastically altered American society. The ten- and twelve-hour workday left many children without parental supervision; family disorganization was becoming widespread. Many children lived in the streets, where they encountered the disorder and rampant vice of the new urban environment.

Concern for the plight of children led to the establishment of the House of Refuge in New York in 1825, quickly followed by others in Boston and Philadelphia. These institutions provided housing and care for troublesome children who might otherwise be left in the streets or, if their behavior brought them into serious conflict with the law, sent to jail or prison. The philosophy embodied in the state charters that established these institutions was that of *parens patriae,* originally referring to the feudal duties of the king to his vassals and later the legal duties of the king to his subjects who were in need of care, particularly children and the mentally incompetent. Herbert Lou (1972: 4) notes that "with the independence of the American colonies, and the transplanting of the English common-law system, the state in this country has taken the place of the crown as the *parens patriae* of all minors." In the United States, *parens patriae* also includes minors who are delinquent.

Age at which criminal courts gain jurisdiction of young offenders ranges from 16 to 18 years old.

Age of offender when under criminal court jurisdiction

16	17	18		
Connecticut	Georgia	Alabama	Kansas	Oklahoma
New York	Illinois	Alaska	Kentucky	Oregon
North Carolina	Louisiana	Arizona	Maine	Pennsylvania
Vermont	Massachusetts	Arkansas	Maryland	Rhode Island
	Michigan	California	Minnesota	South Dakota
	Missouri	Colorado	Mississippi	Tennessee
	South Carolina	Delaware	Montana	Utah
	Texas	District of	Nebraska	Virginia
		Columbia	Nevada	Washington
		Florida	New Hampshire	West Virginia
		Hawaii	New Jersey	Wisconsin
		Idaho	New Mexico	Wyoming
		Indiana	North Dakota	Federal
		Iowa	Ohio	districts

All states allow juveniles to be tried as adults in criminal courts. Juveniles are referred to criminal courts in one of three ways—
• Judicial waiver—the juvenile court waives its jurisdiction and transfers the case to criminal court (the procedure is also known as ''binding over'' or ''certifying'' juvenile cases to criminal courts).
• Concurrent jurisdiction—the prosecutor has the discretion of filing charges for certain offenses in either juvenile or criminal courts.
• Excluded offenses—the legislature excludes from juvenile court jurisdiction certain offenses, usually either very minor, such as traffic or fishing violations, or very serious, such as murder or rape.

Thirteen States authorize prosecutors to file cases in either the juvenile or criminal courts at their discretion. This procedure, known as concurrent jurisdiction, may be limited to certain offenses or to juveniles of a certain age. Eight of the thirteen states provide concurrent jurisdiction options in the trial of youth for serious crimes.

Forty-six states, the District of Columbia, and the federal government have judicial waiver provisions.

Youngest age at which juvenile may be transferred to criminal court by judicial waiver

No specific age	10	13	14	15	16
Alaska	South Dakota	Georgia	Alabama	District of	California
Arizona		Illinois	Colorado	Columbia	Hawaii

Florida	Mississippi	Connecticut	Idaho	Kansas
Maine		Delaware	Louisiana	Kentucky
New Hampshire		Indiana	Maryland	Montana
Oklahoma		Iowa	Michigan	Nevada
South Carolina		Massachusetts	New Mexico	North Dakota
Washington		Minnesota	Ohio	Oregon
West Virginia		Missouri	Tennessee	Rhode Island
Wyoming		New Jersey	Texas	Wisconsin
Federal		North Carolina	Virginia	
districts		Pennsylvania		
		Utah		

Note: Many judicial waiver statutes also specify offenses that are waivable. This chart lists the States by the youngest age for which judicial waiver may be sought without regard to offense.

Source: U.S. Bureau of Justice Statistics.

As both immigration and urbanization continued unabated, the spectre of masses of undisciplined and uneducated children gave rise to the *child-saving movement*. Led by middle- and upper-class women of earlier American stock, the child-savers were influenced by the nativist prejudices of their day and, later, by social Darwinism. Something had to be done to save the children from their environment of ignorance and vice, or they would become progenitors of the same. The asylum, the house of refuge, and the reformatory were all parts of this movement, but the most important accomplishment was the establishment of the juvenile court.

Juvenile Court

While a minor might be sent to the house of refuge or the reformatory instead of jail or prison, he or she could be arrested, detained, and tried as would any adult accused of a crime. A few jurisdictions modified their trial process for children in the decades after the Civil War in an attempt to separate them from adult offenders, but, records Herbert Lou (1972: 19), "it was left to Illinois to pass the first comprehensive law to create the first specially organized juvenile court." That this occurred in Chicago was no coincidence. Chicago was the scene of rapid urbanization; from 1890 to 1900, the population increased almost 50 percent, with 70 percent of the residents being foreign born (Pettibone et al. 1981). In 1893 there was an economic panic, and as conditions of the poor continued to deteriorate, reforming juvenile justice became the primary goal of the child-savers, women who "were generally well-educated, widely-traveled, and had access to political and financial resources" (Platt 1974: 77).

The first juvenile court was established in Cook County (whose county seat is Chicago) on July 1, 1899, as the result of the Juvenile Court Act of April

14, 1899. Consistent with the concept of *parens patriae,* in addition to children who were delinquents (persons under sixteen who violate the law), the juvenile court was given jurisdiction over neglected and dependent children, that is, over children who presented "behavior problems" but who were not delinquents. This special category became known as *status offenders.*

Because the purpose of the juvenile court was to aid—not to punish—children, the due-process guarantees of the adult criminal court were absent. The court with its informal and unstructured system of justice quickly became the standard for other juvenile courts established throughout the United States; by 1924, all but two states had special courts for children (Finckenauer 1984). The noncriminal nature of the proceedings extended to the nomenclature used:

Adult Criminal Court	*Juvenile Court*
defendant	respondent
information/indictment	petition
arraignment	hearing
prosecution	adjudication
verdict	finding
sentence	disposition

Legal Developments

The nature of the juvenile court process remained unchanged into the 1960s when the Warren Court began to pay increasing attention to questions of due process as indicated by decisions in the cases of *Gideon, Mapp,* and *Miranda* (discussed in chapter 6). In 1966 the Court granted certiorari in the case of *Kent v. United States.* Morris Kent, age sixteen, had been convicted in criminal court of raping a woman in her Washington, D.C., apartment; he was sentenced to a term of thirty to ninety years in prison. In conformity with federal statutes, the case had first been referred to the juvenile court where, over the objections of defense counsel, jurisdiction was waived to the criminal court. The Supreme Court ruled that before a juvenile can be tried in adult court, he or she is entitled to a waiver hearing with counsel, and, if jurisdiction is subsequently waived, a statement of the reasons must be provided by the judge for the record.

The Gault decision. In 1967 the Court decided the most important case affecting the juvenile court when it agreed to consider a writ of habeas corpus in the case of *In re Gault.* Gault was an Arizona case that reached the Court without benefit of a lower-court review. In general, an appellate court will not consider a case unless all other remedies have been exhausted. However, Arizona law did not permit a review of juvenile court decisions, and, furthermore, no record had been made of the juvenile court proceedings upon which to base an appeal. Gerald Gault, age fifteen at the time, and a friend were arrested by the police on the complaint of a female neighbor that they had made lewd and indecent remarks over the telephone. The youngster's parents were not notified of their son's arrest and did not receive a copy of the petition. Juveniles were not entitled to many due process guarantees in juvenile court proceedings. Gerald was not advised of his right to remain silent or his right to counsel. At a second juvenile court hearing, Gerald was declared to be a juvenile delinquent and committed to the state industrial school for a maximum of six years—until his twenty-first birthday. Had Gerald been over the age of eighteen, the maximum sentence would have been a fine of not more than $50 or imprisonment for not more than sixty days. The complainant was not present at either hearing and the judge did not speak with her on any occasion, and no record was made of the court proceedings.

In its decision, the Supreme Court acknowledged the helping—that is, non-criminal—philosophy that led to the establishment of the juvenile court. But it also revealed a sense of outrage over what had transpired in this case: "Under our Constitution, the condition of being a boy does not justify a kangaroo court." The Court ruled that a youngster being adjudicated in juvenile court is entitled to certain rights and procedures, which include the following:

1. *Notice.* The child and parents or guardians shall receive a notice "in writing, of the specific charge or factual allegations to be considered at the hearing, and . . . such written notice [shall] be given at the earliest practicable time, and in any event, sufficiently in advance of the hearing to permit preparation."

2. *Right to counsel.* This requires that "the child and his parents must be notified of the child's right to be represented by counsel retained by them, or if they are unable to afford counsel, that counsel will be appointed to represent the child."

3. *Protection against self-incrimination.* This guarantee "is applicable in the case of juveniles as it is with respect to adults." The Court added, "It would be surprising if the privilege against self-incrimination were made available to hardened criminals but not to children."

4. *Right to confront and cross-examine adverse witnesses.* This, like the right to remain silent, was found to be essential: "No reason is suggested or appears for a different rule in respect to sworn testimony in juvenile courts than in adult tribunals."

5. *Right to appellate review and transcripts of proceedings.* The Court held that this cannot be denied: "As the present case illustrates, the consequences of failure to provide an appeal, to record the proceedings, or to make findings or state the grounds for the juvenile court's conclusion may be to throw the burden upon the machinery for habeas corpus, to saddle the reviewing process with the burden of attempting to reconstruct a record, and to impose upon the Juvenile Judge the unseemly duty of testifying under cross-examination as to the events that transpired in the hearings before him."

Other juvenile justice decisions. In 1971 (*McKeiver v. Pennsylvania*), the Court ruled that a juvenile court proceeding is not a criminal prosecution within the meaning of the Sixth Amendment and, therefore, the child is not entitled to a jury trial. Because of the noncriminal nature of the juvenile court, instead of the proof-beyond-a-reasonable-doubt standard, the level of evidence required for a finding of delinquency was the civil standard of the preponderance of evidence. In 1979, however, the Supreme Court ruled (*In Re Winship*) that "the reasonable-doubt standard plays a vital role in the American scheme of criminal procedure. It is a prime instrument for reducing the risk of conviction resting on factual error." Accordingly, the Court determined that "the constitutional safeguard of proof beyond a reasonable doubt is as much required during the adjudicatory stage of a delinquency proceeding as those constitutional safeguards applied in *Gault.*"

In 1975, the Court, in *Breed v. Jones,* ruled on the issue of double jeopardy for juveniles. Breed was seventeen years old when he was arrested for armed robbery, and a juvenile petition alleging the same was filed. After taking testimony from two witnesses presented by the prosecutor and the respondent, the judge sustained the petition. At a subsequent disposition hearing, however, the judge ruled that the respondent was not "amenable to the care, treatment and training program available through the facilities of the juvenile court" and ordered that he be prosecuted as an adult. Breed was subsequently found guilty of armed robbery in superior court. In its decision, the Supreme Court held "that the prosecution of respondent in Superior Court, after an adjudicatory proceeding in Juvenile Court, violated the Double Jeopardy Clause of the Fifth Amendment, as applied to the States through the Fourteenth Amendment."

In 1984, in a strong affirmation of the concept of *parens patriae,* the Court upheld the constitutionality of a New York statute that permits the preventive detention of juveniles when there is a "serious risk" that before trial the juvenile may commit an act which if committed by an adult would constitute a crime. In *Schall v. Martin,* the Court found that juveniles, unlike adults, "are always in some form of custody," and that by definition, they "are not assumed to have the capacity to take care of themselves." In more recent years, there has been a dramatic shift away from the concept of *parens patriae* and toward a model based on *just deserts* for juvenile offenders. While this clearly defeats the purpose of a separate court for juveniles whose raison d'être is help, not punishment, it has proven politically popular.

The Juvenile Court Process

The juvenile court process differs from state to state and even jurisdiction to jurisdiction—and even the name can vary, but all juvenile courts approximate the model that is presented below and is seen in figure 7.1.

Figure 7.1. Juvenile court process for cases of delinquency and status offenses.

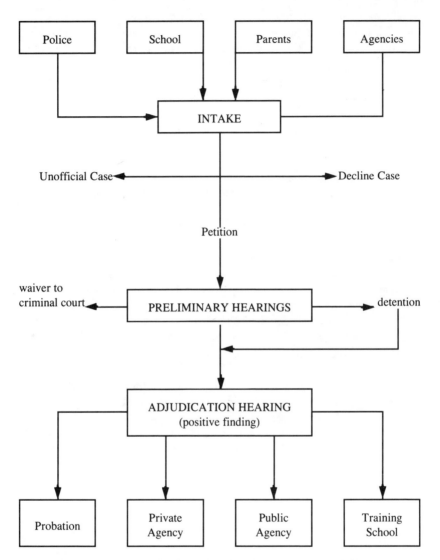

The definition of a juvenile is statutory, that is, the age of adulthood is determined by the legislature. In most states, it is sixteen. The juvenile court has responsibility for four types of cases:

1. *Delinquency*, or behavior that if engaged in by an adult would constitute a crime. In the case of certain very serious criminal behavior, for example,

murder, the law may require a transfer of the case for prosecution in adult criminal court.

2. *Status offense,* or behavior that if engaged in by an adult would not constitute a crime, but that (based on *parens patriae*) provides the basis for governmental intervention in the life of a child, for example, truancy, being beyond the control of parents, being addicted to drugs or alcohol, running away from home, sexual promiscuity (almost invariably referring to the behavior of girls).

3. *Neglect or abuse,* or the cases of children who are neglected or abused by parents or guardians.

4. *Dependency,* or the cases of children who do not have parents or guardians available to provide proper care.

Most cases that come to the attention of the juvenile court involve delinquent acts, and the referrals are typically made by the police. Status offenders (called MINS—Minors in Need of Supervision—or PINS—Persons in Need of Supervision—or CHINS—Children in Need of Supervision) are referred to the juvenile court by the police, school officials, and parents or guardians who complain the subject is beyond their control.

Most cases involving abused, neglected, or dependent children are referred to the juvenile court by the department of child welfare after it has been notified by the police, neighbors, or certain responsible professionals. The law usually requires medical doctors, teachers, social workers, and nurses to report cases of suspected abuse or neglect to the child welfare agency for investigation. A caseworker may then draft a petition and refer the case to juvenile court, which has the authority to ensure the protection and treatment of the child through various judicial orders. In order to qualify for federal funds, states must appoint an attorney (*guardian ad litem*) to represent and act as an advocate on behalf of an abused or neglected child.

Instances of less serious delinquency and of status offense, neglect, abuse, or dependency that come to the attention of the authorities are often handled in a manner that does not involve the formal justice apparatus. School officials or the police, for example, may refer such cases directly to public or private social welfare or child protective agencies without any involvement of the juvenile court.

Cases that are referred to the juvenile court enter by way of the *intake section,* which is staffed by probation officers. The intake officer determines if the court has jurisdiction, and if the case is to be referred to a courtroom for a hearing or if services should be provided by another source. He or she will interview the child, the child's parents or guardians, and any other interested parties, for example, victim or witness. The files of any previous court contact will be reviewed, and the officer will often consult (especially in serious cases) with the prosecutor's office before making a determination.

In less serious cases, a nonjudicial alternative is often the first choice, making it an *unofficial case*. If all parties are amenable, the child and parents will be referred to a social service agency, and he or she may be placed on unofficial probation for ninety days.

If unofficial handling is not successful, or if the case is too serious for such treatment, it will be sent to court by way of a petition. The *petition* sets out the allegations in the case, and filing results in a court hearing during which an assistant corporation counsel (municipal attorney) or assistant prosecutor will represent "the people." Children whose families are unable to pay for legal services are represented by an assistant public defender.

As opposed to the adult courts, juvenile proceedings are closed to the general public, and the records and transactions are confidential. In most states the records of a juvenile court proceeding are sealed and access to them requires a court order. Juveniles are not routinely fingerprinted and photographed, and their names are usually not printed in the newspapers.

The juvenile court may be part of a division of a superior court (for example in Illinois), but more frequently it is a lower court. Judges usually sit at a table, instead of the more traditional high bench, and they usually do not wear judicial robes.

Preliminary hearings. The preliminary hearing is held to inform the parties of the charges in the petition and of their rights in the proceedings as per the *Gault* decision. If the case involves an abused, neglected, or dependent child, a guardian will be appointed to act as an advocate for the child, usually a social worker from a child welfare agency. If appropriate, the hearing will be used to determine whether an alleged delinquent child should remain in detention or custody. This *custody hearing* is usually held within twenty-four hours of the apprehension. If it is determined that there is an "urgent and immediate necessity" to continue detention, the judge issues a *hold-in-custody order.* Otherwise, the child is released to parents or guardians or to shelter care.

Dependent, neglected, or abused children, and status offenders may be placed into foster care or a residential shelter. Within a few days, a *shelter hearing* is held at which a judge determines if continued out-of-home placement is necessary. If it is, the judge will appoint a temporary guardian for the child, usually from a child welfare agency, but sometimes a relative or friend of the family. The judge may also issue an *order of protection,* which allows the penalties for contempt of court (summary imprisonment) if violated. An order of protection will usually contain specific restrictions on a potential abuser or assailant to refrain from further abuse and/or contact with the child or others in danger.

During a custody or shelter hearing, probable cause must be established, that is, the judge must determine if there is enough evidence to believe that the allegations stated in the petition justify a full hearing.

Adjudicatory hearings. The adjudicatory hearing parallels an adult trial, and its purpose is to provide the judge with a basis for determining whether the child should be made a ward of the juvenile court because he or she is delinquent, a status offender, abused, neglected, or dependent. There are three phases common to adjudicatory hearings:

1. First, a plea is entered in the form of an admission or denial of the allegations made in the petition.
2. If a denial is made, then evidence must be presented to prove beyond a reasonable doubt that a delinquent act was committed by the respondent or, in the case of a status offense, with a preponderance of the evidence that the child is a MINS (or CHINS or PINS), or abused, neglected, or dependent.
3. If the allegations are sustained, the judge enters a *finding* that the child is an adjudicated delinquent, a MINS (or CHINS or PINS), abused, neglected, or dependent and declares him or her to be a ward of the court.

Dispositional Hearings. If the judge makes a positive finding, the probation department will prepare a *predisposition or social investigation report* containing the social and psychological factors affecting the child and his or her family; it parallels the presentence report used in criminal court. The report will include the probation officer's recommendation as to what disposition would best serve the child and the community. In special cases the judge may declare the child a temporary ward of the court and order services prior to an adjudicatory hearing, or the judge may place the child under supervision and require restitution, regular school attendance, and so forth.

The purpose of the dispositional hearing is to determine what outcome will best serve the interests of the child, his or her family, and the community. There are a number of different dispositions available to a juvenile court judge, but some depend on the resources available in the jurisdiction. In cases of delinquency, these include:

1. *Commitment to the juvenile division of the department of corrections* for children who are at least thirteen and whose offense would be punishable with incarceration if tried under the criminal law. The period of this commitment is indeterminate, but may not last longer than the delinquent youth's twenty-first birthday. The actual date of release is determined by department of corrections juvenile officials.
2. *Probation* for adjudicated delinquent children of any age for a period not beyond the age of twenty-one. A child placed on probation will be released to parents or placed out of the home and receive supervision and services by a probation officer. As a condition of probation, juveniles are usually required to obey their parents, attend school regularly, be home at an early hour in the evening, avoid disreputable companions and places, and refrain from alcoholic

beverages and controlled substances. In some cases there will also be a requirement for restitution and/or community service.

3. *Conditional discharge* and release to parents on the condition that no further delinquent acts will take place.

4. *Out-of-home placement*, often in the form of a commitment to the child welfare agency, which will arrange for a foster home or residential treatment setting that can provide counseling and education to help the child to behave in a more constructive manner.

5. *Referral* to a public or private agency with specialized services such as a drug treatment program for children who are addicted to controlled substances or alcohol.

6. *Detention*, usually for no more than thirty days, in a juvenile facility and then release to probation supervision, perhaps in combination with one of the other alternatives listed above.

If appropriate, the judge may also order protective supervision of the parents or guardians to whose custody the child was released.

The dispositional alternatives for status offenders include probation supervision, out-of-home placement, referral, or emancipation of the child as a mature minor. For children who are abused or neglected, the court will choose the disposition that is best able to provide protection and overcome the ill effects of the neglect or abuse. The dependent child is by definition without parents or guardians available to provide proper care, and dispositions are limited to an out-of-home placement with the assignment of a guardian or emancipation. As in cases involving other categories of children, the judge may also order protective supervision.

Juveniles in Criminal Court

Under certain circumstances juveniles can be tried in criminal court as long as the process is in accord with the *Breed* decision. There are three basic mechanisms for accomplishing the transfer of a juvenile to criminal court (Wizner 1984):

1. *Legislative exclusion.* Most states have statutory provisions that exclude certain crimes from the jurisdiction of the juvenile court. These are usually the most serious criminal acts such as murder and forcible rape.

2. *Judicial waiver.* Almost every state grants the juvenile court judges discretionary power to *waive* (transfer) their jurisdiction over certain juvenile offenders. This discretion is limited by statutory criteria with respect to factors such as age, prior record, amenability to treatment, and degree of dangerousness.

3. *Prosecutorial discretion.* A few states empower prosecutors to charge juveniles in either juvenile or criminal court. This discretion is usually limited by statutory criteria with respect to age and type of offense.

Researchers Inger Sagatun, Loretta McCollum, and Michael Edwards report a lack of any significant difference in sentence outcome for youngsters adjudicated in juvenile court and those tried in criminal court after controlling for the severity of offense. They point out that

> minors are likely to be looked upon as special persons by prosecutors, probation officers, and judges in the criminal courts. They are younger than the main population of defendants before the criminal courts. Even jurors may view the young person in criminal court differently. In the cases examined, there were more findings of "not guilty" in the criminal court than in the juvenile court. The labeling process may be different in the two courts. While a minor may be looked upon as a hardened criminal in the juvenile court, (s)he may be viewed as a mere innocent youngster in criminal court. (1985: 87)

Issues of Controversy

There has been a great deal of controversy over juvenile justice, particularly with respect to the role of the juvenile court judges, attorneys, status offenses, and treatment.

Role of the juvenile court. As noted above, the raison d'être of a separate court for juveniles has historically been based on *parens patriae* and the juvenile court as a vehicle for providing social services to children in need. In many jurisdictions, however, the juvenile court has moved toward dispensing punishment—not merely providing social services. In some jurisdictions the line between the criminal court and the juvenile court has become blurred as the latter moves toward a *justice model:* dispositions based on what the youngster *deserves,* rather than what a youngster *needs.* The State of Washington, for example, in 1977 abrogated the doctrine of *parens patriae* and adopted a model based on *just deserts* (Schram et al. 1981: 65): "(1) Make juvenile offenders accountable for their criminal behavior; and (2) provide for punishment commensurate with age, crime, and criminal history. Nowhere is the rehabilitation of the juvenile offender mentioned as a purpose or intent [in the Washington statute]."

Judges. While a judicial post requires knowledge of law and legal procedure, the juvenile court judge, in addition, needs a working knowledge of several other disciplines, including psychology, sociology, and social work. Judges in general come to the bench without any special training for their position, and this can be a particular problem in juvenile court. Legal education provides very little in the way of training for practice in juvenile justice, and the judge typically comes to the juvenile court bench with a background in civil or criminal law, and with little knowledge of the philosophy and practice of the juvenile court. Furthermore, many, if not most judges, have little or no experience with children of lower-class groups, those youngsters most likely to be found in juvenile court.

In many jurisdictions the juvenile court is a bench with low prestige, and those receiving juvenile court appointments often aspire to a higher court, one with more prestige (and perhaps a greater salary). This can have a destabilizing influence on the juvenile court, one that can be corrected by a unified court system. In order to deal with the other shortcomings, some states have mandated training for juvenile court judges, and the National Council of Juvenile Court Judges sponsors a national college located on the campus of the University of Nevada at Reno. Some jurisdictions are utilizing *referees* or *masters,* specialists trained in law and juvenile justice who hold hearings and make recommendations to juvenile court judges.

Attorneys. The role of defense counsel in the juvenile court can be fraught with ambivalence. In a criminal case, the role is clear: advocacy, bringing to bear all of one's professional skills to gain the best possible outcome for a client. The "best possible outcome" in juvenile court, however, is often a matter of opinion, and the role of the attorney in a *parens patriae* proceeding is not clear. Most children entering the juvenile court are in need of help. Should defense counsel become an agent mediator between the court, the youngster, and his or her parents, so that the client receives this help? Or should the lawyer argue vigorously against the allegations in the petition in order to free the client of all judicial incumbrances? While the canons of legal ethics do not require that an attorney accept the client's view of a particular situation, how far can counsel go in disregarding the wishes of a youngster facing action in juvenile court? The issue remains one of controversy.

Status offenses. Juvenile court jurisdiction over status offenders has long been controversial. In 1976 this writer argued against such jurisdiction, and similar positions have been taken by the National Council on Crime and Delinquency and the American Society of Criminology. Since, by definition, a status offender has not been accused of a crime, punitive intervention—use of arrest, detention, the court process, training schools—is inappropriate, and the stigma is potentially harmful (Abadinsky 1976). Edwin Schur (1973: 120) states that an initial appearance in juvenile court can set in motion a potentially damaging series of events, "a complex process of response and counterresponse beginning with an initial act of rule-violation and developing into elaborated delinquent self-conceptions and a full-fledged delinquent career."

In Scandinavian countries and in Belgium, social agencies have responsibility for status offenders without the need for court intervention. Proponents of continued juvenile court jurisdiction over status offenders argue, however, that these youngsters are not essentially different from those youngsters committing delinquent acts; they are all children in need of services, and without the intervention of the juvenile court, these services would not be forthcoming.

Treatment. In the field of juvenile justice, there is general agreement that services for children are inadequate. Judges are often faced with very few options at an adjudication hearing, something that accounts for the frequent use of probation even when this disposition is not in the best interests of the child and the community. Treatment facilities for children are quite expensive, especially residential facilities where operating expenses can easily run in excess of $35,000 per year per youngster. This unfortunate situation shows no signs of improving in the future.

With these surveys of civil and juvenile justice, we have completed our examination of the formal methods of adversarial justice used in the United States. In the final chapter, we will examine the more frequently used alternatives to formal processing.

Notes

1. One of the guarantees that does apply, *res judicata*, is similar to the prohibition against double jeopardy. Once a party loses a suit he or she cannot raise the same cause of action again even if there are new grounds for the claim. The defendant, likewise, is prevented from bringing an action to defeat an adverse judgment. Plaintiff and defendant, of course, can appeal an adverse decision.

2. In cases where there is concern that a defendant may move or otherwise dispose of his or her property prior to the outcome of a trial, the plaintiff can request an *attachment* that prevents any disposition of property which may prevent the satisfaction of an adverse judgment. For a full discussion of attachment, civil arrest, levies, liens, and other methods for securing and enforcing civil judgments, see Friedenthal, Kane, and Miller (1985: ch. 15).

8

Negotiated Justice: Plea Bargaining, Mediation, and Arbitration

Most court cases in the United States, criminal and civil, are settled not by trial but by negotiation. In the criminal justice system, negotiated settlements are referred to as *plea bargaining*, an ad hoc exchange between a defendant who agrees to plead guilty to a criminal charge and a prosecutor who, in return, offers leniency. The degree of leniency depends upon a variety of factors that are the subject of the first part of this chapter. Later in this chapter we will examine alternatives to the court process in criminal and civil disputes: mediation and arbitration.

Plea Bargaining

Plea bargaining has a history in the United States that dates back more than one hundred years (Friedman 1979) and "appears to have become fairly well entrenched in a number of United States jurisdictions by the 1880's" (Sanborn 1986: 134). In New York City, for example, guilty pleas comprised as much as 85 percent of the total number of convictions during the last two decades of the nineteenth century (Sanborn 1986). Peter Nardulli (1978) notes that in the 1920s plea bargaining was criticized as a device for enabling politically connected defendants to gain preferential treatment. When it emerged as an issue again during the 1950s, however, its condemnation centered around the coercion involved in "forcing" a defendant to plead guilty. In more recent debates, plea bargaining is criticized for providing criminals with excessive leniency *and* coercing defendants to waive their constitutional rights to a trial.

William McDonald (1985: 6) observes that plea bargaining occurs "when a defendant enters a guilty plea with the reasonable expectation of receiving some consideration from the state." He notes, however, that in some jurisdictions a trial can be more like a plea bargain than the adversarial proceeding it is supposed to be: "Defendants learn that if they agree not to contest the trial they will receive more lenient sentences than they might if they challenge the cases against them." Although such cases are essentially plea bargains, they are counted as trials and help maintain the appearance of a trial system. Paul Wice (1985: 24) notes that consideration from the state can take two forms: "being charged with a less serious crime, which will usually result in a lighter sentence, or receiving the minimum punishment allowable for the originally charged offense."

Plea bargaining is often criticized as an abuse of discretion that results in leniency for serious criminals. On the other hand, it is also criticized as unfair to defendants, who must either waive their constitutional rights or run the risk of a substantially higher sentence if found guilty after a trial. Popular perceptions of plea bargaining fall short of reality. In order to better understand the reality of plea bargaining, we will examine two opposing views.

The Negative View

Critics argue that plea bargaining is a symptom of a system operated to further the needs of the principal actors rather than the needs or interests of the public. Heavily funded police departments bring an abundance of cases into a judicial system that does not have the resources necessary to provide individualized justice. Justice requires a deliberately slow and exacting concern for due process; it is a luxury the system cannot afford—cases resulting in trials take about twice as long as cases disposed of by guilty pleas (Bureau of Justice Statistics 1986). In response to this dilemma, the key actors—judges, prosecutors, defense attorneys—disregard the goal of justice and, instead, tailor their activities to enable the system to function with a minimum of difficulty or disruption.

Due process is ensured through the adversarial method, an ideal characterized by a vigorous prosecutor for the state, who is opposed by an equally vigorous advocate for the defendant, in a courtroom battle before judge and jury. In the view of Abraham Blumberg, the requirements of the judicial system have led to an abandonment of the adversarial ideal, and the practice of criminal law has instead been reduced to a confidence game:

> Organizational goals and discipline impose a set of demands and conditions of practice on the respective professions in the criminal court, to which they respond by abandoning their ideological and professional commitments to the accused client, in the service of these higher claims of the court organization. All court personnel, including the accused's own lawyer, tend to be coopted to be-

Figure 8.1. Typical outcome of 100 felony arrests brought by the police for prosecution.

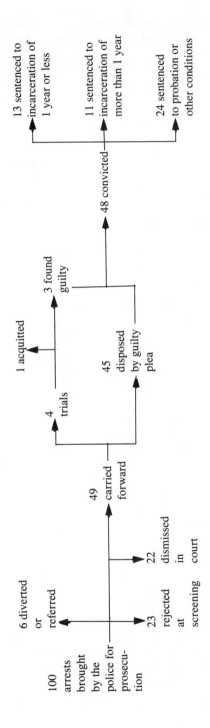

Source: Barbara Boland and Ronald Sones, *The Prosecution of Felony Arrests* Washington, DC: U.S. Government Printing Office, 1986.

come agent-mediators who help the accused redefine his situation and restructure his perceptions concommitant with a plea of guilty. (1967: 19–20)

How does the system "help" the defendant to "redefine" his or her situation in a manner that induces a plea of guilty? The scenario begins with criminal statutes that prescribe lengthy terms of imprisonment for many felony crimes. Although these sentences are rarely imposed, they serve to generate a great deal of fear in a defendant. This fear is aided by the police and prosecutors who engage in *overcharging,* vertical and horizontal. *Vertical overcharging* means charging a single offense at a higher level than the circumstances in the case would appear to support; for example, charging murder in a case where the evidence seems to indicate manslaughter, or charging as a felony the kind of case routinely disposed of as a misdemeanor. *Horizontal overcharging* means charging the arrestee with every conceivable crime even remotely related to his or her actions.

Thus, at their first meeting the defense counsel tells the defendant that if convicted on the highest count or on all of the counts alleged by the police, he or she will be ready for Social Security before being released from prison. The unsettling prospect of a lengthy prison term signals the beginning of a softening-up process. As part of this, overcharging means a higher bail, which can cause the defendant to remain in jail while awaiting adjudication.

If the system is to function efficiently, the occasional recalcitrant defendant must be made to serve as an example for others who might be contemplating a jury trial. Joseph Tybor and Mark Eissman (1985: 1) recount that "after Ron Baker was arrested for robbery, prosecutors offered him probation in return for a guilty plea. The public defender assigned to handle his case urged him to accept the offer. But Baker, a delivery man with no criminal convictions, pleaded innocent and asked for a chance to prove it in a jury trial. Eventually he was convicted, and the same judge who had earlier approved the probation offer sentenced Baker to six years in prison." The judicial attitude behind such treatment is summed up in the statement: "He takes some of my time; I take some of his" (Uhlman and Walker 1980).

If the defendant is able to secure private counsel, in addition to being concerned about the outcome of the case, he or she must be concerned about paying legal fees. As noted in chapter 5, because their clients are generally poor and unreliable, criminal attorneys depend on quantity rather than quality and demand "upfront money," which in most cases will not be sufficient for the hours typically required for a jury trial.

> Most attorneys who specialize in criminal cases depend on a high turnover of clients who can afford only modest fees. Without high volume and the investment of a modest amount of time in each case, many a private defense counsel would go broke. (Jacob and Eisenstein 1977: 26)

Under such circumstances, private defense counsel is likely to recommend that his or her client plead guilty in exchange for leniency. For a defendant facing the prospect of a lengthy term of imprisonment, this may appear to be sound advice.

In order to better manipulate the client, Michael Cox points out, defense counsel is assisted by the prosecutor:

> Prosecutors have great leverage; they draft the charges and generally make recommendations on sentencing. These prosecutorial prerogatives put the defendant at a disadvantage. A prosecutor may "overcharge," either horizontally (e.g., in a bad check case charge uttering, obtaining by false pretenses, and forgery, even though they may overlap and be multiplicious for sentencing), or vertically (e.g., always charge homicides as first degree murder). Through overcharging, an accused is immediately put on the defensive. If the case is tried on the merits, a jury will often react by thinking (even if only subconsciously), "There are so many charges and they are so serious; the defendant must be guilty of something." The number of charges/specifications and the "degree" [e.g., robbery in the first degree or burglary in the second degree] are at the heart of plea negotiations. As an added incentive to deal, a prosecutor may threaten to recommend a high sentence if conviction is obtained after a trial on the merits. (1975: 34)

Summarizing the purpose of these plea-bargaining practices, Albert Alschuler states that

> overcharging and subsequent charge reduction are often the components of an elaborate sham, staged for the benefit of defense attorneys. The process commonly has little or no effect on the defendant's sentence, and prosecutors may simply wish to give defense attorneys a "selling point" in their efforts to induce defendants to plead guilty. (1968: 95)

While private defense counsel must depend on client fees, the public defender is a salaried employee who is paid regardless of how many cases he or she handles. Nevertheless, as Herbert Jacob and James Eisenstein (1977: 26) point out, "Public defender organizations charged with representing all indigent defendants prefer a quick disposition because their manpower barely suffices to handle their case load." A 1985 report for the City Bar Association revealed that indigent defendants in New York City were not being adequately represented; legal aid lawyers were seeking to process as many cases as possible instead of providing vigorous advocacy for clients. The report stated that barely .5 percent of the cases handled by society attorneys resulted in a trial and more complex cases were referred to court-appointed counsel, many of whom were incompetent, if not senile (Margolick 1985).

Albert Alschuler notes that public defenders experience pressure from trial judges, who are concerned with disposing of as many cases as possible as quickly as possible:

The process may begin with a judge's suggestion that a certain plea agreement would be fair and if a defender accepts this suggestion, the matter is at an end. Defenders who resist judicial suggestions too often, however, are frequently forced to endure abusive remarks from the bench:

You're a quasi-public agency. You should be interested in *justice*.

Haven't you got any client control?

You spend too much time on hardened criminals.

No private attorney would take this case to trial.

You must be awfully eager for experience.

When will you guys bend to reality?

You guys believe your clients too much.

You're acting like a private lawyer. (1975: 1237)

The counsel for the defense—whether private, public defender, or assigned—has a great deal in common with prosecutors and judges: a similar educational, professional and, often, political background. Defense attorneys are socialized into a closed system, and they learn that a price must be paid for failing to understand and abide by system norms. Milton Heumann (1978: 57) describes how this socialization takes place: "In the process of handling their cases, new defense attorneys learn that the reality of the court differs from what they had expected; through rewards and sanctions, they are taught to proceed in a certain fashion." In particular, he points out, they learn to avoid legal challenges that may be seen as frivolous to prosecutors and judges—and that can gain the enmity of both:

The hostility of prosecutors and judges to these time-consuming motions is communicated to the new attorney. First, the prosecutor or judge may simply call the defense attorney into his office and explain that the motions are needless formalities. If this advice is insufficient to dissuade the newcomer, sanctions such as "hassling" the attorney by dragging the case out over a long period of time, closing all files to the attorney, and even threatening to go to trial on the case, ensue. (1978: 62)

The prosecutor can also keep a private attorney hopping by objecting to continuances when the lawyer overbooks. Usually, if counsel requests a continuance, and the prosecutor does not object, it will be routinely granted. If the prosecutor objects, however, and the judge is also opposed, an attorney with several cases scheduled for the same day is in a serious dilemma. Alan Dershowitz (1983: 355), a Harvard law professor and prominent defense attorney, lists some of the ways the prosecutor can make the defense attorney's life pleasant or miserable: "by agreeing to or opposing continuances; by opening or closing files for discovery; by waiving or insisting on technical requirements; by recommending or denigrating the attorney to prospective clients; by being generally agreeable or disagreeable."

Thus, defense attorneys are forced to abandon their adversarial stance in favor of accommodation. Alschuler (1975: 1179) states that the system of plea bargaining "leads even able, conscientious, and highly motivated attorneys to make decisions that are not really in their clients' interests." Defendants are finessed or coerced, sometimes both, into cooperating with a system that not only is seeking to inflict punishment on them, but also lacks the resources to insure that the innocent do not plead guilty.

The Benign or Positive View

When asked to explain the existence of plea bargaining, even informed observers point to the crush of cases that threaten to overwhelm the judicial system; they say, "Nobody *likes* plea bargaining, but it's the only way the system can survive." This typical view is contested by Milton Heumann (1978: 157), who points out that guilty pleas have been the outcome of most criminal cases for almost one hundred years, even when courts were not overburdened with too many cases. Trials have not been the central means for resolving criminal (or civil) cases for nearly a century. Heumann describes the reasons each of the parties have for preferring a guilty plea to a trial:

> Court personnel simply recognize the factual culpability of many defendants, and the fruitlessness, at least in terms of case outcome, of going to trial. From these perceptions flows the notion that if the obviously guilty defendant cops a plea, he will receive some award. Whether the defendant believes this results from his show of contrition, or, more prosaically, from saving the state time and money, is not of concern here; the fact that he perceives that he receives a reward is the key point. Similarly, prosecutors and judges do not believe that they accord this reward simply to "move the business." They feel that by giving considerations to the defendant who pleads guilty, they are furthering their own professional goals (sorting serious from nonserious cases, obtaining certain [prison] time in serious cases, and so on.) . . . [I]t is not at all simply an expedient to dispose of "onerously large case loads." (1978: 156)

William McDonald (1985) corroborates this view and reports that, contrary to popular belief, his research indicates that prosecutors are not concerned with the question of case backlog or caseload when they evaluate what to do with specific cases. With respect to overcharging, he points out that it is considerably easier to drop or reduce charges than to add or increase them. The police are likely to charge up, not simply to provide room for bargaining but because the amount of information available early in a case is often limited. (It should also be noted, however, that the credit received by an officer who makes an arrest is dependent on the seriousness of the charges, another reason for charging up.)

Malcolm Feeley (1979) explains plea bargaining by noting that one of the norms of the legal profession is a preference for events that have a relatively high level of predictability. (This is not unique to lawyers; in most businesses, from grocery stores to auto manufacturers, uncertainty is problematic.) But the trial process lacks predictability; it requires a professional (prosecutor or defense counsel) to relinquish control over the outcome of a case to a jury, a panel of twelve persons without any legal training. Whether it is a civil or criminal matter, lawyers do not normally find this situation appealing. Research by Celesta Albonetti (1986:640) revealed that ''prosecutorial screening following felony indictment is influenced by decision makers' attempts to avoid uncertainty.''

The prosecutor has additional concerns. First, the longer a case takes, the greater the likelihood of an outcome in favor of the defendant. Witnesses may fail to appear, or they forget important items, and files are sometimes misplaced or lost. Gathering the necessary elements for the trial, including the defendant and witnesses, all at the same time in the same courtroom can be troublesome. Nancy Jacobs and Ellen Chayet (1986: 15) found that in New York City ''trouble in delivering an incarcerated defendant, while not a regular occurrence, consumes nearly two months, on average, when it is a factor. Witness production problems, for either the prosecution or defense, typically adds an average of a month to case processing time.''

Another reason for preferring the certainty of plea bargaining is that the gathering of physical evidence at the crime scene and crime lab shortcomings can undermine a prosecutor's case. Joseph Peterson (1974) found significant shortcomings in the gathering of physical evidence by police agencies at the scene of a crime. In 1985 the state of Illinois ordered the shutdown of a laboratory that regularly botched tests involving drug and drunk-driving cases (Franklin 1985). A study by the Chicago Crime Commission in 1986 revealed that the failure to complete tests on suspected contraband drugs substantially hampered the prosecution of drug cases in that city (Tybor and Eissman 1986). A three-year study of the 240 government-operated crime laboratories at the federal, state, county, and municipal levels revealed that 70 percent failed to perform even a simple blood test correctly (Grunson 1983). Investigations of the medical examiner's offices in New York and Chicago in 1985 revealed numerous errors in determining the causes of death.

The norms of the legal profession require cordiality between adversaries. As in the case of professional boxers, attorneys are expected to shake hands before and after a bout, an act that does not reduce their efforts to emerge victorious. David Neubauer explains that

> if defense and prosecution are on good terms, this does not mean the adversary process has broken down. It may be only a reflection of the normal rules of conduct expected of lawyers. The ''cooperation'' of defense and prosecution is a product of such general expectations about how lawyers should conduct themselves. (1974: 78)

Although defense attorneys, private or public defender, are typically on good terms with their counterparts in the prosecutor's office, each is a professional who is expected by the other, as well as by the rest of their legal peers, to behave in a professional manner. This requires lawyers to engage in vigorous advocacy; anything less can lead to a loss of respect, which can devastate a legal career.

In place of a trial as the epitome of the adversarial ideal, private plea negotiation has evolved, and as Suzann and Leonard Buckle (1977) argue, plea negotiation is adversarial. In place of two opposing attorneys meeting in a highly dramatic and time-consuming courtroom confrontation, they negotiate in private settings, such as the judge's chambers. Attorneys review the case, pointing out the strengths of their own position as opposed to the weaknesses of the opponent's; the process continues until an agreement—a "deal"—can be struck. The process is that of a mini-trial without the time-consuming formalities required in a courtroom.

Pamela Utz (1979) found in Alameda County, California, early discussion between defense and prosecution was encouraged by an informal discovery process during which both sides reviewed the case together before the preliminary hearing. It was understood that cases that were not prison material should not go to trial, while serious cases with good evidence were inappropriate for plea bargaining—non-negotiable cases. Utz reports that the prosecutor met with the defense attorney as a fellow professional rather than as an adversary, ready to share in reviewing and evaluating the case. "Using the facts of the case, including what is known about the offender," she says (1979: 112), "the two sides try to determine 'what really happened,' and what is an equitable disposition for the particular defendant." According to the unwritten policy that has evolved,

> the parties must assess the evidence according to the norms of rational inquiry, and each side is there to hold the other accountable. Thus, negotiation continues to presume vigorous advocacy, although the assessment binds both sides who must refrain from threatening a trial. If, after settling the facts, the defendant is judged guilty, the seriousness of the offense is judged according to community interests and a penalty that is realistically related to seriousness and case worth is jointly decided on the basis of established norms.[1] (1979: 112)

Does the prevalence of plea bargaining indicate that the adversarial method has been abandoned in favor of expediency in the attempt to reduce uncertainty? Malcolm Feeley states an emphatic no!

> To infer the lack of an adversarial stance and the existence of bargained settlements—for the pure purpose of administrative convenience—from the absence of trials is to ignore altogether the importance of these other "truth testing" and highly combative processes. . . . [In other words] combativeness—short of trial does in fact exist. (1979: 29)

Figure 8.1. Variables influencing a prosecutor's charging decision.

	Weak Case	Strong Case
Not Serious	I	II
Very Serious	III	IV

Extralegal factors

Offender characteristics
• prior criminal history
• age, health
• marital status, children

Community sentiments
• publicity about case
• attitude toward defendant

Victim characteristics
• criminal record
• status in community

The Process and the Law

The accomplishment of a plea bargain depends on many factors, particularly the prosecutor's assessment of the case and agreement among the judicial actors about the appropriate charges.

Case screening. When a prosecutor receives a case from the police, there is an evaluation of its strengths and weaknesses. This is usually made by an assistant prosecutor assigned to an intake (screening) unit. A prosecutor's office frequently has to deal with dozens of state, county, and municipal police agencies (and even more in metropolitan areas such as Cook County, Illinois, which has 125). As would be expected, some perform better than others; some police officers are well trained and conscientious; some are poorly trained and lack motivation. The prosecutor receives cases from them all.

Rather than waste scarce resources on prosecuting petty or weak cases, prosecutors employ a screening system that generally follows a scheme (outlined in figure 8.1) with four categories for rating cases:

Category I: A case in which the charges are not serious and the evidence is weak will usually not be prosecuted.

Category II: A case in which the charges are not serious but the evidence is strong is a good candidate for plea bargaining.

Category III: A case in which the charges are serious but the evidence is weak is a good candidate for rejection, dismissal, or plea bargaining. According to the Bureau of Justice Statistics (1985: 14), "Evidence-related deficiencies and witness problems account for more than half the rejections by prosecutors at screening. In most jurisdictions, evidence and witness problems are also the most common reasons for dismissals in court."[2]

Category IV: A case in which the charges are very serious and the evidence is strong is a candidate for vigorous prosecution.

In addition to the legal factors that influence a prosecutor's charging decision, there are *extralegal factors:* the defendant's prior criminal record; his or her age, health, marital status, work history; publicity about the case; and the background and status of the victim. In some cases, the defendant will assist the police or the prosecutor, for example, by providing information about other criminals. These factors combine with the evidentiary aspects of a case to determine the charging decision.

The degree of case screening accomplished by a prosecutor's office differs from jurisdiction to jurisdiction. A jurisdiction that subjects cases to an early and vigorous review, McDonald (1985: 46) notes, "increases the degree of confidence we can have that the guilty plea process is convicting *probably* guilty defendants." Where such screening is not used, guilty pleas may be made without those "values associated with ideas about legality and the requirement of proof beyond a reasonable doubt." On the other hand, says McDonald, vigorous screening programs

> reject cases that could have been convicted through plea bargaining. For those that believe that a little bit of punishment for a lot of offenders regardless of the seriousness of their crimes or their prior records deters more crime than the selective prosecution of a smaller number of serious offenders, rigorous screening is not regarded as positive reform. (1985: 46-47)

Floyd Feeney, Forest Dill, and Adrianne Weir (1983: 243) point out that it is difficult to evaluate prosecutorial performance on the basis of a conviction rate since "it may be a sign of excellent prosecutorial performance or a sign of overly conservative charging policies."

Strong cases are built on quality investigations in which all the available evidence has been gathered and all of the witnesses have been found and interviewed. Cases brought in by the police may fail to meet the evidentiary standard necessary to justify prosecution and be rejected at screening. A high rejection rate "may be a sign of lax performance by either the police or the prosecutor, illegal or highly aggressive police work" (Feeney et al. 1983: 243). Barbara Boland and her colleagues (1983) note that a small fraction (8 to 19 percent) of police officers account for about half of the arrests that end in convictions. These officers are apparently more adept at gathering evidence than their peers.

Serious cases that appear strong at intake can begin to weaken as time passes. They are either dropped after charges have been filed or plea bargained down to secure a guilty plea. The Vera Institute of Justice notes that the main reason that many of the cases that begin as felonies are not prosecuted as felonies is that

> a high percentage of them, in every crime category from murder to burglary, involve victims with whom the suspect has had prior, often close relations. Logically, suspects who are known to their victims are more likely to be caught than strangers because they can be identified more easily by the complainants. And this very fact of a previous personal relationship often leads a complainant to be reluctant to pursue prosecution through adjudication. (1977: 134)

This reluctance can be the result of tempers that cool with the passage of time; or informal mediation, conciliation and/or restitution may have been effective; or the complainant may have been intimidated.

Because, as the Vera Institute of Justice (1977: 134) notes, "criminal conduct is often the explosive spillover from ruptured personal relations among neighbors, friends and former spouses," prosecutors are sometimes reluctant to prosecute as full-scale felonies cases that erupted from quarrels between friends, neighbors, relatives, or lovers. Often the primary purpose of an arrest in such situations is to defuse a potentially violent situation, and these cases are frequently candidates for rejection at screening or subsequent dismissal in court.

Boland and her colleagues point out that prosecutors who utilize a more intensive case-screening policy drop fewer charges after filing:

> One effect of a rigorous screening policy is that crimes that are in essence private disputes are prevented from taking up costly court time and resources. A number of studies have shown that many crimes against persons involve individuals who had some kind of prior relationship. At the time of the incident, police intervention may be necessary to quell a potentially explosive situation. But by the time the case is brought to court, the victim often no longer wants to prosecute. With experience, prosecutors learn to identify such cases and can prevent them from getting into the court system only to be dropped later in the proceedings. (1983: 6)

Illene Bernstein and her colleagues (1977: 374) found that in cases of assault investigated in New York City, an overwhelming majority "were alleged to have occurred between friends and relatives," and these cases were typically treated quite leniently.

Hans Zeisel states that plea bargaining may result from a perception on the part of the prosecutor that the case is unlikely to be won at trial due to the failure of a complainant to cooperate because of intimidation or

> because the burden of further cooperation exceeds his ebbing anger, or his sense of civic duty, or his tolerance of the treatment he received in court. He . . . may live far from the courthouse, and his presence is required on a great many occasions along the enforcement route—when he files the complaint, at the preliminary hearing, before the grand jury, and finally at trial. While not all cases travel the whole route, some of these occasions require repeated appearances because of unforeseen adjournments and other managerial obstacles. (1982: 27)

Barbara Boland and Elizabeth Brady (1985: 18) report, however, that reduced charges are often "not the result of negotiations between prosecutor and defense counsel but rather reflect the unilateral decision on the part of the prosecutor that the appropriate conviction charge should be a less serious crime than the initial arrest or court charges.'' Such decisions are normally made quite early in case processing.

"Normal crimes." Cases that are not screened out at intake or dropped after charges have been filed usually result in a guilty plea. While the guilty plea is most often the result of some form of exchange, the actual process may be so simple that it cannot be accurately described as "negotiation." David Sudnow (1965: 163) explains such transactions by introducing the concept of *normal crimes:* those whose typical features (the ways they usually occur, the characteristics of persons who commit them, as well as the typical victims) are so common that they can be classified as "normal." For example, a "normal burglary" involves a nonprofessional violator who is black or Hispanic, no weapons, low-priced items, little property damage, and a lower-class victim. Possession of firearms, harm to the occupants, victims who are not lower class, or white perpetrators, for example, would remove the incident from the category of "normal burglary." If defense attorney and prosecutor agree that a burglary is a normal one, custom and precedent provide for a settlement without the need for negotiation. Although the statutes provide a penalty for each crime, judicial actors have established their own unwritten penalties for each "normal crime," which, because they mitigate statutory penalties, serve to encourage pleas of guilty and thus insure a penalty for the perpetrator at a minimum expenditure of scarce legal resources.

William McDonald (1985: v) reports that when presented with the same hypothetical cases, "prosecutors and defense counsel were in remarkable agreement in their estimates of the probability of conviction in those versions of the cases where the evidentiary strength of the case was strong." He also noted that in weaker cases, however, there were significant differences among and between them.

In order to facilitate plea bargaining, judges, prosecutors and defense attorneys must constitute a *workgroup* (Jacob and Eisenstein 1977). This requires *regular players* who interact frequently and share the common goal of disposing of cases with a minimum of resource expenditure and uncertainty. Only a stable workgroup can develop the patterns necessary to make behavior predictable. Judicial systems in which personnel—judges, assistant prosecutors, defense attorneys—are shifted frequently lack the stability necessary for the formation of workgroups, and plea bargaining will be more difficult to accomplish.

The role of the judge. The role of the judge in plea bargaining differs from jurisdiction to jurisdiction. Federal district court judges are prohibited by the *Federal Rules of Criminal Procedure,* Rule 11e(1)c from participating in plea negotiations. In Illinois, however, circuit court judges are routinely involved in plea negotiations. In states where judges exercise a great deal of discretion in the sentencing process, they tend to be more involved in plea negotiations; in states where the judge has only limited options, their role is less important. For example, as noted in chapter 6, Illinois utilizes a determinate sentencing system in which the judge has wide discretion. The charging decision, which is controlled by the prosecutor, does not carry with it a specific sentence. Therefore, before a prosecutor can offer a sentence to the defendant in return for a plea of guilty, the judge must be in agreement. In practice, a pre-plea conference is held at the request of defense counsel. When the prosecutor and judge agree, a sentence is conveyed to the defendant by his or her counsel. If agreed upon, the principals return to the courtroom and formalize the agreement. In many cases the judge will request a pre-plea report (which provides background information on the defendant) from the probation department before agreeing to a particular sentence.

Martin Levin (1977: 33) notes that in Minneapolis plea negotiations do not involve the prosecutor, who "is present but merely as a 'third party' witness." Instead, the judge leads the discussions which center on the sentence, not the charges. Levin found the same situation in Pittsburgh, where negotiations center on the sentence, not the charges, and typically involve the judge and defense counsel.

In some jurisdictions there is a "plea court," an arrangement whereby one or more judges who specialize in "moving cases" preside at calendar hearings, which are held to dispose of as many cases as possible by pleas of guilty. In New York City, supreme court (a trial court) judge, Harold J. Rothwax, developed a reputation for moving cases, usually one every two to ten minutes. As each case is called, an assistant district attorney hands him a sheet indicating the details of the crime, the recommended bail, and the plea offer. As an example of how the judge expedites the cases before him, Sam Roberts provides this vignette:

> Two repeated felons appear before Judge Rothwax, one without counsel. Instead of adjourning the case, he assigns a lawyer sitting in the front row reserved for attorneys. The district attorney's offer was a sentence with a minimum of two years and a maximum of four years. "After today," the judge states, "it's three to six; after that it's four to eight." To the lawyer he states: "If they're ever going to plead, today is the time to do it." (1985: 13)

The wide discretion over sentencing enjoyed by judges in New York obviously facilitates plea bargaining.

Limiting or Abolishing Plea Bargaining

Attempts have been made to limit or exclude plea bargaining from criminal justice, and the results have been mixed. Prosecutors have enormous discretionary powers and have been able to adjust to changes designed to undermine plea bargaining. In states that implemented sentencing guidelines for judges in order to bring about greater uniformity, in Pennsylvania, for example, "prosecutors tended to charge on more offenses and on slightly more serious offenses," note John Kramer, Robin Lubitz, and Cynthia Kempinen (1986:21).

"Clearly such behavior gives prosecutors more flexibility when it comes to plea bargaining. The prosecutor can offer to drop charges or reduce the statutory grade of offenses in exchange for a plea." Some states have also implemented *mandatory minimum sentences* for certain crimes in order to reduce judicial discretion, but this has merely served as another chip in the game of plea bargaining. In New York, laws passed at the behest of Governor Nelson Rockefeller, known locally as the "Rockefeller Laws," severely limited the ability of prosecutors to plea bargain. The result was a substantial increase in the number of defendants demanding jury trials, and prosecutors and judges soon found ways to circumvent the law (Joint Committee on New York Drug Law Evaluation 1977; Aaronson et al. 1977). In Alaska, on the other hand, when the attorney general (that state's chief prosecutor) issued an order prohibiting the state's district attorneys from engaging in plea bargaining, the number of defendants pleading guilty remained about the same. Prosecutors did not have to waste time on negotiations, and the system became more efficient. There were, however, unanticipated results of the policy (Rubinstein, Clarke, and White et al. 1980):

—there was absolutely no change in sentences for cases involving violent crimes such as rape, robbery, and felonious assault;
—there was little change in sentences for most serious property offenders, particularly those with prior felony convictions; and
—the major change was longer sentences for less serious property offenders.

Belinda McCarthy and Charles Lindquist (1985) found that robbery defendants in Jefferson County (Birmingham), Alabama, frequently pled guilty even in the absence of significant benefits. Martin Levin (1977) found that in Minneapolis judges discouraged plea bargaining, but defendants pled guilty at a high rate nevertheless. A study in Cook County (Chicago) revealed no significant difference between the penalties given to violent offenders who pled guilty and those convicted by judges at bench trials (Eissman and Tybor 1985).

Legal Issues

In order for a plea bargaining agreement to be legally binding on the defendant, the trial judge is required to determine if he or she fully understands the ramifications of a plea of guilty. Rule 11(c) of the *Federal Rules of Criminal Procedure* require a judge to determine that the defendant understands:

1. the nature of the charge to which the plea is offered, the mandatory minimum penalty provided by law, if any, and the maximum possible penalty provided by law including the effect of any special parole terms;

2. if the defendant is not represented by an attorney, that he has the right to be represented by an attorney at every stage of the proceeding against him and, if necessary, one will be appointed to represent him;

3. that he has the right to plead not guilty or to persist in that plea if it has already been made, and that he has the right to be tried by a jury and at that trial has the right to the assistance of counsel, the right to confront and cross-examine witnesses against him, and the right not to be compelled to incriminate himself;

4. that if he pleads guilty or *nolo contendere* [no contest], there will not be a further trial of any kind, so that by pleading guilty or *nolo contendere* he waives the right to a jury trial; and

5. that if he pleads guilty or *nolo contendere,* the court may ask him questions about the offense to which he has pleaded, and if he answers these questions under oath, on the record, and in the presence of counsel, his answers may later be used against him in a prosecution for perjury or false statement.

Figure 8.2 is an example of the kind of document used to prove that the judge has ascertained that the defendant understands the ramifications of a guilty plea.

The Supreme Court has ruled (*Brady v. United States,* and *North Carolina v. Alford,* 1970) that a determination must be made as to the voluntary nature of a plea of guilty and, furthermore, the plea must be made knowingly and intelligently. Accordingly, Rule 11(d) provides:

> The court shall not accept a plea of guilty or *nolo contendere* without first, by addressing the defendant personally in open court, determining that the plea is voluntary and not the result of force or threats or of promises apart from a plea agreement. The court shall also inquire as to whether the defendant's willingness to plead guilty or *nolo contendere* results from prior discussions between the attorney for the government and the defendant or his attorney.

Figure 8.3 is an example of the document used by the judge to prove that a guilty plea is voluntary.

If a defendant refuses a prosecutor's offer of leniency in return for a plea of guilty, can the prosecutor reindict the defendant on more serious charges? In 1978, the Supreme Court (*Bordenkircher v. Hayes*) said yes. In this case, Paul Hayes declined to plead guilty to a lesser charge in return for a sentence of five years. He was subsequently convicted of forgery and sentenced as an "habitual offender" to a term of life imprisonment. The Court reasoned that since plea bargaining had been ruled constitutional in prior decisions, the Court must also accept the "simple reality that the prosecutor's interest at the bargaining table is to persuade the defendant to forego his right to plead not guilty." As long as procedural safeguards have been adhered to, charging the defendant with a

Figure 8.2. An example of a document used to prove that a judge has ascertained that a defendant understands the ramifications of a guilty plea.

GUILTY PLEA PROCEEDING

The defendant personally appearing before me, I have ascertained the following facts, noting each by initialing it.

Judge's
Initial

———————   1. That the defendant understands the nature of the charges against him ———————

———————   2. That the defendant understands the range of possible sentence for the offenses charged, from a suspended sentence to a maximum of ——————————— and that the mandatory minimum (if any) is ———————

———————   3. That the defendant understands the following constitutional rights which he gives up by pleading guilty:

———————   (a) His right to trial by jury, if any.

———————   (b) His right to the assistance of an attorney at all stages of the proceeding, and to an appointed attorney, to be furnished free of charge, if he cannot afford one.

———————   (c) His right to confront the witnesses against him and to cross-examine them as to the truthfulness of their testimony.

———————   (d) His right to present evidence on his own behalf, and to have the state compel witnesses of his choosing to appear and testify.

———————   (e) His right to remain silent and to be presumed innocent until proven guilty beyond a reasonable doubt.

———————   4. That the defendant wishes to give up the constitutional rights of which he has been advised.

———————   5. That there exists a basis in fact for believing the defendant guilty of the offenses charged.

———————   6. That the defendant and the prosecutor have entered into a plea agreement and that the defendant understands and consents to its terms.

———————   7. That the plea is voluntary and not the result of force, threats or promises other than a plea agreement.

On the basis of these findings, I conclude that the defendant knowingly, voluntarily and intelligently pleads guilty to the above charges, and accept his plea.

_____   _____
Date   Judge

CERTIFICATION BY DEFENDANT

I certify that the judge personally advised me of the matters noted above, that I understand the constitutional rights that I am giving up by pleading guilty, and that I desire to plead guilty to the charges stated.

_____   _____
Defense-Counsel, if any   Defendant

Figure 8.3. An example of the document used by a judge to prove that a guilty plea is voluntary.

PLEA AGREEMENT

The state of Arizona and the defendant hereby agree to the following disposition of this case:

Plea: The defendant agrees to plead guilty/no contest to:

Terms: On the following understandings, terms and conditions:
1. That the defendant will receive a sentence no greater than ———————————————— and no less than ————————— and consistent with the following additional terms: —————————

2. That the following charges are dismissed, or if not yet filed, shall not be brought against the defendant. —————————

3. That this agreement, unless rejected or withdrawn, serves to amend the complaint, indictment, or information to charge the offense to which the defendant pleads, without the filing of any additional pleading. If the plea is rejected or withdrawn the original charges are automatically reinstated.

4. If the defendant is charged with a felony, that he hereby gives up his right to a preliminary hearing or other probable cause determination on the charges to which he pleads. In the event the court rejects the plea, or the defendant withdraws the plea, the defendant hereby gives up his right to a preliminary hearing or other probable cause determination on the original charges.

5. Unless this plea is rejected or withdrawn, that the defendant hereby gives up any and all motions, defenses, objections or requests which he has made or raised, or could assert hereafter, to the court's entry of judgment against him and imposition of a sentence upon him consistent with this agreement.

6. That if after accepting this agreement the court concludes that any of its provisions regarding the sentence or the term and conditions of probation are inappropriate, it can reject the plea, giving the defendant an opportunity to withdraw the plea.

I have read and understand the above. I have discussed the case and my constitutional rights with my lawyer. I understand that by pleading (guilty) (no contest) I will be giving up my right to a trial by jury, to confront, cross-examine, and compel the attendance of witnesses, and my privilege against self-incrimination. I agree to enter my plea as indicated above on the terms and conditions set forth herein. I fully understand that if, as part of this plea bargain, I am granted probation by the court, the terms and conditions thereof are subject to modification at any time during the period of probation in the event that I violate any written condition of my probation.

—————————————
Date

—————————————
Defendant

I have discussed this case with my client in detail and advised him of his constitutional rights and all possible defenses. I believe that the plea and disposition set forth herein are appropriate under the facts of this case. I concur in the entry of the plea as indicated above and on the terms and conditions set forth herein.

—————————————
Date

—————————————
Defense Counsel

I have reviewed this matter and concur that the plea and disposition set forth herein are appropriate and are in the interest of justice.

—————————————
Date

—————————————
Prosecutor

more serious crime when he or she declines to plead guilty does not violate the Due Process Clause of the Fourteenth Amendment.

Does a prosecutor have to live up to the terms of a plea bargain? In 1971 the Supreme Court (*Santobello v. New York*) said yes. In this case the assistant district attorney agreed to permit the defendant to plead guilty to a gambling misdemeanor charge which would carry a maximum prison sentence of one year. The prosecutor agreed to make no recommendation as to the sentence. After the plea of guilty was entered, a sentencing hearing was scheduled at which a different assistant district attorney appeared. In violation of the agreement, this district attorney recommended the maximum sentence. The Court ruled "that when a plea [of guilty] rests in any significant degree on a promise or agreement of the prosecutor, so that it can be said to be part of the inducement or consideration [to plead guilty], such promise must be fulfilled." In 1984, however, the Supreme Court (*Mabry v. Johnson*) ruled unanimously that a defendant has no constitutional right to enforcement of a proposed plea bargain that a prosecutor withdraws before it becomes official.

Alternative Dispute Resolution

There is widespread dissatisfaction with the administration of justice in the United States which Lawrence Cooke (1982: 3) summarizes: "The processes themselves are described as incomprehensible, the products of lawyers who profit from obfuscation and complexity so that the lay person is incompetent to seek redress in the courts without professional guidance." But even lawyers are finding the system problematic, and as James Alfini (1986: 252) notes, "Attorneys more frequently are considering alternatives such as mediation in divorce cases, arbitration in commercial cases, and private courts or rent-a-judge programs in cases where there is a need for speedy resolution or confidential treatment of certain matters."

In practice, few persons make use of the entire process of justice; most cases, civil or criminal, are settled without resorting to trials. On the civil side, a trial can be painstakingly slow and expensive, and the outcome may create new problems for the principals. These outcomes are always zero-sum decisions; that is, there is a winner and a loser. On the other hand, the cases that do not go to trial—the minor cases, both civil and criminal—are typically given short shrift as part of the mass that enters the justice system. For these reasons, Associate Supreme Court Justice Sandra Day O'Connor stated (quoted in Roehl and Ray 1986: 2), "The courts of this country should not be the places where the resolution of disputes begins. They should be places where the disputes end—after alternative methods of resolving disputes have been considered and tried."

While the adjudication of serious criminal behavior would be inappropriate for any forum other than the criminal court, interpersonal disputes that do not involve serious criminal behavior and civil disputes have been seen as candidates for alternative processing—alternative dispute resolution—that is, utilizing a forum other than the formal justice system. James Alfini (1986: 252) notes that citizens often have options "such as the mediation services of a community-based program to resolve family, neighborhood, and consumer disputes." Alternative processing can also be beneficial in criminal cases, as David Aaronson and his colleagues point out:

> A central thesis of the alternatives movement is that our criminal courts, patterned on an adversary model for the resolution of social conflicts, are an imperfect—and often inappropriate—societal response to the processing of many offenders, especially those charged with minor criminal offenses or offenses involving no substantial factual disputes. In many lesser criminal cases the process of conventional adjudication may be too time-consuming, too expensive, somewhat irrelevant to, or even inconsistent with, achieving effective

---

Resolving Minor Criminal Disputes

Ronald L. Olson, chairperson of the The ABA Special Committee on Dispute Resolution, provides an example from Clay County, Alabama, of the need for alternate systems of dispute resolution (Ray et al. 1983: 7).

The person who was accused of mule stealing apparently had been a tenant farmer on one of the largest farms in that part of the state, the landowner being a very rich and powerful individual, who not only owned much land and had many tenants but was responsible for getting the prosecutor elected and the judge appointed. When he discovered a mule was missing, it didn't take long for him to push the arm of the law into action. The prosecutor very quickly investigated and arrested one of the tenants. Of course, the prosecutor vigorously prosecuted him. At the conclusion of the presentation by the prosecutor, the tenant decided it wasn't really worth his effort to take the stand.

The judge, knowing whose mule it was, issued some very harsh instructions and sent the jury off to deliberate. The jury came back after about five minutes or ten minutes of deliberations and the judge asked, as is the custom, "Mr. Foreman, have you reached a verdict?" "Yes, we have, your honor." "What is that verdict?" "We find the defendant not guilty provided he returns the mule." Well that caused an uproar. The judge exploded from his seat. The prosecutor jumped up. The judge, red in the face, gave the jury a whole new set of instructions, more harsh than before, and sent them back to bring in a "proper verdict." . . . They came back in about a minute and a half: "Have you reached a verdict, Mr. Foreman?" "Yes, we have your honor." "What is it?" "We find the defendant not guilty, and he can keep the mule."

dispositions. . . . Alternatives seek immediate relief for the overburdened criminal justice system: through simpler, less expensive, more effective and fairer dispositions. (1977:3)

Christine Harrington describes the alternative movement as a response to

(1) criticism of lower courts for not providing procedural or substantive justice to minor offenders, and (2) the claim that courts cannot effectively address social demands expressed in complex disputes because such disputes require a more flexible negotiation process that involves the parties more directly in decision making. (1985: 34)

While dissatisfaction with the courts as a vehicle for adjudicating minor criminal matters is often due to the need to expedite the handling of such cases—rough justice—dissatisfaction in civil disputes is usually due to inability of persons with grievances to afford access to the courts. Most people cannot afford the cost of litigation unless there is a provision for a contingency fee. In cases that do not promise a financial settlement, or where the amount of money in dispute is relatively small, such as in tenant-landlord or consumer-merchant disputes, litigants have no easy way to gain any level of satisfaction. The frustrations arising out of this reality can result in bitter resignation, alienation, or even violence.[3] In fact, in addition to the interpersonal level, alternative dispute resolution is being used extensively at the corporate and government regulatory levels.

Mediation and Arbitration

Alternatives to formal adjudication of civil and criminal disputes make use of either mediation or arbitration. Both share a common goal, which Fred Delappa (1983: 9) defines as "trying to resolve the underlying problems that exist between parties in a manner that will result in an avoidance of future disputes." These systems, which focus on harmony as opposed to vindication, have predominated in primitive societies since time-immemorial, but it is only in more recent decades that they have been studied and adapted to such complex societies as the United States.

Mediation. The mediation process utilizes an impartial third party who assists the disputants in reaching a voluntary settlement of their differences. It is non-adversarial, devoid of any attempt to determine right or wrong. Lawrence Cooke (1982: 5) says that the most notable feature of mediation is "its dedication to the parties' self-resolution of their disagreement"; the mediator "encourages communication, assists in the identification of areas of disagreement, as well as agreement, and then works to bring both parties to a resolution, but a resolution reached and defined by the parties themselves." Fred Delappa (1983: 8) points out that the mediation process "attempts to discover and resolve the underlying cause of the dispute. This may result from consideration and airing of the feelings and attitudes of the individual disputants in addition to the facts." Instead of the adversarial method whose product is "justice"—determining who is right and who is wrong—mediation has as its goal reconciliation, a more harmonious relationship between the parties. Daniel McGillis and Joan Mullen (1977: 11) note that the role of a mediator "can range from minor involvement in which an individual who is essentially a conciliator offers some advice to the disputants regarding a possible resolution, to highly structured interaction with disputants."

John Cooley (1986) describes this highly structured interaction. The typical mediation process, he explains, begins with an introduction by the mediator, who explains the procedures and attempts to establish some rapport with the two parties. The complaining party is then asked to present his or her story. The mediator takes copious notes, sometimes asking for restatement or clarification of material from the complainant. At the conclusion of the statement, the mediator summarizes the presentation, omitting any disparaging remarks, and determines if the responding party understands the complaining party's story. The second party is then asked to present his or her story, and the mediator once again takes notes, asks for restatement or clarification, and summarizes.

The mediator now attempts to clarify the underlying issues in the dispute by talking privately with each party. In subsequent joint sessions the mediator summarizes areas of agreement and disagreement, carefully avoiding the disclosure of material given in confidence. The mediator then employs two fundamental principles of effective mediation: "creating doubt in the minds of the parties as to the validity of their positions on issues; and suggesting alternative approaches which may facilitate agreement" (Cooley 1986: 267). He or she then continues meeting individually and collectively with the disputants to narrow the areas of disagreement and to urge a settlement with which each side can live more harmoniously.

Arbitration. The arbitration process utilizes one or more (sometimes panels of three) persons whose decision is binding on both parties. Fred Delappa (1983: 9) notes that although arbitration is less formal than the judicial process, it is nevertheless "a formal proceeding following the standard adversary process, often involving rules of evidence and written briefs." It does, however, promise a more speedy resolution of a dispute than could be expected in the judicial process. It is also conducted in private, an important advantage for parties who wish to preserve confidentiality. Unless the arbitration has been ordered by a court, however, there is no power of subpoena. The disputants must agree to arbitration and to the arbitrators. Directories from which arbitrators can be selected are produced by the American Arbitration Association, the Federal Mediation and Conciliation Service, and the National Mediation Board, as well as the Bureau of National Affairs (*Directory of Arbitrators*) and Prentice-Hall (*Who's Who of Arbitrators*). As in the handling of civil cases in the judicial process, there may be discovery, prehearing conferences, submission of briefs, and oral arguments in an adversarial spirit. As opposed to the mediation process, ex parte conferences, that is with only one party present, are not permitted. At the conclusion of the arbitration process, the arbitrator(s) makes his or her decision orally and, usually, in writing. On occasion, these may be accompanied by lengthy opinions on which the decision was based (Cooley 1986).

Other Means of Dispute Resolution

In cities with large Jewish or Chinese populations, there are often rabbinical courts or mediation forums for the private resolution of personal disputes involving members of these communities. There are a variety of other organizations that provide mediation or arbitration in specific disputes; the Chamber of Commerce, Better Business Bureau, or trade associations may sponsor forums for settling certain types of consumer disputes.

At the other end of the spectrum, California enacted legislation in 1872 providing for a "private" judicial system, although it has only been since the 1970s that the law has been extensively utilized. Los Angeles uses dozens of retired superior court judges as arbitrators for civil litigants who opt for a more speedy resolution of their claims. In California, however, these arbitrators have judicial authority, and their decisions are enforceable by the state. The arbitrators are paid by the parties involved, and they set their own fees, which can range from $150 to $300 an hour or $750 a day. That the fee can hasten the parties to settle is obvious. The most famous of these "private justice" judges is Joseph Wapner, star of television's "The People's Court," which is limited to disputes in which damages do not exceed $1,500 (Chambers 1986).

Georgia Dullea (1986) reports that attorneys are frequently turning to mediators to resolve family disputes over questions such as, Should an elderly relative be placed in a nursing home? What happens when three siblings inherit a piece of property? Should a child attend a private or public school? In 1984 the ABA adopted "Standards of Practice for Lawyer Mediators in Family Disputes"; the preamble reads:

> For the purposes of these standards, family mediation is defined as a process in which a *lawyer* helps family members resolve their disputes in an informative and consensual manner. This process requires that the mediator be qualified by training, experience, and temperament; that the mediator be impartial; that the participants reach decisions voluntarily; that their decisions be based on sufficient factual data; and that each participant understands the information upon which decisions are reached. *While family mediation may be viewed as an alternative means of conflict resolution, it is not a substitute for the benefit of independent legal advice.* (Emphasis added)

There are also *court-annexed dispute resolution programs.* In some jurisdictions, all civil cases involving disputes under a certain fixed amount must be submitted to arbitration. In 1952 the Pennsylvania legislature granted trial courts the power to establish compulsory arbitration programs (Johnson 1977). In Philadelphia, for example, as of 1985 all cases (except real estate and equity) under $20,000 are referred to panels of three attorney-arbitrators. The panel awards are binding unless the loser requests a trial—and the litigant whose trial does not improve the size of the award is penalized. Jonathan Marks, Earl Johnson, Jr., and Peter Szanton (1985: 31) report that "other jurisdictions employ mandatory screening panels in particular subject areas such as medical malpractice. These panels listen to informal presentations of both sides' cases and recommend settlements." There are at least sixteen states that have authorized court-ordered arbitration programs, as do a number of federal districts.

In 1978 the United States District Court for the Western District of Washington established a local rule that provides for the designation of any civil case for a mandatory mediation process. In such cases the attorneys for all parties must meet at least once to engage in a good-faith attempt to negotiate a settlement without mediation within two months of notification. If the parties are unable to reach a settlement, they must agree upon a mediator, a volunteer attorney serving *pro bono*. Each side presents the mediator with a memorandum of contentions relative to both liability and damages, not to exceed ten pages. The mediator may respond with a memorandum of settlement recommendations and meet with the parties individually and jointly to promote the settlement. If these efforts are unsuccessful, the plaintiff must file with the clerk of the court a certificate showing compliance with the requirements of the mediation process. The court then convenes a conference of attorneys to consider the appointment of an arbitrator. The arbitrator, also a volunteer attorney serving *pro bono,* is empowered to make a decision or award in the case. Unless the right to a trial has been waived beforehand, however, the losing party is entitled to a trial *de novo*—the mediation/arbitration proceedings being privileged (confidential) in all respects (Tegland 1984).

One of the earliest alternative dispute programs involving criminal cases was established in Columbus, Ohio, in 1971. The *Night Prosecutor's Program* (NPP) handles cases involving interpersonal disputes that are referred by the police or prosecutor's office. Respondents are informed by program staff that failure to appear for a hearing "may bring further legal action," and the notification is signed "by order of the police prosecutor." The NPP relies on mediation and utilizes law students who act as hearing officers. No records of the cases handled are kept on official documents, although records are maintained for statistical purposes and in the event the parties return. The hearings are informal, with each side being allowed to tell his or her own story without interruption. The goal is to get the disputants to arrive at a mutual agreement on a solution for their problem. In order to emphasize that the program is unable to enforce settlements, no written resolutions are maintained by NPP. If requested, however, a summary will be provided to the parties by the hearing officer (Palmer 1974; McGillis and Mullen 1977).

A similar program for juveniles was established in 1973 in Anne Arundel County, Maryland: the *Community Arbitration Project* (CAP). In Anne Arundel County, police officers, in place of an arrest, are authorized to issue a juvenile citation for certain offenses. The citation must be signed by the youngster and parent or guardian, and if there is a civilian complainant, he or she receives a copy of the citation. The citation directs the youngster and parents to appear for a hearing, which is conducted in a courtlike setting. Instead of a judge, however, an arbitrator presides; he or she is authorized to close the case for insufficient evidence, to issue a warning, or to require the youngster to participate in a counseling and/or community service project which may involve restitution. If appropriate, the arbitrator may refer the case to the prosecutor's office for possible prosecution (Blew and Rosenblum 1977).

In 1974, the American Bar Association provided grants for the establishment of programs that provide alternatives to the court system. One of these programs was sponsored by the Orange County (Florida) Bar Association with support from the city of Orlando. The *Citizen Dispute Settlement Program* (CDS) was established to provide "impartial hearings to residents of Orange County, Florida, who had complaints involving ordinance violations and misdemeanors" (Conner and Surette 1977: xiii). In addition to salaried staff, CDS utilizes volunteer attorneys who serve as hearing officers. Most of the complainants are referred by the police or prosecutor's office. Ross Conner and Ray Surette describe the CDS process:

> A citizen presenting a complaint to CDS is interviewed by the program staff. A hearing date is set, usually within the coming week. The other party involved in the dispute, the respondent, is notified by mail of the date, place, and purpose of the hearing.
>
> Each hearing is unique. Some are as short as 30 minutes, others extend for two or three hours. The complainant, respondent, and a hearing officer are present at some hearings; at others, if it is permitted by the hearing officer, the complainant and respondent are joined by family, friends, and witnesses. If the parties reach an agreement, they sign a statement listing the terms of the agreement. Copies of the statement are given to both the complainant and respondent. (1977: 3)

A Sample CDS Case: A Neighbor's Barking Dogs

On Friday night, Mr. Merkle was awakened for the third time that night by the sound of barking dogs. A telephone call to his neighbor, Mr. Stearns, only resulted in a heated exchange, and the dogs continued to bark throughout the night. The next morning Merkle confronted Stearns about the dogs and about their phone conversation the night before. Tempers flared but this time Stearns assaulted Merkle. Mr. Merkle stormed off to call the Orange County Sheriff's Department, while Mr. Stearns put the dogs inside his house. When the deputy arrived, he saw no barking dogs. Because Merkle did not want to press assault charges, the deputy referred him to the Citizen Dispute Settlement Program.

Mr. Merkle decided to visit the program office where he explained his problem to the CDS staff. CDS then scheduled a hearing for the following Thursday night and sent Mr. Stearns a notice to come to the hearing. Both parties arrived at the local traffic court (where CDS hearings are held) that Thursday evening to attend the informal hearing. Mr. Trees, a local attorney who had volunteered to serve as their arbitrator, was introduced to them by the project director.

TREES: Both of you gentlemen will have a chance to speak your piece so don't interrupt each other please. I'll have some questions and we'll try to get a clear view of the issue. Now, this is not a trial and I'm not a judge, we're trying to avoid that. What transpires here is not legally binding on anyone, so it doesn't prevent anyone from pursuing the traditional legal process. But, hopefully, you will take advantage of this opportunity. We'll try to reach some sort of a compromise agreement tonight.

Mr. Merkle started by stating that Mr. Stearns' dogs were keeping him awake at night. His bedroom window faced the yard where the dogs were kept. All he wanted, he said, was some peace and quiet at night.

Now it was Mr. Stearns' turn to tell his side of the story. He explained that he had gotten the dogs for protection because his house had been broken into several times. Mr. Stearns said that he had not heard the dogs barking. This only happened, he explained, when someone or something was in the yard. And, he added, no one is in the yard at night. Then the discussion started:

MERKLE: I hear them *very* clearly! You must be a heavy sleeper. Why should *I* have to listen to your dogs?

STEARNS: I have the right to protect my home!

TREES: OK, listen. Would you agree that Mr. Merkle has a right to enjoy his home and not be disturbed by dogs at unreasonable hours? And would you, Mr. Merkle, agree that Mr. Stearns has a right to have pets?

(Both nod in agreement)

Good, then let's start working toward a solution where you both can enjoy your rights and live next to each other in relative peace.

Within half an hour both parties agreed that Stearns would keep the dogs in the enclosed porch at night in an effort to reduce the barking. Both parties also agreed to stop threatening and yelling at each other. At the conclusion of the hearing, these agreements were written down and signed by both parties as a sign of good faith; each party received a copy of the agreement. Before they left, Merkle and Stearns separately rated their satisfaction with their hearing, and both stated they were quite satisfied.

Source: Ross F. Conner and Ray Surette, *The Citizen Dispute Settlement Program* (Chicago: American Bar Association, 1977), 4. Used with permission.

The most extensive effort to provide alternative mechanisms for resolving interpersonal and civil disputes using mediation was initiated by the Law Enforcement Assistance Administration (LEAA), a federal funding program for local justice agencies that was discontinued during the administration of President Jimmy Carter. Some of these *Neighborhood Justice Centers* (NJC) were sponsored (with federal funding) under private auspices such as that of the American Arbitration Association, and others by public agencies such as the police or in Columbus, Ohio, the city attorney's office. Some folded with the LEAA, while others continued their operations with local funding. Private sponsorship has the advantage of avoiding the stigma that attaches to official justice agencies such as the police department or the prosecutor's office; as Daniel McGillis and Joan Mullen (1977: 47) state: "Any project which is attached to criminal justice system agencies has the automatic problem of being viewed by some as presumptively biased in favor of the complainant." However, those attached to public agencies have an automatic source of referrals and have the authority to compel appearances and even enforce settlements.

In an evaluation of NJC projects in Atlanta, Kansas City, and Los Angeles, Royer Cook, Janice Roehl, and David Sheppard (1980) found that they all operated quite well, handling large numbers of cases that were diverted out of the formal justice system within one or two weeks from intake, with about half the cases reaching an agreement through mediation. Most of the respondents indicated that they were satisfied with the program and the outcome of their cases and would return again should the need arise. After six months most of the settlements were still in place and being upheld. It was noted that the NJCs connected to justice agencies attracted and resolved more disputes than those programs without such referral sources. The researchers concluded that "Neighborhood Justice Centers appear to handle most minor interpersonal disputes more efficiently than the courts" (1980: 21).

Criticism of Alternative Dispute Resolution

A less positive view is expressed by Stephen Schulhofer (1986: 86), who declares that while the idea of neighborhood justice is appealing, "what we have learned about the operation of these centers does not afford much basis for an optimistic assessment of their potential." He states that there are no significant differences in satisfaction levels expressed by those using an NJC and those resorting to the courts. "There is no evidence," he states, to indicate that "neighborhood mediation, when it occurs, has been more successful than adjudication in reaching the underlying causes of conflict. In practice, mediators have tended to deal only with the superficial aspects of disputes" (1986: 88). He points to the professionalization of mediators, who tend to be lawyers—the

ABA is quite interested in mediation programs—and notes that dispute resolution is fast becoming another specialty for attorneys.

There is also the problem of *participation,* of creating dispute processes that both parties will participate in. Whereas in the lower criminal court, it is often the complainant who withdraws from participation, in the ADR programs, it is frequently the respondent. It is Christine Harrington's (1985: 170) observation that "the coercion and authority of police, prosecutors, and judges are essential elements to the institutional existence of neighborhood justice centers." The need to resort to these coercive elements "suggests that mediation *reproduces* the participation problems reformers sought to resolve with alternatives."

Other criticisms have centered on the question of disparity: forcing the poor to resolve disputes in lesser forums while the wealthy continue to have access to, and make use of, the formal systems of justice. "By diverting poor people's cases to less formal forums do we lessen the chance that the courts will be made fairer to poor people—as by requiring that adequate representation be provided to those who cannot afford to hire their own lawyers?" ask Marks, Johnson, and Szanton (1985: 52). On the other hand, they note, there is also concern "that corporations and other major litigants will create 'luxury class justice' outside the courts." Freed from having to deal with cumbersome delays and the other shortcomings of formal justice, elite litigants will desert the courts, and "just as public schools deteriorate when affluent parents send their children to private schools, so the argument goes, court performance will deteriorate further when affluent litigants no longer have to face delays and costs which burden the rest of the litigating populace."

Then there is the issue of *uncertainty.* As noted in chapter 1, a rational system of law promotes commerce and industry, which require a high level of predictability—capitalists require a reasonable expectation of outcome for the myriad of transactions with which they are involved. Alternative dispute resolution mechanisms—often informal justice—do not necessarily follow the legal norms, "but mediate mutually acceptable agreements or apply common notions of justice to decide disputes" (Marks, Johnson, Szanton 1985: 55). Alternative dispute mechanisms represent a move toward kadi or ad hoc justice and may render outcomes less predictable, which could have an impact on our economic system.

From more primitive and informal systems of justice we moved to the complexity and strictures of common law; and the latter gave rise to the need for a system of equity. Case law and the attendant system of adversarial justice have become so complex, time-consuming, and expensive, that they have led to a renewed interest in more informal systems of resolving disputes: mediation and arbitration. We have come full circle in our examination of law and justice.

Notes

1. Monroe Freedman (1975: 88) argues that a prosecutor "cannot properly go forward with a case unless [he or she] is satisfied beyond a reasonable doubt that the accused is guilty." Furthermore, "a prosecutor should be professionally disciplined for proceeding with a prosecution if a fair-minded person could not reasonably conclude, on the facts known to the prosecutor, that the accused is guilty beyond a reasonable doubt."

2. In his research, however, William McDonald (1985) found that prosecutors were likely to take weak cases to trial or dismiss them rather than to engage in a plea bargain. The reason for this is unclear.

3. Posner (1985: 6) states that the trial with all of its surprises and confrontations—adversary zeal—"all seem related to the function of judicial dispute resolution as a substitute for retribution."

Glossary

absolute liability: Fault without qualification.

actus reus: Behavior that constitutes a specific crime.

adjudicatory hearing: Trial in juvenile court.

administrative law: Rules that govern the operations of regulatory agencies.

adversarial method: System of fact-finding used in American trials in which each side is represented by an attorney acting as an advocate.

affirmative defense: Without denying the charge, defendant raises extenuating or mitigating circumstances such as insanity, self-defense, or entrapment.

appeal: Legal challenge to a decision by a lower court.

appellate review: Consideration of a case by a court of appeals.

arbiter dicta: Judicial opinion which is not part of the ratio decidendi.

arbitration: A method for resolving disputes utilizing a neutral third-party who renders a decision that is binding on the disputants.

arraignment: Early stage in the judicial process at which the defendant hears the charges and enters a plea of not guilty, nolo contendere, or guilty.

arrest: Physical taking into custody of a suspected criminal or juvenile.

arrest warrant: Document issued by a judicial or administrative officer authorizing the arrest of a specific person.

assumption of risk: Common-law doctrine that renders employers in dangerous occupations liability-free.

attachment: Court order that prevents any disposition of property which may prevent the satisfaction of an adverse judgment.

bail: Money or other security placed in custody of the court in order to insure the return of a defendant to stand trial.

bench trial: Trial conducted without benefit of a jury.

bill of particulars: Motion by the defense to obtain the details of the prosecution's charges or the occurrences to be investigated at trial.

Blackstone, William: Influential English legal scholar who organized the common law into four volumes.

bond: Document signed by a defendant in which he or she agrees to return to court at a subsequent date to stand trial.

bond hearing: An appearance before a judicial officer who determines the conditions of release—bail—pending trial.

booking: Process of photographing, fingerprinting, and recording of identifying data subsequent to a suspect's arrest.

case law: That which is based on the previous decisions of appellate courts, particularly the Supreme Court.

case method: Teaching device using case law and the Socratic method to educate students in law school.

certiorari: Requirement that four justices must agree to hear a case before it can be considered by the Supreme Court.

chain of custody: Need to prove that physical evidence being presented at trial is without any doubt that which was retrieved at the crime scene or during a subsequent investigation.

challenge for cause: Objection to using a prospective juror raised by counsel at a *voir dire* hearing.

charge to the jury: Instructions of a judge to the jury after a trial is complete and deliberations are about to begin.

child-saving movement: Activities of mostly middle- and upper-class women of the late nineteenth century that led to the establishment of the juvenile court.

circumstantial evidence: Indirect evidence, such as fingerprints, from which an inference can be drawn.

civil law: Statutes and court decisions that involve noncriminal matters.

civil law code: Detailed enumeration of rules and regulations designed by legal scholars to provide the basis for settling all possible disputes without relying upon precedent.

class action: Mass tort in which there are a few nominal plaintiffs who represent a much larger number of victims.

classical theory: An outgrowth of Enlightenment philosophy which stresses equality before law—"all men are created equal"—and provides a basis for the determinate sentence.

closing arguments: Summary statements to a judge or jury by opposing attorneys at the end of a trial.

common law: Legal system inherited from England based on tradition or precedent rather than civil law codes.

comparative negligence: Assessing liability on the basis of shared blame.

conditional release: Release from prison based on the accumulation of time off for good behavior and requiring the releasee to abide by certain regulations.

contingency fee: A portion of the settlement/judgment in a tort action received by the plaintiff's attorney in lieu of a fee.

contributory negligence: Legal concept that limits or nullifies liability when the plaintiff is not totally without blame.

corpus delicti: Proof that a crime has been committed.

courtroom workgroup: Regular participants in the day-to-day activities of a particular courtroom: judge, prosecutor, defense attorney, and often clerk and bailiffs.

Craveth System: Method used by national law firms to train the graduates of elite law schools in the practice of corporate law.

crime: Any violation of the criminal law.

crime control model: Theoretical construct which conceives of efficiency as vital to the detection, apprehension, and conviction of criminal offenders, and views due process as impeding this efficiency.

criminal law: Statutes defining certain acts of commission and/or omission as crimes.

criminalistics: Science of crime detection; refers to the examination of physical evidence of a crime such as footprints, weapons, and bloodstains.

cross-complaint: An action by the defendant that asks for relief or damages from the plaintiff.

cross-examination: Questions by an attorney aimed at discrediting the courtroom testimony of an opposition witness.

default: Failure of a defendant in a civil action to respond to allegations.

delinquent: Person found to have violated the law, but whose age prevents defining him or her as a criminal.

demurrer: Motion for a directed verdict of acquittal based on an assertion that the prosecution did not present sufficient evidence to allow the case to go to the jury.

detainer: Judicial or administrative document ordering an inmate to be turned over to specific authorities whenever his or her sentence or period of detention is over.

determinate sentence: Term of imprisonment imposed by a judge that has a specific number of years, for example 9–0–0 (nine years), as opposed to indeterminate sentences.

determinism: A construct stressing the lack of choice, particularly the belief that one's behavior is "determined" by physiological or environmental variables, devoid of mens rea.

direct evidence: Evidence supported by eye-witness testimony.

direct examination: Questions asked of a friendly witness by counsel at trial.

directed verdict: Motion requesting a trial judge to render a verdict of not guilty based on insufficient evidence having been presented by the prosecutor.

discovery: Pretrial procedure allowing access to the information held by opposing counsel.

discretion: Lawful ability of an agent of government to exercise choice in making a decision.

dismiss: Motion that argues the court lacks jurisdiction or that the plaintiff has not presented a legally sound basis for a cause of action.

disposition: Decision of a juvenile court judge after a positive finding has been made, for example, placing the respondant on probation.

diversion: Permitting a person charged with an offense to avoid prosecution in exchange for participation in a rehabilitative or restitution program.

diversity of citizenship: Provides the basis of federal jurisdiction in disputes between citizens of different states and/or foreign nations.

double jeopardy: Trying a defendant a second time for the same offense after he or she has already been found not guilty.

due process: Those procedural guarantees to which every defendant is entitled under the Constitution as interpreted by the judicial branch.

due process model: Theoretical construct which brings into question the ability of law enforcement officials to correctly identify criminals; it stresses painstaking procedures to ensure that errors are avoided, that the innocent are not found guilty, that the police do not abuse their authority.

entrapment: Behavior of an agent of government which encourages the committing of a criminal act by a person who was not predisposed to do so. Constitutes an affirmative defense.

equity: Refers to a legal concern for fairness of outcome. Often implemented through the use of injunctive relief and judicial review.

exclusionary rule: Legal doctrine prohibiting the use of evidence secured in an improper manner from being used at trial.

executive clemency: Refers to the power of a governor or president to grant pardons, commutations, and reprieves.

federal system: Governmental scheme used in the United States in which power is divided between a central (federal) and state governments, with the central government ultimately being supreme.

fellow-servant rule: Legal doctrine that prevents an employee from recovering damages from an employer if an accident is the result of the negligence of a fellow employee.

felony: The more serious of the two basic types of criminal behavior, usually bearing a possible penalty in excess of one year in prison.

field interrogations: Questioning of civilians by law enforcement officers in the street or other locations outside of a governmental facility.

finding: Verdict in a juvenile court.

fleeing felon rule: In common law, allows a peace officer to use deadly force to prevent the escape of a suspect in a felony case. Has been voided by a Supreme Court decision.

free will: According to classical theory, each person has the opportunity to be law-abiding or criminal and, therefore, the person who opts to commit a crime is deserving of punishment commensurate with the offense.

garnishment: Judicial order requiring a certain amount of money to be taken out of each paycheck from a defendant.

general deterrence: Belief that punishing an individual criminal has the effect of deterring other would-be criminals.

good time: Reduction of the time served in prison as a reward for not violating prison rules; usually from one-third to one-half off the maximum sentence.

grand jury: Group of citizens, usually numbering twenty-three, who are assembled in secret to hear or investigate allegations of criminal behavior.

group home: Residential treatment facility for a small number of young offenders.

guardian *ad litem:* Attorney appointed to represent and act as an advocate on behalf of an abused or neglected child.

guilty but insane: Legal concept according to which a person who was suffering from a mental illness, but was not insane, at the time of the commission of a crime is not relieved of criminal responsibility.

***habeas corpus*, writ of:** Legal document challenging custody and designed to force authorities holding a person to produce him or her and justify the custody.

halfway house: Residential facility housing offenders who have been released from jail or prison—halfway out—or those who have been placed on probation in lieu of incarceration—halfway in.

hearsay evidence: Testimony from a third party about a statement made out of court by someone else.

hung jury: A jury which cannot reach a verdict.

immunity: Legal protection against prosecution.

impaneling: The selection and swearing in of a jury.

incapacitation: Physically preventing an offender from committing further criminal acts; in the United States by imprisonment.

indeterminate sentence: A sentence which has both a minimum and maximum term of imprisonment, with the actual length determined by a parole board.

indirect evidence: Evidence that does not prove a proposition directly (circumstantial).

individual deterrence: Refers to the belief that once punished, a criminal will tend not to engage in further criminal behavior.

inevitable discovery: A legal doctrine that permits the use of evidence even though it was secured in an improper manner on the belief that it would have eventually been discovered anyhow—an exception to the exclusionary rule.

infancy: A legal age below which a person cannot be held criminally responsible.

information: Accusatory document detailing the charges and filed by the prosecutor which serves to bring a defendant to trial.

injunction: In equity, a judicial order restraining a party from a particular act.

inquisitorial system: Judicial procedure in which the judge is at the center of the fact-gathering process.

insanity: In law, refers to the lack of criminal responsibility.

insanity defense: Affirmative defense offered to avoid being held accountable for criminal behavior.

integrated bar: Compulsory membership in a bar association as a condition of legal practice.

interrogatories: Written questions presented to the opposing side in a civil action requiring answers under oath.

irresistible impulse test: An affirmative defense in which the subject is considered to have known that his or her actions were wrong, but nevertheless was unable to control them.

jail: A local (municipal or county) institution used to house those awaiting trial, those convicted of a misdemeanor, and those convicted of a felony and awaiting transfer to a prison.

joinder of offenses: Combining indictments or informations that are somehow connected into a single case.

judgment: Determination by a judge or jury in a civil case of the remedy or damages to be assessed.

judgment notwithstanding the verdict: A determination by the trial judge that a civil jury determination is excessive or unreasonable.

judicial comity: A courtesy according to which the courts of one state defer to the laws and judicial decisions of another state. Also serves to protect the independence of the state courts from federal interference (i.e., the Eleventh Amendment).

judicial notice: Refers to matters subject to common knowledge or verification which the judge instructs the jury to take as fully established without the need to present formal proof (e.g., calendars, medical dictionaries).

judicial realism: A school of legal thought that challenges the case method focus on precedent.

judicial review: The power of the judicial branch to declare acts of the executive and legislative branches unconstitutional.

jury pool: Those persons who have been summoned and sworn to serve on a jury, but who have not yet been subjected to a *voir dire* hearing.

just deserts: Refers to a criminal receiving punishment that fits the crime.

justice of the peace: A judicial official authorized to try minor cases.

labeling: A concept which views the societal reaction to behavior, the stigma that results from an arrest or conviction, as exerting a controlling influence on the future behavior of those who are labeled.

law review: A journal edited by law school students containing legal articles.

legal aid society: Private agency that provides (usually civil) legal services to indigents.

legal realism: A school of legal thought that challenged the case method focus on precedent.

make more definite: A motion to require the plaintiff to be more specific about the complaints that are alleged.

mala in se: Bad in itself—behavior that is universally criminal (e.g., murder).

mala prohibita: Behavior that is criminal only because a society defines it as such (e.g., manufacture of alcoholic beverages).

mandatory release: The release of an inmate at the end of his or her sentence less any good time.

mediation: System of reconciling disputes in which the disputants assign a neutral party to help reach a settlement.

medical model: Referring to attempts to rehabilitate criminals by an analogy to the methods used by medical doctors: study diagnosis, treatment.

mens rea: The "guilty mind" necessary to establish criminal responsibility.

merit system: A process of selecting judges that utilizes a nominating commission in an attempt to remove partisan politics from the court system.

misdemeanor: Lesser of the two basic types of crime; usually punishable by no more than one year of imprisonment.

Missouri Plan: The "merit selection" of judges using a panel whose members are appointed by the governor or selected by the bar association; the panel submits three candidates to the governor who must pick one for a judicial vacancy. After serving for one year, the judge must stand for retention at a general election.

M'Naghten Rule: A test of criminal responsibility based on English common law: Did the offender know that what he or she was doing was wrong?

moot court: A body set up to provide a forum for the purpose of arguing a case which has no official standing; usually part of legal education.

natural law: Refers to a law superior to man-made enactments; rules binding on all societies.

nolle prosequi: A decision by the prosecutor to decline to prosecute a particular defendant.

nolo contendere: No contest; statement that a defendant declines to defend against the charges.

normal crimes: A concept that recognizes that there are certain frequent and routine patterns that result in categories of crime being viewed as "normal" by prosecutors and defense attorneys.

opening statements: Statements made to the jury by attorneys at the start of a trial.

original intent: A position that requires determining the collective intention of the framers whenever applying a constitutional provision to a specific case.

overcharging: A police practice of alleging an excessive number of criminal violations when they arrest a suspect.

pardon: An act of executive clemency which has the effect of releasing an inmate from prison or removing certain legal disabilities from persons convicted of crimes.

parens patriae: Common law concept that refers to the obligation of the state toward persons who are unable to care for themselves, such as children or the mentally ill.

parole: The release of a prison inmate by a board authorized to make such a decision, followed by a period of supervision by a parole officer.

parole board: An administrative body the members of which are chosen by the governor to review the cases of prisoners eligible for release on parole. The board has the authority to release such persons and to return them to prison for violating the conditions of parole.

parole guidelines: An attempt to structure the discretionary release powers of parole boards by providing a grid which sets the time to be served by inmates based on the seriousness of the crime and the parole prognosis or salient factors score.

pat-down: Refers to frisking, placing the hands about the body of a suspect in order to detect any weapons that he or she may be carrying.

peremptory challenge: The ability of opposing attorneys to excuse prospective jurors without having to state a reason.

plain view doctrine: Legal concept that allows the police to seize evidence without a warrant if they view it from a place in which they had a legal right to be, for example, looking through the window of an automobile stopped for a traffic infraction.

plea bargain: A legal transaction in which a defendant pleads guilty in exchange for some form of leniency.

pleadings: Formal written statements that constitute the plaintiff's cause of action and the defendant's grounds for defense.

positive law: Human enactments resulting from the popular consent of individuals who form themselves into a sovereign people.

positivism: The use of scientific methods to study crime; the belief that such methods will enlighten society about the nature of crime and criminals and that crime is not simply the result of free will.

presentence investigation report: A document containing information about the offender, submitted by a probation department to a judge, upon which the latter can base his or her sentencing decision.

presumptive sentence: A determinate form of sentencing which allows for some discretion in the form of mitigation or aggravation.

pretrial release: The setting free of a defendant without having to provide bail—ROR (release on recognizance).

preventive detention: The holding of a defendant in custody pending trial on the belief that he or she is likely to commit further criminal acts.

prima facie **case:** A case that is sufficient, has a minimum amount of evidence necessary to allow it to continue in the judicial process.

probable cause: The minimum level of evidence needed to make a lawful arrest or secure certain warrants: a level of information that would lead a prudent person to believe that a crime was being, or had been, committed by a specific perpetrator.

probable cause hearing: A court hearing to determine if an arrest was justified—did the officer have probable cause?

probation: A sentence in lieu of imprisonment under which a defendant is supervised in the community by a probation officer.

pro bono: Refers to the provision of free legal services by a private attorney.

prosecutor: A public official who represents the state in a criminal action.

protective search: A search by law enforcement officers without the benefit of a search warrant to insure that there are not weapons about that could endanger them, or to secure items in possession of a suspect who has been placed under arrest.

public defender: A public official who represents indigent defendants.

public interest law: A name given to nongovernmental efforts to provide legal representation in matters of wide concern, such as the environment or product safety.

public safety exception: An exception to the exclusionary rule on the grounds that the action which resulted in securing evidence that would normally be suppressed was necessary to protect the public from some immediate danger.

ratio decedendi: The legal principle on which a case is based.

rational law: A system in which there is an application of general principles to specific facts.

reasonable mistake exception: Legal argument raised to justify the admission of evidence that might otherwise be suppressed as per the exclusionary rule.

recall: A statutory provision whereby voters can petition to have the name of an elected official appear on a ballot for removal by the electorate.

recidivism: The repetition of criminal behavior.

reformatory: A correctional facility for young offenders.

regulatory law: Rules promulgated by administrative agencies.

released on own recognizance (ROR): Releasing a defendant without the need to post bail.

reporter system: The publication of state and federal appellate decisions in a manner that allows research and retrieval by attorneys.

reprieve: A temporary stay of the execution of a sentence to allow more time for judicial review.

residential treatment center (RTC): A private facility for the treatment of juveniles.

res judicata: Prohibits a losing plaintiff from raising the same cause of action again even if there are new grounds for the claim.

restitution: Reimbursing the victim of a crime.

retribution: That portion of a criminal penalty which is based on vengeance or just deserts.

scientific jury selection: Using the tools of the social sciences in the jury selection process.

self-defense: Affirmative defense claiming that physical force was used to protect oneself or others in imminent danger.

self-incrimination: Providing evidence against oneself; forcing a suspect to do so is prohibited by the Fifth Amendment.

senatorial courtesy: Unofficial rule that, under certain conditions, allows a U.S. senator to veto a federal judicial appointment in his or her state.

sentencing council: A device to reduce sentencing by having judges meet to decide jointly on the proper sentences for various crimes.

sentencing disparity: The phenomenon of offenders who commit similar crimes receiving vastly different sentences.

sentencing guidelines: An attempt to reduce sentencing disparity; a structure to guide judges' decisions in a manner that will coincide with the other judges in the same jurisdiction.

separation of powers: The division of government into three branches: executive, legislative, and judicial.

sequestering: Placing a jury in protective custody in a hotel until they complete their deliberations.

shelters: Temporary residential facilities for children in need of emergency care.

side-bar: During trial, a private conversation between the judge and attorneys conducted in court but out of hearing of the jury.

social investigation: A study prepared by a probation officer in juvenile court to provide the judge with information on which to base a disposition.

special verdict: Charge by a trial judge which requires a jury to respond to a series of written questions of fact upon which the judge will determine the outcome of the case.

standing: Requirement in a civil action that the plaintiff have a personal stake in the outcome.

stare decicis: To abide by, or adhere to, decided cases and not to distort settled points. A concept requiring a court to recognize and honor its own previous decisions and those of higher courts; rule of precedent.

status offense: Actions that would not constitute a crime if the actor was an adult, for example, truancy, but, in accord with *parens patriae*, can subject a youngster to the juvenile court process.

statutory law: The enactments of legislative bodies.

stipulation: Agreement between opposing attorneys on certain uncontested factual issues.

strike: A motion that asks the court to excise parts of a civil petition as irrelevant, improper, or prejudicial.

substantial capacity test: A legal test for criminal responsibility that has replaced the M'Naghten test in many states.

summary judgment: A motion based on the claim that there is no genuine issue of material fact and, therefore, the undisputed portion of a case should be eliminated from trial.

supremacy clause: The constitutional provision that the federal government has powers which cannot be exercised by the states or to which the states must conform.

suppression: Motion seeking to invoke the exclusionary rule.

tangible evidence: Any physical exhibit or visual aid.

testimonial evidence: That which is presented orally by a witness in court under oath; occasionally takes the form of a sworn pretrial disposition.

tort: A private wrong which is the subject of a lawsuit.

training school: A residential facility operated by the state or the county for juvenile delinquents.

trial: A fact-finding process which uses the adversarial method.

true bill: Refers to the handing up of an indictment by a grand jury.

venire: Process by which jurors are summoned to service.

venue: Proper jurisdiction for considering a particular case.

voir dire **hearing:** The judicial procedure by which opposing attorneys have an opportunity to challenge prospective jurors.

References

Aaronson, David E., Nicholas N. Kittrie, David J. Saari, and Carolina Cooper
  1977   *Alternatives to Conventional Adjudication: Guidebook For Planners and Practitioners.* Washington, DC: U.S. Government Printing Office.

Abadinsky, Howard
  1987   *Probation and Parole: Theory and Practice.* 3d ed. Englewood Cliffs, NJ: Prentice-Hall.
  1985   *Organized Crime.* 2d ed. Chicago: Nelson-Hall.
  1976   "The Status Offense Dilemma: Coercion and Treatment." *Crime and Delinquency* 22 (October): 456–60.

Abraham, Henry J.
  1975   *The Judicial Process: An Introductory Analysis of the Courts of the United States, England, and France.* New York: Oxford University Press.

Albonetti, Celesta A.
  1986   "Criminality, Prosecutorial Screening, and Uncertainty: Toward a Theory of Discretionary Decision Making in Felony Case Processings." *Criminology* 24 (November): 623–44.

Alfini, James J.
  1986   "Alternative Dispute Resolution and the Courts: An Introduction." *Judicature* 69 (February-March): 252–53, 314.

Alschuler, Albert
  1975   "The Defense Attorney's Role in Plea Bargaining." *Yale Law Review* 84: 1179–1314.
  1968   "The Prosecutor's Role in Plea Bargaining." *University of Chicago Law Review* 36: 50–112.

American Bar Association
> 1980   *Law Schools and Professional Education.* Chicago: American Bar Association.

American Bar Association Task Force on Lawyer Competency and the Role of Law Schools
> 1979   *Lawyer Competency and the Role of Law Schools.* Chicago: American Bar Association.

Andreski, Stanislav, ed.
> 1971   *Herbert Spencer: Structure, Function and Evolution.* New York: Scribner's.

Andrews, Lori B.
> 1982   "Mind Control in the Courtroom." *Chicago Tribune* (March 28): Section 2: 1, 2.

Aspen, Marvin E.
> 1987   "Let's Select Judges on Their Merit, Not Their Politics." *Chicago Tribune* (January 21): 17.

Aubert, Vilhelm
> 1983   *In Search of Law: Sociological Approaches to Law.* Totowa, NJ: Barnes and Noble.

Auerbach, Carl A.
> 1983   "Administrative Agency." In the *Guide to American Law,* pp. 74–75. St. Paul, MN: West.

Auerbach, Jerold S.
> 1976   *Unequal Justice: Lawyers and Social Change in America.* New York: Oxford University Press.
> 1971   "Enmity and Amity: Law Teachers and Practitioners, 1900–1922." In *Law in American History,* edited by Donald Fleming and Bernard Bailyn, pp. 549–601. Boston, MA: Little, Brown.

Axelrod, David
> 1983   "Judicial Bench No Place to Practice Party Loyalty." *Chicago Tribune* (August 28): Section 4: 4.

Balbus, Isaac D.
> 1973   *The Dialectics of Legal Repression: Black Rebels Before the American Criminal Courts.* New York: Russell Sage.

Baldwin, Scott
> 1984   "The Sure Way to Protect the 'Little Guy.' " *New York Times* (December 2): F2.

Barzilay, Jonathon
> 1983   "The D.A.'s Right Arms." *New York Times Magazine* (November 16): 119–23.

Beard, Charles A.
> 1913   *An Economic Interpretation of the Constitution of the United States.* New York: Macmillan.

Beccaria, Cesare
 1963   *On Crime and Punishments.* Indianapolis, IN: Bobbs-Merrill. Originally published in 1764.
Bellows, Randy I.
 1983   "Notes of a Public Defender." Paper prepared for the Program on the Legal Profession, Harvard University Law School.
Berman, Harold J.
 1961   "The Historical Background of American Law." In *Talks on American Law,* edited by Harold J. Berman, pp. 3–17. New York: Vintage Books.
 1958   *The Nature and Functions of Law.* Brooklyn, NY: Foundation Press.
Bernstein, Illene N., Edward Kick, Jan T. Leung, and Barbara Schultz
 1977   "Charge Reduction: An Intermediate Stage in the Process of Labeling Criminal Defendants." *Social Forces* 56 (December): 362–84.
Bickel, Alexander M.
 1962   *The Least Dangerous Branch: The Supreme Court at the Bar of Politics.* Indianapolis, IN.: Bobbs-Merrill.
Blew, Carol H. and Robert Rosenblum
 1977   *The Community Arbitration Project: Anne Arundel County, Maryland.* Washington, DC: U.S. Government Printing Office.
Blodgett, Nancy
 1986   "A Look at Today's Lawyer." *ABA Journal* (September 1): 47–52.
Blumberg, Abraham S.
 1967   "The Practice of Law as Confidence Game: Organizational Cooptation of a Profession. *Law and Society Review* 1: 15–39.
Blumrosen, Alfred W.
 1962   "Legal Process and Labor Laws." In *Law and Sociology: Exploratory Essays,* edited by William Evan, pp. 185–225. Glencoe, IL: Free Press.
Bok, Derek
 1983   *Annual Report to the Board of Overseers,* Harvard University.
Boland, Barbara and Elizabeth Brady
 1985   *The Prosecution of Felony Arrests, 1980.* Washington, DC: U.S. Government Printing Office.
Boland, Barbara, Elizabeth Brady, Herbert Tyson, and John Bassler
 1983   *The Prosecution of Felony Arrests, 1979.* Washington, DC: U.S. Government Printing Office.
Boland, Barbara and Ronald Sones
 1986   *The Prosecution of Felony Arrests.* Washington, DC: U.S. Government Printing Office.
Brennan, William J., Jr.
 1986   "Guaranteeing Individual Liberty." *USA Today* (September): 40–42.
Brown, Richard Maxwell
 1971   "Legal and Behavioral Perspectives on American Vigilantism." In *Law in American History,* edited by Donald Fleming and Bernard Bailyn, pp. 93–144. Boston, MA: Little, Brown.

1969   "The American Vigilante Tradition." In *The History of Violence in America: Historical and Comparative Perspectives,* edited by Hugh D. Graham and Ted R. Gurr, pp. 154–226. New York: Bantam.

Buckle, Suzann R. and Leonard Buckle
1977   *Bargaining for Justice: Plea Disposition in the Criminal Courts.* New York: Praeger.

Bureau of Justice Statistics
1986   *Felony Case-Processing Time.* Washington, DC: U.S. Government Printing Office.
1985   *Crime and Justice Facts, 1985.* Washington, DC: U.S. Government Printing Office.

Caldeira, Gregory A.
1986   "Neither Purse nor the Sword: Dynamics of Public Confidence in the Supreme Court." *American Political Science Review* 80 (December): 1209–26.

Cannon, Mark W.
1982   "Innovation in the Administration of Justice, 1969–1981: An Overview." In *The Politics of Judicial Reform,* edited by Philip L. Dubois, pp. 35–48. Lexington, MA: D.C. Heath.

Cardozo, Benjamin N.
1924   *The Growth of the Law.* New Haven, CT: Yale University Press.

Carp, Robert A. and Ronald Stidham
1985   *The Federal Courts.* Washington, DC: Congressional Quarterly.

Carson, Gerald
1978   *A Good Day at Saratoga.* Chicago: American Bar Association.

Carter, Lief H.
1985   *Contemporary Constitutional Lawmaking.* New York: Pergamon.
1984   *Reason in Law.* 2d ed. Boston, MA: Little, Brown.
1983   *Administrative Law and Politics.* Boston, MA: Little, Brown.

Case, Stephen
1984   "Lawyers Are Often Grossly Overpaid." *New York Times* (December 2): F2.

Casper, Jonathan
1978   *Criminal Courts: The Defendant's Perspective: Executive Summary.* Washington, DC: U.S. Government Printing Office.

Cavalier, Richard
1986   "Strong Medicine: It Could Prove to Be a Cure for the Nation's Malpractice Malise—But Some May Find It Hard to Swallow." *Chicago Tribune Magazine* (December 7): 58–67, 72.

Central Office of Information
1976   *The Legal System of Britain.* London, England: Her Majesty's Stationery Office.

Chambers, Marcia
    1986   "California's Private Courts Are Swift." *New York Times* (February 24): 9.

Chapin, Bradley
    1983   *Criminal Justice in Colonial America: 1606–1660.* Athens, GA: University of Georgia Press.

Chayes, Abram and Antonia H. Chayes
    1984   "Corporate Counsel and the Elite Law Firm." Paper presented at the Conference on the Law Firm as a Social Institution, Stanford University Law School, February 24–25.

Chroust, Anton-Hermann
    1965   *The Rise of the Legal Profession in America. Vol. 2.* Norman, OK: University of Oklahoma Press.

Clymer, Adam
    1986   "Public Evenly Split Over Supreme Court." *New York Times* (July 13): 11.

Conner, Ross F. and Ray Surette
    1977   *The Citizen Dispute Settlement Program: Resolving Disputes Outside the Courts—Orlando, Florida.* Chicago: American Bar Association.

Conti, Samuel D. and David C. Steelman
    n.d.   *Early History of Sheriffs and County Clerks.* North Andover, MA: National Center for State Courts.

Cook, Royer F., Janice A. Roehl and David I. Sheppard
    1980   *Neighborhood Justice Centers Field Test: Executive Summary.* Washington, DC: U.S. Government Printing Office.

Cooke, Lawrence H.
    1982   "Mediation: A Boon or a Bust?" In *Mediation in the Justice System,* edited by Maria R. Volpe, Thomas F. Christian and Joyce E. Kowalewski, pp. 3–17. Chicago: American Bar Association.

Cooley, John W.
    1986   "Arbitration Vs. Mediation—Explaining the Differences." *Judicature* 69 (February-March): 263–69.

Costikyan, Edward
    1966   *Behind Closed Doors.* New York: Harcourt, Brace and World.

Council for Public Interest Law (CPIL)
    1976   *Balancing the Scales of Justice: Financing Public Interest Law in America.* Washington, DC: Council for Public Interest Law.

Cox, Michael P.
    1975   "Discretion: A Twentieth Century Mutation." *Oklahoma Law Review* 28: 311–32.

Criminal Defense Systems
    1984   Washington, DC: U.S. Government Printing Office.

Curran, Barbara A.
  1986   "American Lawyers in the 1980s: A Profession in Transition." *Law and Society Review* 20: 19–52.
  1983   "The Legal Profession in the 1980's: The Changing Profile of the Legal Profession." Paper presented at a research seminar sponsored by the Fellows of the American Bar Foundation, July 30, Atlanta, GA.

Currie, David P.
  1985   *The Constitution in the Supreme Court: The First Hundred Years: 1789–1888.* Chicago: University of Chicago Press.

Curtis, Michael K.
  1986   *No State Shall Abridge: The Fourteenth Amendment and the Bill of Rights.* Durham, NC: Duke University Press.

Dawson, John P.
  1961   "The Functions of the Judge." In *Talks on American Law,* edited by Harold J. Berman, pp. 18–29. New York: Vintage Books.

Delappa, Fred
  1983   *Resolving Disputes: An Alternative Approach.* Chicago: American Bar Association.

Dershowitz, Alan M.
  1983   *The Best Defense.* New York: Vintage Books.

De Tocqueville, Alexis
  1956   *Democracy in America.* New York: New American Library. Originally published in 1835.

Dictionary of Criminal Justice Data Terminology
  1981   Washington, DC: U.S. Government Printing Office.

Dorsett, Lyle W.
  1968   *The Pendergast Machine.* New York: Oxford University Press.

Dubois, Philip L., ed.
  1982   *The Politics of Judicial Reform.* Lexington, MA: D. C. Heath.
  1982   *The Analysis of Judicial Reform.* Lexington, MA: D. C. Heath.

Dullea, Georgia
  1986   "Using Mediators to Resolve Family Disputes." *New York Times* (April 21): 17.

Dworkin, Ronald
  1986   *Law's Empire.* Cambridge, MA: Harvard University Press.
  1985   *A Matter of Principle.* Cambridge, MA: Harvard University Press.

Earle, Edward Meade
  1937   "Introduction" to *The Federalist.* New York: New Modern Library.

"Editorial"
  1964   *Journal of the American Judicature Society* 48: 124–25.

Eisenstein, James
  1978   *Counsel for the United States: U.S. Attorneys in the Political and Legal Systems.* Baltimore, MD: Johns Hopkins University Press.

Eissman, Mark and Joseph R. Tybor
  1985   "Plea Bargaining Declines." *Chicago Tribune* (November 3): 1, 18.
Elias, T. Olawale
  1956   *The Nature of African Customary Law*. Manchester, England: Manchester University Press.
Emerson, Deborah D.
  1984   *The Role of the Grand Jury and the Preliminary Hearing in Pretrial Screening*. Washington, DC: U.S. Government Printing Office.
  1983   *Grand Jury Reform: A Review of Key Issues*. Washington, DC: U.S. Government Printing Office.
Evan, William M., ed.
  1962   *Law and Sociology: Exploratory Essays*. Glencoe, IL: Free Press.

Federal Judicial Center
  1985   *The Roles of Magistrates: Nine Case Studies*. Washington: U.S. Government Printing Office.
Federalist, The
  1937   New York: Modern Library. Originally published in 1788.
Feeley, Malcolm
  1984   "Legal Realism." In *The Guide to American Law: Everyone's Legal Encyclopedia*, pp. 129–31. St. Paul, MN: West.
  1979   *The Process Is Punishment: Handling Cases in a Lower Court*. New York: Russell Sage Foundation.
Feeney, Floyd, Forrest Dill and Adrianne Weir
  1983   *Arrests without Conviction: How Often They Occur and Why*. Washington, DC: U.S. Government Printing Office.
Feldstein, Thomas M. and Stephen B. Presser
  1984   "David Dudley Field." In *The Guide to American Law: Everyone's Legal Encyclopedia*, pp. 238-40. St. Paul, MN: West.
Finckenauer, James O.
  1984   *Juvenile Delinquency and Corrections: The Gap Between Theory and Practice*. New York: Academic Press.
Fishman, James J.
  1979   "The Social and Occupational Mobility of Prosecutors: New York City." In *The Prosecutor*, edited by William F. McDonald, pp. 239–54. Beverly Hills, CA: Sage.
Fiske, Edward B.
  1986   "Law Schools Turn to Competing to Win Students." *New York Times* (July 7): 1, 9.
Flanders, Steven
  1977   *Case Management and Court Management in United States District Courts*. Washington, DC: U.S. Government Printing Office.

Fleming, Donald and Bernard Bailyn, eds.
    1971   *Law in American History.* Boston, MA: Little, Brown.
Frank, Jerome
    1970   *Law and the Modern Mind.* Garden City, NY: Anchor Books. Glouces-
              ter, MA: Peter Smith. Originally published in 1930.
Frankel, Marvin E. and Gary P. Naftalis
    1977   *The Grand Jury: Institution on Trial.* New York: Hill and Wang.
Franklin, Tim
    1985   ''State to Seek Funds to Replace Bungling Lab.'' *Chicago Tribune* (Au-
              gust 18): Sec. 3, p. 1.
Freedman, Monroe H.
    1975   *Lawyers' Ethics is an Adversary System.* Indianapolis, IN: Bobbs-
              Merrill.
Freund, Paul A.
    1961   ''The Supreme Court.'' In *Talks on American Law,* edited by Harold J.
              Berman, pp. 71-84. New York: Vintage Books.
Friedenthal, Jack H., Mary Kay Kane, and Arthur R. Miller.
    1985   *Civil Procedure.* St. Paul, MN: West.
Friedman, Lawrence M.
    1979   ''Plea Bargaining in Historical Perspective.'' *Law and Society Review*
              7: 247–59.
    1973   *A History of American Law.* New York: Simon and Schuster.
Frug, Jerry
    1986   ''Henry James, Lee Marvin and the Law.'' *New York Times Book Re-
              view* (February 16): 1, 28–30.
Fuller, Lon L.
    1961   ''The Adversary System.'' In *Talks on American Law,* edited by Harold
              J. Berman, pp. 30-43. New York: Vintage Books.
Fund for Modern Courts
    1986   *The Illusion of Democracy: New York City Civil Court Elections,
              1980-1985.* New York: Fund for Modern Courts, Inc.
    1984   *Judicial Elections in New York.* New York: Fund for Modern Courts,
              Inc.

Gilmore, Grant
    1977   *The Ages of American Law.* New Haven, CT: Yale University Press.
Glick, Henry R.
    1983   *Courts, Politics, and Justice.* New York: McGraw-Hill.
    1982   ''The Politics of State-Court Reform.'' In *The Politics of Judicial Re-
              form,* edited by Philip L. Dubois, pp. 17–33. Lexington, MA: D. C.
              Heath.
Gluckman, Max
    1955   *The Judicial Process among the Bartose of Northern Rhodesia.* Man-
              chester, England: Manchester University Press.

Goldberg, Nancy A. and Marshall J. Hartman
  1983   "The Public Defender in America." In *The Defense Council,* edited by William F. McDonald, pp. 67–102. Beverly Hills, CA: Sage.
Goldberg, Stephen B., Eric D. Green, and Frank E. A. Sander
  1985   *Dispute Resolution.* Boston: Little, Brown.
Goldman, Sheldon and Thomas P. Jahnige
  1985   *The Federal Courts as a Political System.* New York: McGraw-Hill.
Gould, Carole
  1986   "When to Turn to a No-Frills Law Firm." *New York Times* (November 9): F15.
Grunson, Lindsey
  1986   "Tiny Delaware's Corporate Clout." *New York Times* (June 1): F6.
  1983   "Second Opinions on Medical Examiners." *New York Times* (May 15): E6.

Haar, Charles M.
  1986   "Need Services? Try Common Law." *New York Times* (May 14): 25.
Hamilton, Alexander, John Jay, and James Madison
  1937   *The Federalist.* New York: Modern Library. Originally published in 1788.
Handlin, Oscar and Lilian Handlin
  1982   *A Restless People: Americans in Rebellion, 1770–1787.* Garden City, NY: Doubleday.
Hans, Valerie P. and Neil Vidmar
  1986   *Judging the Jury.* New York: Plenum.
Harrell, Mary Ann and Burnett Anderson
  1982   *Equal Justice Under Law: The Supreme Court in American Life.* Washington, DC: The Supreme Court Historical Society.
Harrington, Christine B.
  1985   *Shadow Justice: The Ideology and Institutionalization of Alternatives to Court.* Westport, CT: Greenwood.
Hart, H. L. A.
  1961   *The Concept of Law.* Oxford, England: Clarendon Press.
Hastie, Reid, Steven D. Penrod, and Nancy Pennington
  1983   *Inside the Jury.* Cambridge, MA: Harvard University Press.
Heinz, John P. and Edward O. Laumann
  1982   *Chicago Lawyers: The Social Structure of the Bar.* Chicago: Russell Sage Foundation and the American Bar Association.
Henderson, Thomas A., Cornelius M. Kerwin, Randall Guynes, Carl Baar, Neal Miller, Hildy Saizow, and Robert Grieser
  1984   *The Significance of Judicial Structure: The Effect of Unification on Trial Court Operations.* Washington, DC: U.S. Government Printing Office.
Henson, Ray D., ed.
  1960   *Landmarks of Law.* Boston, MA: Beacon.

Heumann, Milton
    1978   *Plea Bargaining.* Chicago: University of Chicago Press.
Heymann, Philip B. and William H. Kenety
    1985   *The Murder Trial of Wilbur Jackson.* 2d ed. St. Paul, MN: West.
Hoebel, E. Adamson
    1974   *The Law of Primitive Man.* New York: Atheneum.
Hoffman, Paul
    1982   *Lions of the Eighties: The Inside Story of the Powerhouse Law Firms.*
              Garden City, NY: Doubleday.
Hogue, Arthur R.
    1966   *Origins of the Common Law.* Bloomington, IN: Indiana University
              Press.
Holland, Kenneth M.
    1982   "The Twilight of Adversariness: Trends in Civil Justice." In *The Analy-*
              sis of Judicial Reform, edited by Philip L. Dubois, pp. 17–29. Lex-
              ington, MA: D. C. Heath.
Horowitz, Donald L.
    1977   *The Courts and Social Policy.* Washington, DC: Brookings Institution.
Horowitz, Morton J.
    1977   *The Transformation of American Law, 1780–1860.* Cambridge, MA:
              Harvard University Press.
Howard, J. Woodford, Jr.
    1981   *Courts of Appeal: A Study of the Second, Fifth, and District of Columbia*
              Circuits. Princeton, NJ: Princeton University Press.
Hunt, Morton
    1982   "Putting Juries on the Couch." *New York Times Magazine* (November
              28): 70–72, 78, 82, 86, 88.
Hurst, James Willard
    1956   *Law and the Conditions of Freedom in the Nineteenth-Century United*
              States. Madison, WI: University of Wisconsin Press.
    1950   *The Growth of American Law: The Law Makers.* Boston, MA: Little,
              Brown.

Israel, Jerold H. and Wayne LaFave
    1980   *Criminal Procedure: Constitutional Limitations.* St. Paul, MN: West.

Jacob, Herbert
    1984   *Justice In America: Courts, Lawyers, and the Judicial Process.* Boston,
              MA: Little, Brown.
Jacob, Herbert and James Eisenstein
    1977   *Felony Justice.* Boston, MA: Little, Brown.
Jacobs, Nancy F. and Ellen F. Chayet
    1986   "Court Dynamics and Disposition Time: The Realities of Case Delay."

Paper presented at the annual meeting of the American Society of Criminology, October 30, in Atlanta, GA.

Jacoby, Joan
1982   *Basic Issue in Prosecution and Public Defender Performance.* Washington, DC: U.S. Government Printing Office.

Jaffe, Louis L.
1961   "Administrative Law." In *Talks on American Law,* edited by Harold J. Berman, pp. 112–23. New York: Vintage Books.

Jenkins, John A.
1984   "Betting on the Verdict." *New York Times Magazine* (November 25): 86–99.

Johnson, Charles A. and Bradley C. Canon
1984   *Judicial Policies: Implementation and Impact.* Washington, DC: Congressional Quarterly.

Johnson, Dirk
1986   "Lawyer Hires an Ex-Juror for Retrial." *New York Times* (January 31): 15.

Johnson, Earl, Jr.
1977   *Outside the Courts: A Survey of Diversion Alternatives in Civil Cases.* Denver, CO: National Center for the State Courts.
1974   *Justice and Reform: The Formative Years of the OEO Legal Services Program.* New York: Russell Sage.

Joint Committee on New York Drug Law Evaluation
1977   *The Nation's Toughest Drug Law: Evaluation of the New York City Experience.* New York: Association for the Bar of the City of New York.

Kairys, David, ed.
1982   *The Politics of Law: A Progressive Critique.* New York: Pantheon.

Kairys, David
1982   "Legal Reasoning." In *The Politics of Law: A Progressive Critique,* edited by David Kairys, pp. 11–19. New York: Pantheon.

Kamisar, Yale, Wayne R. LaFave, and Jerold H. Israel
1986   *Basic Criminal Procedure.* St. Paul, MN: West.

Katz, Stanley M.
1971   "The Politics of Law in Colonial America: Controversies Over Chancery Courts and Equity Law in the Eighteenth Century." In *Law in American History,* edited by Donald Flemming and Bernard Bailyn, pp. 257–84. Cambridge, MA: Harvard University Press.

Kaufman, Irving R.
1986   "What Did the Founding Fathers Intend." *New York Times Magazine* (February 23): 42, 59–60, 67–69.

Kennedy, Duncan
1982   "Legal Education as Training for Hierarchy." In *The Politics of Law: A*

Progressive Critique, edited by David Kairys, pp. 40–61. New York: Pantheon.

Kirby, Michael P.
1977   *The Effectiveness of the Point Scale.* Washington, DC: Pretrial Services Resource Center.

Kirchheimer, Otto
1961   *Political Justice.* Princeton, NJ: Princeton University Press.

Koenig, Thomas and Michael Rustad
1985   ''The Challenge to Hierarchy in Legal Education: Suffolk and the Night Law School Movement.'' In *Research in Law, Deviance and Social Control,* volume 7, edited by Steven Spitzer and Andrew T. Scull, pp. 189–212. Greenwich, CT: JAI Press.

Kramer, John, Robin L. Lubitz, and Cynthia A. Kempinen
1986   ''An Analysis of Prosecutorial Adjustments to Sentencing Guideline Reform in Pennsylvania.'' Paper presented at the annual meeting of the American Society of Criminology, October 31, in Atlanta, GA.

Kreindel, Burton, Robert H. Adams, Robert V. D. Campbell, Susan P. Hobart, and John P. Moreschi
1977   *Court Information Systems.* Washington, DC: U.S. Government Printing Office.

Kress, Jack M.
1976   ''Progress and Prosecution.'' *Annals of the American Academy of Political and Social Science* 423 (January): 99–116.

Kristof, Nicholas D.
1986a   ''The Rush to Hire L.A. Lawyers.'' *New York Times* (September 21): F14.
1986b   ''Theories Expand Concept of Liability.'' *New York Times* (October 14): 10.

Kurland, Philip B. and Ralph Lerner, eds.
1987   *The Founder's Constitution.* 5 vols. Chicago, IL: University of Chicago Press.

Ladinsky, Jack
1963   ''Careers of Lawyers, Law Practice, and Legal Institutions.'' *American Sociological Review* 28: 47–54.

Lefcourt, Robert, ed.
1971   *Law against the People: Essays to Demystify Law, Order and the Courts.* New York: Random House.

Lempert, Richard and Joseph Sanders
1986   *An Invitation to Law and Social Science.* New York: Longman.

Lerner, Max, ed.
1943   *The Mind and Faith of Justice Holmes: His Speeches and Judicial Decisions.* New York: Modern Library.

Levi, Edward H.
1955   *An Introduction to Legal Reasoning*. Chicago: University of Chicago Press.

Levin, Martin A.
1977   *Urban Politics and the Criminal Courts*. Chicago: University of Chicago Press.

Levin, Tamar
1987a   "Law Firms Add Second Tier." *New York Times* (March 11): 29, 31.
1987b   "Law Firms Expanding Scope." *New York Times* (February 11): 25, 29
1986a   "A Legal Curb Raises Hackles: It Punishes the Frivolous." *New York Times* (October 2): 25, 31.
1986b   "Leaving the Law for Wall Street: The Faster Track." *New York Times Magazine* (August 10): 14–19; 42, 48, 53.
1983   "A Gentlemanly Profession Enters a Tough New Era." *New York Times* (January 16): Section 3, pp. 1, 10–12.

Lewis, Peter W. and Kenneth D. Peoples
1978   *The Supreme Court and the Criminal Process: Cases and Comments*. Philadelphia, PA: W. B. Saunders.

Lieberman, Jethro K.
1981   *The Litigious Society*. New York: Basic Books.

Llewellyn, Karl N.
1960   *The Common Law Tradition: Deciding Appeals*. Boston, MA: Little, Brown.
1951   *The Bramble Bush*. Dobbs Ferry, NY: Oceana Press.

Locke, John
1952   *The Second Treatise of Government*. Indianapolis, IN: Bobbs-Merrill. Originally published circa 1688.

Loh, Wallace D.
1984   *Social Research in the Judicial Process: Cases, Readings, and Text*. New York: Russell Sage.

Lombroso, Cesare
1968   *Crime, Its Causes and Remedies*. Montclair, NJ: Patterson Smith.

Loss, Louis
1961   "Business Enterprise and the Law." In *Talks on American Law*, edited by Harold J. Berman, pp. 137–50. New York: Vintage Books.

Lou, Herbert H.
1972   *Juvenile Courts in the United States*. New York: Arno Press. Reprint of a 1927 edition.

Lynn, Frank
1984   "Group Finds Voters Lack Choices in Many Supreme Court Elections." *New York Times* (October 14): 18.

MacDonald, H. Malcolm
1961   "Government under Law." Pages 3–21 In *The Rule of Law*, edited by

Arthur L. Harding, pp. 3–21. Dallas, TX: Southern Methodist University Press.

Macy, John W., Jr.
1985   *The First Decade of the Circuit Court Executive: An Evaluation.* Washington, DC: Federal Judicial Center.

Madden, Richard L.
1985   "Part-Time Magistrates Aid Connecticut Judges." *New York Times* (December 8): 34.

Madison, James
1987   *Notes of Debates in the Federal Convention of 1787.* New York: Norton.

Maine, Henry S.
n.d.   *Ancient Law: Its Connection with the Early History of Society, and Its Relation to Modern Ideas.* New York: Cockcroft and Co.

Margolick, David
1985   "The Legal Aid Society on the Defensive." *New York Times* (August 4): E4.
1983a   "The Trouble with America's Law Schools. *New York Times* (May 22): 20–25; 30–37.
1983b   "The Blue-Chip Firms Remain Mostly White." *New York Times* (February 13): E18.

Marks, Jonathan B., Earl Johnson, Jr., and Peter L. Szanton
1985   *Dispute Resolution in America: Processes in Evolution.* Washington, DC: National Institute for Dispute Resolution.

Mayer, Martin
1969   *The Lawyers.* New York: Dell.

McCarthy, Belinda R. and Charles A. Lindquist
1985   "Certainty of Punishment and Sentence Mitigation in Plea Behavior." *Justice Quarterly* 2 (September): 363–83.

McDonald, William F.
1985   *Plea Bargaining: Critical Issues and Common Practices.* Washington, DC: U.S. Government Printing Office.
1983   "In Defense of Inequality: The Legal Profession and Criminal Defense." In *The Defense Counsel,* edited by William F. McDonald, pp. 13–38. Beverly Hills, CA: Sage.
1979   "The Prosecutor's Domain." Pages 15–51 In *The Prosecutor,* edited by William F. McDonald, pp. 15–51. Beverly Hills, CA: Sage.

McDowell, Gary L.
1982   *Equity and the Constitution: The Supreme Court, Equitable Relief, and Public Policy.* Chicago: University of Chicago Press.

McGillis, Daniel and Joan Mullen
1977   *Neighborhood Justice Centers: An Analysis of Potential Models.* Washington, DC: U.S. Government Printing Office.

McGillis, Daniel and Lake Wise
1976   *Court Planning and Research.* Washington, DC: U.S. Government Printing Office.

McKean, Dayton
1963   *The Integrated Bar.* Boston, MA: Houghton, Mifflin.

McLaughlin, Charles H.
1984   "Common Law." In *The Guide to American Law: Everyone's Legal Encyclopedia,* pp. 102-7. St. Paul, MN: West.

Meese, Edwin
1986   "Interpreting the Constitution." *USA Today* (September): 36–39.

Menand, Louis
1986   "What Is 'Critical Legal Studies'? Radicalism for Yuppies." *New Republic* (March 17): 20–23.

Merryman, John Henry
1969   *The Civil Law Tradition.* Stanford, CA: Stanford University Press.

Michalowski, Raymond J.
1985   *Order, Law and Crime: An Introduction to Criminology.* New York: Random House.

Millar, Robert Wyness
1952   *Civil Procedure of the Trial Court in Historical Perspective.* New York: The Law Center of New York University.

Miller, Henry G.
1985   "The Lawyer is No. 2, Not No. 1," *New York Times* (January 26): 17.

Morello, Karen B.
1986   *The Invisible Bar: The Woman Lawyer in America: 1638 to the Present.* New York: Random House.

Morris, Richard B.
1964   *Studies in the History of American Law.* New York: Octagon Books.

Mosely, Ray
1986   "For the Record, Domesday Book Is Going on 900." *Chicago Tribune* (January 13): 14.

Murphy, Walter F. and C. Herman Pritchett
1986   *Courts, Judges, and Politics.* New York: Random House.

Nardulli, Peter F.
1978   "Plea Bargaining: An Organizational Perspective." *Journal of Criminal Justice* 6 (Fall): 217–31.

Neeley, Richard
1986   *Judicial Jeopardy: When Business Collides with the Courts.* Reading, MA: Addison-Wesley.
1981   *How the Courts Govern America.* New Haven, CT: Yale University Press.

Neubauer, David W.
1974   *Criminal Justice in Middle America.* Morristown, NJ: General Learning Press.

Noonan, John T., Jr.
 1976   *Persons and Masks of the Law.* New York: Farrar, Strauss, and Giroux.
"No Trial—and No Punishment Either"
 1986   *New York Times* (March 17): 20.

O'Brien, David M.
 1986   *Storm Center: The Supreme Court in American Politics.* New York: Norton.

Packer, Herbert L.
 1968   *The Limits of the Criminal Sanction.* Stanford, CA: Stanford University Press.
Palmer, John W.
 1974   "Pre-arrest Diversion: Victim Confrontation." *Federal Probation* 38 (September): 12–18.
Peters, William
 1987   *A More Perfect Union.* New York: Crown.
Peterson, Joseph L.
 1974   *The Utilization of Criminalistics Services by the Police: An Analysis of the Physical Evidence Recovery Process.* Washington, DC: U.S. Government Printing Office.
Pettibone, John M., Robert G. Swisher, Kurt H. Weiland, Christine E. Wolf, and Joseph L. White
 1981   *Major Issues in Juvenile Justice Information and Training: Services to Children in Juvenile Courts: The Judicial-Executive Controversy.* Washington, DC: U.S. Government Printing Office.
Pileggi, Nicholas
 1982   "The Last Liberals." *New York* (September 13): 28, 30–35.
Platt, Anthony M.
 1974   *The Child Savers: The Invention of Delinquency.* Chicago: University of Chicago Press.
Plunkett, Theodore F. T.
 1956   *A Concise History of the Common Law.* 5th ed. Boston, MA: Little, Brown.
Polin, Raymond
 1986   "The Supreme Court's Dilemma and Defense." *USA Today* (September): 43–45.
Porter, Mary Cornelia and G. Alan Tarr, eds.
 1982   *State Supreme Courts: Policymakers in the Federal System.* Westport, CT: Greenwood Press.
Posner, Richard A.
 1985   *The Federal Courts: Crisis and Reform.* Cambridge, MA: Harvard University Press.

Pound, Roscoe
1953   *The Lawyer from Antiquity to Modern Times.* St. Paul, MN: West.
Prelaw Handbook 1982–83
1983   Association of American Law Schools.
Press, Aric
1984   "With Justice for Some." *Newsweek* (June 4): 85–86.

Quinn, Jane B.
1986   "Cutting Back Verdicts." *Newsweek* (July 7): 44.

Ray, Larry, Prudence B. Kestner, Lawrence Freedman, and Anne E. Clare, eds.
1983   *Alternative Dispute Resolution: Mediation and the Law: Will Reason
          Prevail?* Chicago: American Bar Association.
Re, Edward D.
1975a   *Stare Decisis.* Washington, DC: Federal Judicial Center.
1975b   *Appellate Opinion Writing.* Washington, DC: Federal Judicial Center.
Reich, Cary
1986   "The Litigator." *New York Times Magazine* (June 1): 18–24, 48, 50,
          70, 74–76, 84.
Rembar, Charles
1980   *The Law of the Land: The Evolution of Our Legal System.* New York:
          Simon and Schuster.
Roberts, Sam
1985   "For One Zealous Judge, Hard Bargaining Pushes Cases through the
          Courts." *New York Times* (April 29): 13.
Roehl, Janice and Larry Ray
1986   "Toward the Multi-Door Courthouse—Dispute Resolution Intake and
          Referral." *NIJ Reports/SNI* 198 (July): 2–7
Rousseau, Jean Jacques
1954   *The Social Contract.* Chicago: Henry Regnery. Originally published in
          1762.
Rubin, Florence R.
1985   "Citizen Participation in the State Courts." *The Justice System Journal*
          10 (Winter): 292–314.
Rubinstein, Michael L., Stevens H. Clarke, and Teresa J. White
1980   *Alaska Bans Plea Bargaining.* Washington, DC: U.S. Government
          Printing Office.

Saari, David J.
1985   *American Court Management: Theories and Practice.* Westport, CT:
          Quorum Books.
Sagatun, Inger, Loretta McCollum, and Michael Edwards
1985   "The Effect of Transfers from Juvenile to Criminal Court: A loglinear
          Analysis." *Journal of Crime and Justice* 8: 65–92.

Salomone, Rosemary C.
  1986   *Equal Education under Law: Legal Rights and Federal Policy in the Post-Brown Era.* New York: St. Martin's Press.

Sanborn, Joseph B., Jr.
  1986   "A Historical Sketch of Plea Bargaining." *Justice Quarterly* 3 (June): 111–38.

Schram, Donna D., Jill G. McKelvy, Anne L. Schneider, and David B. Griswold
  1981   *Preliminary Findings: Assessment of the Juvenile Code.* State of Washington, mimeo.

Schulhofer, Stephen J.
  1986   "The Future of the Adversary System." *Justice Quarterly* (March) 3: 83–93.

Schur, Edwin M.
  1973   *Radical Non-Intervention: Rethinking the Delinquency Problem.* Englewood Cliffs, NJ: Prentice-Hall.
  1968   *Law and Society: A Sociological View.* New York: Random House.

Schwartz, Bernard
  1974   *The Law in America: A History.* New York: McGraw-Hill.

Schwartz, Richard D. and James C. Miller
  1964   "Legal Evolution and Societal Complexity." *American Journal of Sociology* 70 (September): 159–69.

Seligman, Joel
  1978   *The High Citadel: The Influence of Harvard Law School.* Boston, MA: Houghton Mifflin.

Shapiro, Martin
  1981   *Courts: A Comparative and Political Analysis.* Chicago: University of Chicago Press.

Sigler, Jay A.
  1968   *An Introduction to the Legal System.* Homewood, IL: Dorsey Press.

Sigmund, Paul E.
  1971   *Natural Law in Political Thought.* Cambridge, MA: Winthrop Publishers.

Singer, Linda R. and Eleanor Nace
  1985   *Mediation in Special Education.* Washington, DC: National Institute for Dispute Resolution.

Smead, Howard
  1987   *Blood Justice: The Lynching of Mack Charles Parker.* New York: Oxford University Press.

Smigel, Erwin O.
  1964   *The Wall Street Lawyer: Professional Organization Man.* Glencoe, IL: The Free Press.

Smith, Reginald H.
  1919   *Justice and the Poor.* New York: Carnegie Foundation.

Smith, Rogers M.
   1985   *Liberalism and American Constitutional Law.* Cambridge, MA: Harvard University Press.
Stevens, Charles R.
   1985   "The Legal Profession in Japan." Paper prepared for the Program on the Legal Profession, Harvard Law School.
Stevens, Robert
   1971   "Two Cheers for 1870: The American Law School. In *Law in American History,* edited by Donald Fleming and Bernard Bailyn, pp. 403–548. Boston, MA: Little, Brown.
Stewart, James B.
   1984   *The Partners: Inside America's Most Powerful Law Firms.* New York: Warner.
Stout, Ronald
   1986   "Planning for Unified Court Budgeting." *Judicature* 69 (December-January): 205–213.
Sudnow, David
   1965   "Normal Crimes: Sociological Features of the Penal Code." *Social Problems* 12 (Winter): 255–64.
Sunderland, Edson R.
   1953   *History of the American Bar Association and Its Work.* Published privately by Reginald Heber Smith.
Sutherland, Arthur E.
   1967   *The Law at Harvard: A History of Ideas and Men, 1819–1967.* Cambridge, MA: Harvard University Press.

Task Force on Administration of Justice
   1967   *Task Force Report: The Courts.* Washington, DC: U.S. Government Printing Office.
Taylor, Stuart, Jr.
   1986a   "Vigor in the Court, Laughter in the Court." *New York Times* (October 14): 12.
   1986b   "Tasting the Salty Air of Politics and Criticism." *New York Times* (July 18): 8.
   1986c   "An Inside Look at Supreme Court and Its Cases." *New York Times* (June 24): 10.
Tegland, Karl
   1984   *Mediation in the Western District of Washington.* Washington, DC: Federal Judicial Center.
Texas Criminal Justice Council
   1974   *Model Rules for Law Enforcement Officers.* Gaithersburg, MD: International Association of Chiefs of Police.
Tigar, Michael E. and Madeleine R. Levy
   1977   *Law and the Rise of Capitalism.* New York: Monthly Review Press.

Tribe, Laurence H.
1985   *God Save This Honorable Court: How the Choice of Supreme Court Justices Shapes Our History.* New York: Random House.
Turow, Scott
1977   *One L: An Inside Account of Life in the First Year at Harvard Law School.* New York: Penguin.
Tybor, Joseph R. and Mark Eissman
1986   "Study Confirms Crime Lab's Lag Let Drug Cases Fail." *Chicago Tribune* (March 3): 11.
1985   "Judges Penalize the Guilty for Exercising the Right to Trial." *Chicago Tribune* (October 13): 1, 6.

Uhlman, Thomas M. and N. Darlene Walker
1980   "He Takes Some of My Time, I Take Some of His: An Analysis of Judicial Sentencing Patterns in Jury Cases." *Law and Society Review* 14 (Winter): 323–41.
Unger, Roberto Mangabeira
1986   *The Critical Legal Studies Movement.* Cambridge, MA: Harvard University Press.
1976   *Law in Modern Society: Toward a Criticism of Social Theory.* New York: Free Press.
Utz, Pamela
1979   "Two Models of Prosecutorial Professionalism." In *The Prosecutor,* edited by William F. McDonald, pp. 99–124. Beverly Hills, CA: Sage.

Vera Institute of Justice
1977   *Felony Arrests: Their Prosecution and Disposition in New York City's Courts.* New York: Vera Institute of Justice.
Vorenberg, Elizabeth W.
1982   *A State of the Art Survey of Dispute Resolution Programs Involving Juveniles.* Chicago: American Bar Association.

Wagner, Diane
1986   "The New Elite Plaintiff's Bar." *ABA Journal* (February 1): 44–49.
Walker, Samuel
1980   *Popular Justice: A History of American Criminal Justice.* New York: Oxford University Press.
Waltz, Jon R.
1983   *Introduction to Criminal Evidence.* 2d ed. Chicago: Nelson-Hall.
Warren, Charles
1966   "The Supreme Court in United States History." In *The Historian's History of the United States,* edited by Andrew S. Berk and James P. Shenton, pp. 941–53. New York: Capricon Books.

Warren, Earl
  1977   *Memoirs of Earl Warren.* Garden City, NY: Doubleday.
Wasby, Stephen L.
  1984   *The Supreme Court in the Federal Judicial System.* New York: Holt,
             Rinehart and Winston.
Wasserstein, Bruce and Mark J. Green, eds.
  1970   *With Justice for Some: An Indictment of the Law by Young Advocates.*
             Boston, MA: Beacon.
Wasserstrom, Richard A.
  1961   *The Judicial Decision: Toward a Theory of Legal Justification.* Stan-
             ford, CA: Stanford University Press.
Watson, Richard A. and Rondal G. Downing
  1969   *The Politics of the Bench and Bar.* New York: Wiley.
Weber, Max
  1967   *On Law in Economy and Society.* Edited by Max Rheinstein. New York:
             Simon and Schuster. Translated from the 1925 German edition.
  1958   *The Protestant Ethic and the Spirit of Capitalism.* New York: Scrib-
             ner's.
Weller, Steven and John C. Ruhnka
  1978   "Small Claims Courts: Operations and Prospects." *State Court Journal*
             (Winter); reprinted by the National Center for State Courts.
Wheeler, Russell R. and A. Leo Levin
  1979   *Judicial Discipline and Removal in the United States.* Washington, DC:
             Federal Judicial Center.
White, G. Edward
  1976   *The American Judicial Tradition.* New York: Oxford University Press.
Wice, Paul B.
  1985   *Chaos in the Courthouse: The Inner Workings of the Urban Municipal
             Courts.* New York: Praeger.
  1983   "Private Criminal Defense: Reassessing an Endangered Species." In
             The Defense Counsel, edited by William F. McDonald, pp. 39–64. Bev-
             erly Hills, CA: Sage.
  1978   *Criminal Lawyers: An Endangered Species.* Beverly Hills, CA: Sage.
Wishman, Seymour
  1986   *Anatomy of a Jury: The System on Trial.* New York: Times Books.
Wizner, Stephen
  1984   "Discretionary Waiver of Juvenile Court Jurisdiction: An Invitation to
             Procedural Arbitrariness." *Criminal Justice Ethics* 3 (Summer-Fall):
             41–50.

Zeisel, Hans
  1982   *The Limits of Law Enforcement.* Chicago: University of Chicago Press.

Case Index

Author Index

Subject Index

Absolute liability, 35
Actus reus, 139
Adams, John, 39
Administrative law. *See* Law, administrative
Administrative Office of the United States Courts, 102
Adversarial system, 20–21, 22, 109, 126, 164, 178, 184, 200, 206, 207, 220, 221, 227
Affirmative defense, 140
Alternative dispute resolution, 221–26. *See also* Arbitration; Mediation
American Arbitration Association, 225
American Association for Court Management, 104
American Bar Association (ABA), 12, 47, 59, 60, 68–70, 75, 76, 78, 106, 133, 134
  blacks, attitude toward, 69
  Catholics, attitude toward, 76
  federal judges, role in selecting, 111
  immigrants, attitude toward, 69, 76, 131–32
  Jews, attitude toward, 69, 76
  mediation and arbitration and, 221, 223, 226
American Civil Liberties Union, 136
American Corporate Counsel Association, 73

American Judicature Society, 67, 106
American Medical Association, 22
Amicus curiae, 100
Appeals. *See Courts*, appellate
Appellate courts. *See Courts*, appellate
Aquinas, Thomas, 3
Arbitration, 21–22, 217, 218, 220, 222, 223
Aristotle, 3
Articles of Confederation, 32, 36
Association of American Law Schools, 60, 69, 76
Association of Trial Lawyers, 77
Assumption of risk, 35
Attorneys. *See* Lawyers

Bail, 143–44, 151, 202
Bail bondsmen, 144
Bar associations, 65–70, 75. *See also* American Bar Association
Bar examination, 64, 66–67, 76
Bible, 2, 25, 26, 27
Bill of Rights, 41, 42
Black codes, 42
Blackstone, William, 3, 28, 30, 53, 54
Boston University, 56
Brandeis, Louis D., 69, 112
Brennan, William J., 99
Broadhead, James O., 68
Burger, Warren, 48, 146